THE DISSOLVING ALLIANCE

The Washington Institute for Values in Public Policy

The Washington Institute sponsors research that helps provide the information and fresh insights necessary for formulating policy in a democratic society. Founded in 1982, the Institute is an independent, non-profit educational and research organization which examines current and upcoming issues with particular attention to ethical implications.

ADDITIONAL TITLES

Ideology and American Experience: Essays on Theory and Practice in the United States
Edited by John K. Roth and Robert C. Whittemore (1986)

Beyond Constructive Engagement: United States Foreign Policy Toward Africa
Edited by Elliott P. Skinner (1986)

Human Rights in East Asia: A Cultural Perspective
Edited by James C. Hsiung (1986)

The Nuclear Connection: A Reassessment of Nuclear Power and Nuclear Proliferation
Edited by Alvin Weinberg, Marcelo Alonso, and Jack N. Barkenbus (1985)

Central America in Crisis
Edited by Marcelo Alonso (1984)

Global Policy: Challenge of the 80s
Edited by Morton A. Kaplan (1984)

THE DISSOLVING ALLIANCE
The United States and the Future of Europe

EDITED BY
RICHARD L. RUBENSTEIN

A WASHINGTON INSTITUTE BOOK

PARAGON HOUSE PUBLISHERS
New York

Published in the United States by
Paragon House Publishers
2 Hammarskjöld Plaza
New York, New York 10017

A Washington Institute for Values in Public Policy book.

Library of Congress Cataloging-in-Publication Data

The Dissolving Alliance.

    "A Washington Institute book."
    Includes bibliographies and index.
1. United States—Foreign relations—1981–
2. Europe—Foreign relations—1945–
3. United States—Foreign relations—Europe.
4. Europe—Foreign relations—United States.
5. United States—Foreign relations—Soviet Union.
6. Soviet Union—Foreign relations—United States.
I. Rubenstein, Richard L.
E876.D57   1987   327.7304   86-25191
ISBN 0-88702-216-2
ISBN 0-88702-217-0 (pbk.)

Contents

v

Preface
The Dissolving Alliance:
The U.S. and Its NATO Allies

The papers in this volume were originally presented at a conference on "The Fifth Decade of 'Peace' in Europe" sponsored by The Washington Institute for Values in Public Policy and held in the city of Washington, March 3–5, 1986. The editor served as conference chairman and wishes to thank Robert O. Sullivan, Deputy Director of Programs of the Institute, Mrs. Elaine Kradjan, and the Institute staff for their work in making the conference possible. The editor is also indebted to Professor Alexander Shtromas of the University of Salford, Salford, United Kingdom, who provided invaluable assistance in the selection of both the participants and their topics. When the papers were edited, it was evident that the participants' dominant concern was the highly problematic character of the NATO alliance. It was therefore decided to publish those essays which reflected that concern in a single volume. Since Professor Shtromas' paper was an historical study of the Soviet takeover of the Baltic States during World War II, it was decided that the Institute would publish his paper, "The Nazi-Soviet Alliance and the Fate of the Baltic States (1939–1941)," as a separate monograph.

An international group of scholars and other authorities who were serving or who had served in Poland, the Federal Republic of Germany, the United Kingdom, the Soviet Union and the United States took part in the conference. It was clearly understood that the conference could not possibly explore all of the major problems of the fifth decade of "peace" in Europe. Instead, the participants sought to investigate a representative sample. Nevertheless, in spite of the diversity of background, experience and political commitment of the participants, a consensus did arise concerning the principal problems besetting the alliance. Briefly stated, the following was perceived to be the fundamental problem: absent an American willingness to risk nuclear annihilation, the United States has no credible deterrent against a Soviet attack on western Europe. Were the Soviet Union to attack, the United States would have only the choice of risking nuclear suicide in the defense of her allies or of outright capitulation. In general, the participants found the first option lacking in credibility. The participants also found the asymmetry between the regional interests of the European NATO allies, especially the Federal Republic of Germany, and the global interests of the United States to be a second problem of major importance. The military and political implications of these problems are explored in the essays in this volume.

As a multi-authored effort, this book is the work of many hands. The editor wishes to express his thanks to the contributors for their essays and for their participation at the conference. He also wishes to thank Neil A. Salonen, Director of The Washington Institute, for his administrative supervision of the entire project. The editor is further indebted to Jonathan Slevin, Director of Publications of The Washington Institute, Robert Rand, Production Consultant, and Helen Driller, Production Manager of Paragon House Publishers, for their patient, diligent and expert work in seeing this book through production.

RLR
Tokyo

Introduction
The Dissolving Alliance
RICHARD L. RUBENSTEIN

The world has entered the fifth decade of cold peace in Europe. The end of World War II created a new international order with a new set of problems and conflicts. Europe was divided and became largely dependent upon two non-European superpowers with profoundly competing economic, political, and religious values. Unable to agree on an all-inclusive treaty of peace, the superpower blocs accepted a *de facto* settlement which reflected the new balance of power. That *ad hoc* settlement has lasted, albeit with extraordinary tension and the overhanging threat of nuclear war, for more than forty years.

Now the postwar settlement shows signs of beginning to come apart. The division of Germany and Europe has always been both unnatural and inherently unstable. In spite of extraordinary differences in their political systems, the Federal Republic of Germany and the German Democratic Republic constitute one nation. Their yearning for unification is as natural to them as it is problematic to their neighbors, both in the East and the West.

Sooner or later Europe's present political and social arrangements will give way to an as-yet-unforeseeable new structure. The new European settlement could evolve over a period of decades. Alternatively, a catastrophic explosion of the conflicts underlying the present settlement could suddenly erupt, thrusting Europe and the world into a period of chaos and war.

There are many ways in which the present settlement might unravel. It was arrived at when Europe lay prostrate from the effects of the bloodiest war in its history. Awesome technological innovations such as the microprocessor, the super-computer and the space satellite were as yet distant prospects, as was so radically novel a form of warfare as state-sponsored terrorism. Defeated Japan had yet to begin the rise to its present position as one of the world's two economic superpowers. China was torn asunder by civil war. Third-world anti-Americanism had yet to become a political force of strategic consequence. The Soviet navy had yet to become an effective instrument for the projection of Soviet power. The political and economic conflicts which today beset the NATO allies had yet to manifest themselves.

Clearly, the world of the late 1980s presents a very different constellation of national power than did the world of the late 1940s. Yet, it is well to recall some of the principal elements which shaped that earlier world if we are to understand our own time. As P. Edward Haley, Professor of Political Science and Director of the Keck Institute for Strategic Studies, Claremont-McKenna College, reminds us in his essay, on the eve of the Second World War the Western democracies were militarily outclassed by Germany, the Soviet Union, and Imperial Japan to such an extent that it was impossible for any combination of Western powers to defeat either Nazi Germany or Stalinist Russia without the active aid of the other totalitarian regime. Unfortunately, the word "totalitarian" hardly conveys the tragic choice which then confronted the Western world. The regimes of Adolf Hitler and Josef Stalin were the two most murderous in the entire history of the Western world. This is not the occasion to recount the full story of the horrors inflicted upon European civilization by German National Socialism and Soviet Communism. It is, however, important that we keep in mind that the United States and England could only defeat Nazi Germany or Stalinist Russia in alliance with the other regime hostile to democracy.

Thus, from its inception, World War II was destined to yield a tragic, problematic, and dangerous "peace" even if the Western powers were counted among the victors. Had the West been allied to National Socialist Germany in an effort to destroy Soviet Communism, a scenario which was not regarded as altogether impossible in either the Third Reich or certain circles in the West in the 1930s, millions of Eastern Europeans would have been doomed to enslavement and perhaps ultimate extermination as a victorious National Socialist Reich came to dominate its eastern neighbors. Let us recall Hitler's vision of the postwar world as expressed at his East Prussian headquarters in the winter of 1941–42 and recorded at his express command. This was the period during which he was at the height of his power. Apart from the program for the utter extermination of the Jews and Gypsies, there was to be a Germanic empire stretching from Norway to the

Alps, from the Atlantic to the Black Sea. Russia was to become an area of settlement for Nordic peasants with an Aryan India connected directly with Aryan Germany, 180 million Slavic *Untermenschen* were to die out. While the process of attrition, enslavement, and extermination was going on, the surviving Russians were not to be permitted to learn more than "the meaning of traffic signs" and German commands.[1]

Hitler's plan for a victorious Riech was an expression of his Social Darwinism, the belief that "the survival of the fittest" applies as universally to the evolution of human societies as it does to the evolution of biology. From the beginning to the end of this career, Hitler subscribed to no idea more consistently than to Social Darwinism. This was evident in this statement to Albert Speer on March 19, 1945, in which he expressed the view that, if defeated, the Germans had no right to survive:

> If the war is lost, the people will be lost also. It is not necessary to worry about what the German people will need for elementary survival. On the contrary, it is best for us to destroy even these things. For the nation has proven to be the weaker, and the future belongs to the stronger eastern nation. In any case only those who are inferior will remain after this struggle, for the good have already been killed.[2]

Thus, Hitler's vision of death and destruction did not even exclude his own people. Unlike the ultra-nationalist leader of Germany's World War I armies, Erich Ludendorff, who took measures in 1918 to bring the war to an end *before* it was fought on German soil, Hitler was determined to fight, if necessary, until nothing was left of Germany or the Germans.[3] According to German author Sebastian Hafner, during the period between August 1944 and April 1945, Hitler dedicated all of his energies toward one astonishing goal, *the total ruin of Germany*.[4]

To this day, the myth persists in extreme right-wing circles that the Third Reich was the ultimate defense against the Bolshevik hordes that threatened to engulf Europe. In the final Götterdämmerung days of the Third Reich, the idea was fostered by both Hitler and Goebbels. In recent years the myth has been bolstered by the fact that a truncated Germany, the Federal Republic of Germany, is America's ally in the defense of Western Europe. Apart from the fact that the Federal Republic is morally and politically a totally different kind of state from the Third Reich, it is well to remember that Hitler's final efforts to defeat the enemy were directed at the Western allies, not the Soviet Union. By the end of October 1944 the German armies had stabilized, and both the eastern and western fronts were holding. All German men from the ages of 16 to 60 had been mobilized. The Wehrmacht still had nine million men under arms. Germany had at least a gambler's chance of fighting a long, costly, defensive war that might have preserved its territorial and political unity when defeat finally became unavoidable. Indeed, Chief of Staff General Heinz Guderian urged a strategy of mobile defense upon Hitler, warning him of the dangers of offensive action.

Hitler refused to heed Guderian's warnings. On December 16, 1944, inadequately supplied German forces launched a surprise offensive along a 75-mile front in Belgium's Ardennes Forest which has come to be known as the Battle of the Bulge. The attack was Hitler's enterprise from start to finish. It was also military madness. Instead of the three-to-one ratio required by attacking forces to assure defeat of a defending force, the Germans had a ratio of less than one-to-one and even this ratio required the depletion of badly needed forces from the eastern front. Only surprise and the bad weather which grounded the Allied air force permitted the Germans their initial victories. Shortly before Christmas the weather changed and the Allied air forces were able to stop the German offensive. In spite of Guderian's warnings that the eastern front would collapse if the Russians attacked, Hitler launched two more unsuccessful attacks against the Allies in the Ardennes in early January. On January 12, Marshal Ivan Konev launched a massive Soviet attack across the Vistula. Within a month the Russians were within a hundred miles of Berlin.[5]

The forces needed for the defense of Germany against the invading Russians had largely been squandered by Hitler in the Battle of the Bulge. Instead of using Germany's considerable strength to hold back the Russians, Hitler's strategy made the division of Germany inevitable. Although most Germans had begun to realize that Anglo–American occupation was preferable to Soviet occupation, if for no other reason than the fact that the Germans did not fight a war of extermination and enslavement against the Western powers, Hitler's words and deeds strongly suggest that he preferred that Germany be defeated by the Russians. Toward the end of the war, Hitler even referred to Stalin as that "fellow of genius" for whom he had "unreserved respect."[6]

From the perspective of 1986, *it is important to remember that the*

Introduction

division of Germany was not the inevitable result of East-West rivalry, but of Hitler's conduct of the war. That Hitler's conduct was destructive of the vital interests of his own people was recognized by Albert Speer and other German leaders who sabotaged Hitler's scorched earth policies in the final months of the war. Nevertheless, having freely and overwhelmingly delegated to Hitler absolute leadership, the German people cannot even today escape the long-range consequences of their choice. The fact that people of the Federal Republic have proven to be reliable and steadfast NATO allies cannot obscure the fact that countless generations are often compelled to pay the price of a single generation's political and military folly. The price of military defeat is seldom paid in one installment or by one generation.

Ironically, Germany could easily have been Europe's dominant power today. All that was required in the 1930s was that she *refrain* from going to war. With her highly competent industries, universities and research facilities, her well-educated, skilled, and numerous population, as well as her central position in the heart of Europe, she was better equipped to profit from the technological revolutions of the twentieth century than any other European power. Unfortunately for Germany and the rest of the world, the patient moderation required for such a course of development was rejected for an unwinnable war of immeasurable destructiveness.

In his paper, Klaus Hornung, Professor Political Science at the University of Freiburg in the Federal Republic of Germany, reminds us that peace in Europe is inextricably linked with the still-unresolved question of German unity. He argues that "through the mere passage of time alone unrighteousness and force do not become international law. The acceptance of force, like the expulsion of Germans from their eastern provinces in 1945 or the massive military presence of the Soviet Union in East Germany, would mean sanctioning force as a means of international relations." Among the other consequences of Soviet power which Professor Hornung finds inadmissable are ". . . the expulsion of more than twelve million people from the eastern territories and the annexation of a third of the territory of the Reich of 1937, the refusal of the right of self-determination and of human rights for millions of Germans."

As chairman of the conference, I am grateful to Professor Hornung for the frank exposition of his views. I have little doubt that they reflect the opinions of a considerable number of Germans who currently support NATO and the Western alliance. Professor Hornung is also correct in insisting that the European settlement remains unstable absent a resolution of the German question. Nevertheless, Professor Hornung appears to underestimate the extent to which the reunification of a politically independent Germany could intensify the political instability of Europe and increase the hazards of the outbreak of nuclear war. The 1871 unification of Germany upset Europe's balance of power and eventually compelled Germany's neighbors to subordinate their differences of history, values, levels of economic development, and systems of government to the common project of containing the Reich's awesome power. The political system of Czarist Russia was almost as alien to the systems of Great Britain, France, and the United States during World War I as was that of Stalin during World War II. Nevertheless, in both wars these powers had no choice but to subordinate their differences to the common objective of containing German power.

There is obviously a conflict between Germany's ultimate national aspirations and those of her neighbors which tends to engender an element of tension in the Western alliance. Informed decision makers in England, France, Holland, Belgium, Italy, and perhaps the United States are no less apprehensive concerning the prospect of a reunified Germany than are those in Poland and the Soviet Union.

We are also indebted to Professor Hornung for the candor with which he links the question of German reunification to the question of the return of the territories annexed by Poland at the end of the war. Professor Hornung speaks for those Germans who do not accept the Oder-Neisse line as the permanent German-Polish border. Hornung reminds us that the Moscow and Warsaw treaties of 1970, which normalized relations between the Federal Republic and the USSR and Poland, respectively, committed the Federal Republic to renounce the use of force to change the current borders between it and the German Democratic Republic and Poland. Nevertheless, the treaties did not commit the Federal Republic to renounce other means of bringing about a border change. Characterizing the Oder-Neisse line as Stalin's "devilish plan" to divide Poles and Germans while binding Poland to the USSR, Hornung envisages the eventual peaceful return to a reunified Germany of the territories ceded to Poland at the end of the war. Hornung does not foresee the expulsion of the region's

Polish population after the return of the territories. He assures us that the Poles would enjoy ethnic minority rights in a "Europe of free peoples." It is clear that Poles would not willingly accept minority status in any German state. At the conference, Dr. Zdzislaw M. Rurarz, the former ambassador of Poland to Japan and a bitter opponent of the communist system, insisted that such proposals would only serve to cement the bonds between Poland and the Soviet Union. It is interesting to note that Hornung does not discuss the return to a reunified Germany of Soviet-occupied East Prussia, save to suggest that the leaders of the Soviet Union might someday conclude that their nation's security could best be served by a Soviet withdrawal.

One of the many reasons why Hornung's paper merits study is that he makes it clear that both the Federal Republic and the German Democratic Republic must be reckoned as revisionist states, albeit states which have foresworn the use of force to achieve their objectives, at least for the present. Hornung's paper expresses the aspirations of an influential sector of German public opinion. Nevertheless, it may contain both ahistorical and politically unrealistic elements. Hornung does not connect the mass expulsions of Germans from Eastern Europe and the truncation of German territory with (a) the aggressive war of enslavement and extermination Germany fought in the East and (b) the price any nation must pay for losing a war, especially the kind unleashed by Germany on June 22, 1941. After all, the expulsions and the seizure of German territory were preceded by an extraordinarily bitter history. The German writer Joachim Fest has alluded to that history in the following comment on Germany's war in the East:

> And for all that the campaign was strategically linked with the war as a whole, in its nature and it morality it signified something else entirely. It was so to speak the Third World War.[7]

In view of the kind of war fought by the German army as well as the SS in Eastern Europe, it is hardly surprising that those who were treated as subhuman were not prepared to tolerate the presence in their midst of ethnic Germans who had been entirely willing during the war to accept the role of Master Race in the East. Nor are those Europeans, both eastern and western, for whom the memory and the consequences of German aggression remain very much alive, likely to acquiesce in the reunification of Germany without credible guarantees that a reunified Germany will not replace the Soviet Union as the chief menace to continental peace. Hornung is, of course, sensitive to that issue. However, save for references to a future "Europe of free peoples," he does not spell out in practical terms how his vision can be implemented.

Nor is Hornung's characterization of the postwar fate of divided Germany as contrary to international law particularly cogent, save perhaps as rhetoric which may have a certain appeal to some Americans. A legal system is only functional if it is enforceable. Whatever may be the desirability of a superordinate institution capable of resolving conflicts between sovereign states in accordance with a mutually-agreed-upon, enforceable corpus of international law, no such institution or body of law currently exists. When states are unable to resolve conflicts by diplomatic negotiation, and the issues are crucial, they are likely to resolve them by force or the threat of force. After the defeat of the Third Reich in Eastern Europe, it was inevitable that the fate of Eastern Europe's ethnic Germans and the eastern frontiers of Germany would be determined by the victorious power. Nor can the Western allies be faulted for permitting the Soviets a free hand. They were not prepared to make war against Russia and had no credible means of limiting the exercise of Soviet power in areas occupied by the Soviet armed forces. And, to repeat, the western advance of the Soviet armies was facilitated by the delegated leader of the German people and the willingness of Germany's generals to follow him even after the suicidal consequences of such fidelity were clearly understood.

This is all history. Unfortunately, it is history too often forgotten in the West, which never experienced the kind of war the Germans unleashed in the East. It is further obscured by the distaste and distrust Americans rightly feel toward a communist regime which is the direct heir of the regime of Josef Stalin.

Because of illness, Professor Hornung was unable to attend the conference. His paper was read by Professor Hans-Martin Sass of Bochum University, Federal Republic of Germany, and the Kennedy Institute of Ethics, Georgetown University. In his response to Hornung, Professor Sass argues that the eventual political reunification of the Federal Republic of Germany and the German Democratic Republic in a single nation-state (*Nationalstaat*) is less important than the long-range viability and integrity of the German culture-nation (*Kulturnation*), whose cultural and linguistic boundaries exceed the limits of both states. Sass reminds us that the Germans never had a stable, permanent nation-state or a traditional capital city. Berlin only became a German, in contrast to a Prussian, capital in 1870 with the founding of Bismarck's Reich. Instead of political unification, Sass stresses what he regards as Germany's historic geopolitical role, that of "protecting and defending European (Germanic) Western values continuously against Eastern invasions." At the conference Sass's interpretation of Germany's role was shared by few, if any, of the other participants. Because of Poland's ancient Christian tradition as well as that nation's bitter historical experience with Germany, Dr. Rurarz took especial exception to Sass's characterization of Germany's role as that of a defender of European values against the East. Here again, Rurarz warned that the political consequence of the views of both Hornung and Sass could be to drive even anti-Communist Poles into the Soviet camp.

Taken together, the views of Hornung and Sass point up one of the most important stresses within the NATO alliance: *There is a very real difference between the way Germans perceive themselves and their geopolitical role and how they and their nation are perceived by the Western allies.* This is partially due to the difference between the essentially regional interests of the Federal Republic and the global interests of the American superpower. It is also due to the fact that the allies do not share a common history, especially in the twentieth century, and currently share only a limited number of common aspirations, the most important of which is the need for a common defense against the Warsaw Pact powers.

If the war in the East exceeded in barbarism anything ever experienced in Christian Europe, it cannot be said that Stalin was innocent of responsibility for the disasters. At the conference Alexander Shtromas, Professor of Politics and Contemporary History, University of Salford, Salford, England, put forth the thesis that in 1939 Stalin deliberately sought an alliance with the Third Reich for the purpose of unleashing war in the West.[8] Shtromas further argued that, while Stalin's part in unleashing the war was a long-term communist success, making possible the spead of communism in Eastern and Central Europe, it was an unqualified disaster for the *national* security of the USSR. Acording to Shtromas, a native of Lithuania and an authority on communism and the Soviet Union, communist victories were the only ones that mattered to the Soviet leader. For the sake of communism, Stalin had already caused the murder of millions of

Soviet citizens. Tens of millions of Soviet citizens have lost their lives as a result of the policies of their own government. No other state in history has ever initiated policies designed to eliminate as many of its own citizens as has the Soviet Union.[9]

Stalin and Hitler shared a common indifference to the fate of citizens of their respective countries. In the case of Stalin, it can be argued that his expulsion of more than twelve million ethnic Germans constituted a fate far less harsh than that which he meted out to millions of his own people. Americans trained to view the world through the perspective of a pragmatic, non-ideological liberalism find it difficult to believe that Stalin could deliberately have cooperated with Hitler in plunging Europe into war in spite of the hazards that venture entailed for his own people. Nevertheless, Shtromas' analysis of Stalin's motives is based on the historical record. It is perhaps even harder for most Americans trained in the liberal tradition really to credit Shtromas when he tells us that the most important lesson we must learn is never to mistake the Soviet Union for a normal state that gives priority to Russia's national interests and with whom normal international politics is possible. On the contrary, Shtromas warns us, the key to understanding Soviet policy is that Russian interests will always be subordinated to communist interests when the two conflict.

The defeat of the Third Reich involved the partial fulfillment of the Marxist dream of world revolution. Soviet-style communist regimes were installed in the East European satellite states and, of greatest importance, in East Germany. Shtromas described the process whereby the Soviet takeover of the Baltic states first took place in 1939–40. According to Shtromas, it was possible for members of the miniscule Baltic communist parties to establish effective state administrations by appointing their own members and fully-trusted supporters to office with the aid of some supervisory personnel imported from the Soviet Union. Shtromas further observed that the takeovers were facilitated by the fact that many highly regarded public officials belonging to parties of both the right and the left turned out to be crypto-communists. It is Shtromas' conviction that the crypto-communist phenomenon explains how it was possible to form functioning communist governments in countries with few known communists.

There is, however, a perfectly plausible alternative to Shtromas' "crypto communist" hypothesis, namely, sheer opportunism on the part of the formerly right-wing political leaders and bureaucrats. In the aftermath of the Soviet Union's victory in the most monumental war in all of Europe's history, many East Europeans of both the left and the right may have concluded that it was futile to fight the Soviet Union and, if and when the opportunity presented itself, to cooperate with the newly dominant power. It is also entirely probable that some formerly right-wing politicians found it prudent to read back into their own careers "hidden" evidence of previous communist sympathy. After all, if nations can rewrite their own histories, why not individuals? In East Germany, for example, the Soviet Union was usually less interested in hunting down former Nazis than in coopting them. Those with questionable records had a more powerful incentive to cooperate than those with unblemished records. Indeed, the career of Kurt Waldheim may be a case in point. It is difficult to believe that Waldheim's wartime record was unknown to Yugoslav and Soviet intelligence when he was first considered for the post of U.N. Secretary-General, yet neither communist power raised any objection to Waldheim's appointment. Is it not likely that the Soviet leadership felt that Waldheim could more easily be coopted than someone with a more principled record? In any event, Waldheim's U.N. career seems to have justified such a calculation.

The 1939–40 communist takeovers of the Baltic states were the first successful extensions of communist rule beyond the borders of the Soviet Union. According to Shtromas, the Sovietization of the Baltic states exemplifies the general *modus operandi* of a communist takeover. No matter how small the core of indigenous communists, when such a group is properly supported by the Soviet party and state, it can become a political force capable of seizing and exercising state power. The process, first tried successfully in the Baltic, has recently been repeated in Angola (1975), Ethiopia (1974–78), and Afghanistan (1978). Shtromas warned that the Soviet Union will continue to apply the same scheme whenever and wherever it can.

Shtromas concluded his study with a list of the treaties broken by the Soviet Union in the Baltic takeovers. He argued that the dreary account illustrates the USSR's attitude to treaty obligations. As long as there are credible restraints on the Soviet Union's international behavior, she will honor her treaty obligations. However, should a risk-free occasion arise for the expansion of Soviet power, she will not be deterred by treaty obligations. There is a clear warning to the West in Shtromas' presentation.

While Shtromas described the process whereby a Soviet-sponsored communist takeover occurs, Dr. Rurarz informs us of the economic consequences of such a takeover, specifically the takeover of Poland. Rurarz' account of the Polish economy from 1946 to 1986 makes depressing reading. It should be noted that Rurarz' account lacks the documentation normally expected of a scholarly paper. Nevertheless, Rurarz's paper has been included because he is an eyewitness of unique authority due to his long years of high-level service in the post-war Polish government. Rurarz describes how the Soviet Union treated communist-led Poland as a *de facto* enemy, dismantling and siezing the factories of her newly acquired Western territories, compelling Poland to sell coal, her principal export, to the Soviet Union at ten percent of the world price, forcing Poland to agree to the communist equivalent of the economically exploitative "unequal treaties" imposed by imperialist states on their client states in the latter decades of the nineteenth century. Whereas the United States gave the nations of Western Europe $12 billion under the Marshall Plan, thereby facilitating their return to economic independence, the Soviet Union took $14 billion from the nations of Eastern Europe while preventing them from accepting Marshall Plan aid. Rurarz also describes the stultifying effect on the Polish economy of Soviet strategic interests, a "nationalized economy," and an irresponsible, communist bureaucratic organization. To take but one example, ideological criteria barred the effective utilization of those Poles with entrepreneurial and managerial skills who might have made a real difference in the economic development of postwar Poland.

Moreover, Rurarz shows that the West is partly to blame for Poland's precarious economic condition. Communist economic policies had the effect of impoverishing Poland, but they were useful to the Soviet Union. A command economy is easier to control by a foreign occupier than a free-market economy. The Soviet Union had no interest in ameliorating the condition of the Polish economy. Instead, it encouraged the Polish government to seek loans from Western banks to foster growth and development. The Western credits had the temporary effect of bolstering an unworkable communist economy and further impoverishing the Polish people, hardly a prudent use of credit. Instead of long-term development, the loans yielded an economic crisis in which Poland had a hard currency indebtedness of $23 billion and found herself incapable of servicing her debt.

By the early 1980s, Poland was insolvent. Because of state control of the media, most Poles were unaware of the crisis. The regime had no interest in taking Solidarity's leadership into its confidence. Such a step could have led to a unified national effort to meet the crisis. Rurarz points out that the regime was more interested in creating an impression of chaos which could be blamed on Solidarity than in resolving the crisis.

Rurarz concludes with the observation that at present, martial law has plunged the country into a structural crisis from which there is no way out. In a period in which most West European and Pacific-rim nations have experienced significant development, Poland's current GNP is twenty percent below that of 1978. Faced with growing equipment obsolescence and the need to service a monumental foreign debt, the country is being pauperized. Still, Poland is not an economic liability to the Soviet Union. Weakened and internally divided, the country remains both a strategic asset and a target for large-scale imperialist exploitation. Rurarz warns that the Polish situation threatens to explode sooner or later. If it does, the ensuing disorder could affect all of Europe.

As P. Edward Haley observes in his conference paper, Soviet forces entered Europe as a result of the collapse of the European balance of power and the destruction of the Third Reich. Under the circumstances, the nations of Western Europe had little choice but to unite in alliance with the United States for their common defense. America's nuclear arsenal provided the only hope of countering the threat inherent in the westward projection of Soviet military power. In the first postwar decades, America's decisive nuclear superiority constituted a credible guarantee of Western Europe's security. The situation changed radically when the United States lost that superiority. Haley argues that the West's current Flexible Response strategy, which relies heavily on conventional strength and which removes as many theater nuclear weapons as possible from Europe, replacing them with longer-range, more secure systems, may meet expert approval yet endanger public support for the NATO alliance. According to Haley, even if the West could devise an effective military response, more is required. NATO needs political wisdom and leadership as much as improvements in the quality and quantity of its military forces. It is Haley's opinion that nuclear weapons have reached the limits of their deterrent effectiveness and that the problem of maintaining the peace has now become a question of faith and morale. The contest between East and West could be lost by a collapse of will, perhaps in the German Federal Republic, without employment of a single weapons system. While weapons systems continue to be indispensable to the defense of the West, they can of themselves no longer guarantee the peace and security of Europe.

Peter van den Dungen's paper echoes Edward Haley's conviction that the issues of resolve and political leadership have become central to the continued existence of NATO and the defense of the West. He argues that the nuclear debate has had a profound effect on some of Europe's political parties and that the consensus concerning fundamental aspects of national defense and security policy has broken down in a number of countries. In his view the growing influence of the anti-nuclear movement on the center-left parties spells trouble for the future. At the conference, Haley agreed with van den Dungen and warned that left-wing German nationalists allied to the peace movement are a long-term danger to the Federal Republic's continued participation in the Western alliance.[10] Indeed, there is a very strong anti-American element in the European peace movement.

Van den Dungen further warns against ignoring, belittling, or patronizing of the peace movement by Western governments. He does not exclude the possibility that the peace movement may "objectively" be an unwitting instrument of Soviet policy or that Soviet agents may have infiltrated the movement, an opinion strongly seconded by Rurarz. Nevertheless, he advocates a more conciliatory governmental tone towards the peace movement. According to van den Dungen, most Western governments can be faulted for both the manner and the substance of their response to the movement. He claims that the governments have failed to recognize the extent of their own populations' ignorance concerning the very real threat confronting the West. Far too many people, especially among the young, are unaware of the fact that NATO is the defender of a genuinely free world. Van den Dungen points to the need for large-scale political education. He also counsels moderating official American rhetoric concerning the East-West conflict, which he regards as distinctly counterproductive, especially among groups which must be won over if the Western Alliance is to remain viable.

Introduction

This writer has much sympathy with Professor van den Dungen's call for moderate, informed, and sophisticated political rhetoric. He agrees with van den Dungen on (a) the need to take the peace movement seriously and (b) the need for political education. Apprehensions expressed by the peace movement, such as the threat of a nuclear winter and the extinction of the human race, are matters of universal concern. Nevertheless, one must ask whether there are utopian elements in calls made by leaders of the peace movement for unilateral nuclear disarmament, a nuclear freeze, and even the abandonment of national sovereignty, that are refractory to any kind of realistic political education.[11] There is also the related question of whether some members of the peace movement may have contributed to the poisoning of political debate by the harsh manner in which they have characterized those who are convinced that the safety of the West demands both unrelenting military preparedness and an unwavering resolve to defend the vital interests of the West when challenged by the Soviet bloc.

Finally, there is the question of whether the threat to the human future posed by the use of nuclear weapons understandably fosters religious rather than political responses among the civilian population. The introduction of weapons capable of utterly destroying civilization must inevitably elicit apocalyptic feelings, especially in the United States, with its traditions of sectarian and post-millenial Christianity. Indeed, the situation of humanity in an era of nuclear weapons is potentially apocalyptic. Unfortunately, whether uttered by hawks or doves, the language of the apocalypse and the Manichean dichotomization of the world into the domain of the wholly righteous and the wholly evil is hardly conducive to either constructive political dialogue or the moderation of political rhetoric. I second Professor van den Dungen's appeal for both political education and moderate political rhetoric, Hopefully, the above questions will not be seen as objections, but, rather, illustrative of why van den Dungen's appeal requires an affirmative response.

In his conference paper, Armand Clesse, a citizen of Luxemberg who serves as Professor of Political Science at the University of the Saarland in the Federal Republic of Germany, stresses the conflicts of interest within the Western alliance. Clesse argues that the situation of NATO allies was radically altered in the late sixties when the United States lost its nuclear superiority and became vulnerable to Soviet strategic strikes. According to Clesse, NATO's credibility rests upon the unilateral pledge of the United States to defend its allies, if necessary, with nuclear weapons. As long as America was secure from a Soviet nuclear attack, its nuclear deterrent was credible. When the United States closed the weapons gap, much of the credibility of the American nuclear deterrent was lost. Should the Warsaw Pact powers launch an attack which cannot be stopped by conventional forces, America would be faced with the choice of nuclear retaliation, thereby creating a situation which could result in the mutual annihilation of both superpowers, or of outright capitulation. Clesse reviews the proposals put forth since the sixties to restore the credibility of the American deterrent. He concludes that all are flawed. According to Clesse, many observers believe that the United States could only protect its allies if she regained her invulnerability to a Soviet nuclear attack. Absent such invulnerability, the United States has lost the ability to meet the military commitment which is the very basis of NATO, namely, the ability to defend her allies by whatever means are necessary. Those who hold this view see the United States as having only the choice (a) of attempting to regain her lost strategic invulnerability, perhaps through some form of the Strategic Defense Initiative, or (b) of withdrawing from Europe altogether into a "Fortress America."

The dilemmas inherent in the American loss of power are understood by our European allies whose fears of abandonment have been reinforced by President Reagan's apparent endorsement of Mikhail Gorbachev's proposal for the elimination of all nuclear weapons during the Reykjavik summit. Clesse reviews the American attempts to alleviate European fear of decoupling and to find a way to share responsibility for the nuclear defense of America's European allies. Because of differences in history, geography, national interests, and national aspirations of the NATO allies, Clesse argues that satisfactory solutions to these problems continue to elude NATO. In his conclusion Clesse spells out a fundamental NATO weakness:

> A product of the Cold War, shaped by the feeling of unlimited American power, shaken by the experience of American vulnerability, NATO has never taken up the fundamental challenge raised by the existence of nuclear weapons in the hands of several partially antagonistic powers.

The loss of American nuclear superiority is also a matter of profound concern to Brig. Gen. Robert Richardson, USAF (Ret.).

Introduction

Richardson largely agrees with Clesse's analysis. According to Richardson, the United States is compelled at present either to accept permanent nuclear inferiority or to attempt to overtake the Soviet Union so that a Mutually Assured Destruction (MAD) deterrent strategy may regain credibility. Richardson rejects both alternatives. He sees MAD as a futile and immoral substitute for genuine strategy. MAD, he asserts, risks everything on deterrence. It gives the military the primary task of avenging a nuclear attack rather than defeating it. He sees the proper role of the military to be that of protecting the nation rather than engaging in suicidal revenge attacks.

Richardson looks to President Reagan's Strategic Defense Initiative (SDI) to provide the United States and its allies with a deterrent more credible than MAD. He envisages an environment in which the Soviet Union has or will soon have decisive superiority in offensive ballistic missile systems. Under the circumstances, European peace depends upon America's ability to retaliate effectively with strategic forces. Any diminution in America's retaliatory capability lessens the credibility of America's NATO commitment. Richardson is convinced that SDI will restore that credibility. The protection SDI offers the American public in case of nuclear exchange vastly enhances the American commitment to escalate, if such action be required. Richardson agrees with Clesse that, absent an effective defense against a Soviet strategic attack, an American nuclear retaliatory strike would be tantamount to national suicide.

Similarly, General Richardson argues that if the Soviet Union were to attempt to seize part or all of Western Europe by a sudden conventional attack, SDI would permit the United States to effectively counter the Soviet attempt at a *fait accompli*. With its SDI shield, a United States nuclear threat would be far more creidble than a situation in which the United States must sacrifice New York or Boston to avenge the seizure of Paris.

While General Richardson sees SDI as making possible the continued viability of NATO, Morton Kaplan, Professor of International Relations at the University of Chicago, argues that the postwar settlement is potentially unstable and is likely to unravel in a crisis. Reviewing United States-Soviet relations since 1945, Kaplan suggests three scenarios under which nuclear war might break out:

1. Although averse to undue risk taking, the Soviet Union does test the United States from time to time to ascertain whether a failure of American resolve might lead to a system change in its favor. Kaplan includes Nicaragua and Grenada among recent tests. Kaplan is concerned that the United States might initially fail a future Soviet test, emboldening the Soviet leadership to become overcommitted to a project which, upon reflection, American leaders realize is counter to the nation's vital interests. They would then feel compelled to defend American interests. Under such circumstances, an American defense would risk war with a Soviet Union too committed to retreat.

2. A crisis within the Soviet bloc might convince Soviet leadership that a show of strength or a minor victory over NATO could help it to survive. This could lead to NATO resistance and the outbreak of war. Kaplan sees the Finlandization of Europe as a possible outcome of this scenario.

3. The most dangerous scenario would be the outbreak of a conventional war. Kaplan argues that the losing side would not accept defeat without resorting to nuclear weapons.

Kaplan argues that the threat of nuclear war will exist as long as American and Soviet forces confront each other in the heart of Europe. To overcome this danger, Kaplan advocates that the United States propose a thoroughgoing reconstitution of the World War II settlement in which both the United States and the Soviet Union voluntarily withdraw their forces from Europe. If the Soviet leadership should reject the proposal, the onus for a continuation of present tensions would rest with them. Kaplan advocates that initially both the United States and the Soviet Union massively reduce their European forces. Thereafter, American forces would leave Europe altogether and Soviet forces retire behind the Urals, save for sufficient forces to guard the Soviet frontier. Kaplan argues that both sides would still possess nuclear arsenals and the power to defend their vital interests. Superpower withdrawal would permit a genuinely independent Europe to come into being. The peaceful reunification of Germany would be a possible though not a necessary consequence of the new situation.

It is interesting to compare Kaplan's proposals with Hornung's. Although Hornung does not explicitly state that he looks forward to superpower withdrawal, one must ask how the reunification of Germany and the return of the Oder-Neisse region could take place without it. As noted, Hornung envisages a peaceful process of reunification and territorial restoration. It is, however, difficult to see how Poland could accept a further territorial truncation without a struggle, since the Soviet Union is hardly likely to return the territory seized from Poland at the end of World War II. Although Kaplan regards superpower withdrawal as enhancing the possibility of long-range peace in Europe, withdrawal could lead to a power vacuum and a period of multiple wars among states determined to redefine their borders. Moreover, a genuine United States-Soviet withdrawal could lead to a power vacuum that an independent, unified Germany would probably fill. The European balance of power would once again be changed, as it was in 1871, with little reason to believe that the new Germany would be a greater force for continental stability than it was from 1871 to 1945. In reality, the Soviet Union is hardly likely to agree to any withdrawal of its forces which would lead to a reconstitution of German power.

Whether or not Kaplan's proposals are feasible may be of less importance than the fact that a scholar of his authority and broad international experience feels compelled to set them forth. In reality, the underlying theme of both Kaplan's and Richardson's papers, as well as those of many of the other conferees, is that the current situation is precarious in the extreme. Whereas Richardson looks forward a decade or more to a time when a future technology might give the present settlement a further lease on life, Kaplan is less persuaded that the present settlement can be maintained.

The economic consequences of World War II and the European settlement are discussed by Gordon Bjork, Professor of Economics at Claremont-McKenna College. Bjork points to the internationalization of trade and commerce as the most important single economic development of the postwar period. According to Bjork, this has not been an unmixed blessing for the United States. The gains from international interdependence have been diffused throughout the entire American economy, while the losses have been concentrated in small, powerful groups such as the smokestack industries of the Northeast and the Midwest. Moreover, insofar as there has been economic unification of the Western nations, it has been due to the multinational corporations rather than as a consequence of government action. As a result, we find ourselves in a situation of international interdependence without adequate governmental institutions for sharing defense burdens or reconciling the conflicting economic interests of the Western allies which both reflect and intensify their conflicting political interests.

Bjork sees no fully satisfactory resolution of inter-allied economic tensions. He counsels a policy of incremental improvements in which both governments and responsible multinationals seek ways to promote international trade, stabilize financial flows, and protect the intangible capital embodied in science, technology, and organizational knowledge from unfair competition. Bjork is especially concerned that we avoid simplistic ideological platforms such as "free trade."

The final conference paper was presented by Leo Sandon, Professor of Religion and Director of the American Studies Program at Florida State University. Unlike the other participants, who were primarily concerned with European consequences of the postwar settlement, Sandon focused on the moral and religious values that have historically motivated American action in the arena of international affairs. According to Sandon,

> Americans have no real affinity for mere balance-of-power politics. We have always insisted on the moralizing of the imperial enterprise. . . . Power is always more closely related to values than realists sometimes realize, and Americans characteristically have believed that intervention must be morally justified. That is precisely the reason American leaders have consistently resorted to moral interpretations of imperial policy.

As the title of his paper suggests, Sandon insists that the moralizing of foreign policy is the single most important condition for continued acceptance of a superpower role by the American people. He acknowledges that such moralizing is likely to appear hypocritical and/or unrealistic to most other nations. Nevertheless, America's religious heritage, largely rooted in sectarian Protestantism, precludes popular support for foreign policy efforts based solely on morally neutral calculations of national power. Moreover, Sandon is convinced that ultimately a morally motivated foreign policy will prove to be the most realistic American policy.

Undoubtedly, an important reason for the Vietnam failure was the absence of a national consensus that important moral issues were at stake. Ignoring Hanoi's viciously totalitarian political system, a very large sector of American opinion preferred to see that regime as engaged in an anti-colonial struggle for national liberation. By contrast, an American consensus continues to exist for the support of NATO because of the obvious moral difference between the political systems of all members of the Western alliance and the Soviet-dominated system of the Warsaw Pact nations.

Rejecting "realism" and "neo-isolationism" as foreign policy options, Sandon argues for a "neo-interventionist" American foreign policy. He sees food and freedom as the values for which Americans should exercise power in the eighties. In a world in which hunger threatens large sectors of the developing countries, the production and distribution of food, humanity's basic requirement, is an activity in which the United States can clearly demonstrate the superiority of its system. Sandon further argues that the defense and fostering of freedom, wherever possible, must be the central value component of American interventionism. No other value so clearly distinguishes the Western world from the Soviet bloc. Moreover, no other value is as dependent upon the prudent, worldwide exercise of American power.

We began our discussion with the observation that World War II was destined to yield a tragic, problematic, and dangerous "peace," even if the Western powers were victorious. The conference papers and discussion offered no reason to alter that judgment. No matter which side emerged victorious, World War II was destined to result in the unprecedented enhancement of the power of one of the two most aggressively totalitarian regimes the world has ever known, Nazi Germany and Stalinist Russia. Such a development was in turn bound effectively to shape the character of the "peace" that followed.

During World War II, the American public was presented with an overly optimistic picture of the kind of felicitous postwar world they could expect. The postwar world has largely exceeded the economic and technological expectations of most Americans living at the time. Nevertheless, few Americans had any idea that it would be impossible for their nation to emerge victorious without the simultaneous emergence of a victorious totalitarian power. Nor were there many, even in the military, who understood that even in victory America would soon be compelled to live under the continuous threat of total nuclear destruction.

One can hardly fault the average American for lacking realism about the postwar world when the President of the United States, Franklin Delano Roosevelt, was hopelessly naive in his dealings with Josef Stalin. During the war Stalin predicted that the wartime unity of the Allies would give way to postwar conflict. Stalin had fewer illusions about what lay ahead than did Roosevelt, who appears to have had almost no realistic understanding of the character of Stalin's rule. Once attacked, the United States had no choice but to fight the war against the common foe as an ally of the Soviet Union. Admittedly, hindsight is cheap wisdom. Nevertheless, the long-term interests of the United States would have been better served had its leaders possessed a more realistic understanding of the consequences of the destruction of German power in the heart of Europe, the nature of Stalinist Communism, and the degree to which America's postwar European policy would, of necessity, conflict with that of the Soviet Union. It is unlikely that the postwar settlement would have been any less precarious, but intelligent Americans might have been better prepared for the awesome dangers of a world in which, willy-nilly, the United States succeeded Germany in defining the limits of the westward expansion of the Soviet empire and in which that empire became equal or superior to the United States in strategic nuclear capability.

NOTES

1. See Karl Dietrich Bracher, *The German Dictatorship: The Origins, Structure and Effects of National Socialism,* trans. Jean Steinberg (New York: Praeger Publishers, 1973), pp. 400–09.

2. Albert Speer, *Inside the Third Reich,* trans. Richard and Clara Winston (New York: The MacMillan Company, 1970), p. 440.

3. See A.J. Ryder, *Twentieth-Century Germany from Bismarck to Brandt* (New York: Columbia University Press, 1973), pp. 180–184.

4. Sebastian Hafner, *The Meaning of Hitler,* trans. Ewald Osers (Cambridge, Mass.: Harvard University Press, 1983), p. 151.

5. See Joachim C. Fest, *Hitler,* trans. Richard and Clara Winston (New York: Vintage Books, 1975), pp. 721–23.

6. See Henry Picker, ed., *Hitlers Tischgespräche im Führer Hauptquartier 1941–42,* (Bonn: 1951), pp. 376, 468.

7. Fest p. 648.

8. Alexander Shtromas' paper has been published as an independent monograph, under the title, *The Nazi-Soviet Alliance and the Fate of the Baltic States (1939–1941)*. (Washington: The Washington Institute for Values in Public Policy, 1986.)

9. See Richard Grenier, "The Horror, The Horror," in *The New Republic* (May 26, 1982), pp. 28–29; Robert Conquest, *The Great Terror: Stalin's Purge of the Thirties,* (Harmondsworth, Middlesex: Penguin Books, 1974), pp. 699–713; Gil Eliot, *The Twentieth Century Book of the Dead* (New York: Charles Scribner's Sons, 1972), pp. 218ff.

10. On the German peace movement, NATO and German nationalism, see Kim R. Holmes, *The West German Peace Movement and the National Movement* (Cambridge, Mass.: Institute for Foreign Policy Analysis, 1984).

11. For an especially utopian expression of the aims of the peace movement see Jonathan Schell, *The Fate of the Earth* (New York: Alfred A. Knopf, 1983).

Is the Postwar Settlement Still Viable?

MORTON A. KAPLAN

I believe that the postwar settlement that emerged from World War II and that is represented by Sir Winston Churchill's metaphor of the iron curtain is now potentially unstable, particularly during a crisis. There is undoubtedly some evidence to the contrary. The riots over the installation of the Pershing IIs have faded and the charge that the division of Europe—and in particular the division of Germany—rests equally on the United States and the Soviet Union, if still asserted by some, at least is not asserted by the political leaders of our NATO partners. However, the fading of the protests over the Pershing IIs, for instance, does not necessarily foreshadow what may occur during a crisis if they become visible attractive targets.

Furthermore, as time passes, statesmen will come into office for whom—and particularly for whose younger supporters—the events of the 1940s and the 1950s that clarified the need for NATO fail to be appreciated. We will not then be able to count on the resolute and united support that is needed to sustain our joint interests during a crisis if we do not now formulate and pursue policies that respond to contemporary understandings of the state of world politics and that clarify favorably the real goals of American policy as well as the actual latitude for alternative policies that the state of the world permits. Even if we believe that our critics are on the whole mistaken, despite sometimes-warranted criticisms of particular policies, the art of statecraft requires that we take even mistaken beliefs into account when formulating policies. And perhaps occasionally these criticisms may represent legitimate interests that differ from ours and that we have failed adequately to consider because of our undoubtedly justified preoccupation with the dangers involved in the conflict between NATO and the Warsaw Treaty Organization.

I shall soon attempt to show why this shift in underlying

outlooks has occurred and then suggest how to formulate policies that respond to these conditions. However, a brief personal note may help others to understand my own perspective on these matters.

It is difficult to believe that forty years have passed since I sat on a hill in Saipan and listened to General Marshall's declaration of Germany's surrender. The young man that I was, whose thoughts I can only barely recapture, had gone through dire poverty during the Great Depression and had served, and for nearly a year more would continue to serve, as an enlisted soldier in the American army. I do remember the spirit of optimism with which I approached the world that would emerge from the war, an optimism that has not been shaken by the disasters or the blunders in policy that have occurred in the intervening years. I believed that there were no problems that we could not cope with if we had both the will and the honesty to deal with them.

I retain that optimism, but one additional quality is gravely needed—imagination, a quality that has not been present since the Marshall Plan and NATO were formulated. The type of incremental decision making that serves so effectively more often than not in domestic politics rarely works in international politics, particularly with respect to the most important problems that face us.

I remember running to friends in the Kennedy administration in 1961 and telling them that Vietnam was going to be one of the greatest problems with which they would have to deal and that they could follow either of two courses: get out before they were committed, or do the job right, which would have involved a threat against the North and internal reform in South Vietnam. I preferred the latter alternative but felt that a responsible government would also consider the reform. There was one line of policy that I believed they must not adopt, one that would get them into a dreadful morass if they did, namely, getting involved in a series of escalatory moves. As one of the contributors to the then-young theory of nuclear deterrence, I was fully aware that Vietnam was not a place in which deterrence by small steps would work. Although it is not certain that incremental policy in Europe will fail—and this does distinguish United States policy toward Europe from the case of Vietnam—failure there risks a far greater catastrophe than did failure in Vietnam; and such failure is quite possible, although not foreordained.

The Postwar Settlement

By briefly reviewing the state of affairs that emerged from World War II and examining how that state of affairs led to the initial postwar settlement, I shall now attempt to convey the kinds of considerations that I believe should be taken into account in rethinking our European policies. I will then indicate those factors that have changed sufficiently so that broad new policy lines are mandated allowing us to support with assurance either a new acceptable settlement or a reinforcement of the existing one.

The first thing to understand about postwar Europe is that the United States and the Soviet Union approached the war settlement with concepts that were so dramatically opposed that it is unlikely that either understood the other. The United States saw the war as an outgrowth of fascist aggression. Fascist systems, many American leaders believed, were based upon the combination of a totalitarian party, an industrial elite, and a clique of generals. These fascist regimes arose in societies that had a natural tendency toward fascism as a consequence of historical and sociological conditions. Peace would be kept by remaking these fascist powers into democracies and by maintaining the victorious wartime alliance within the United Nations, a new international organization, to make sure that the defeated states would never again be able to pursue their aggressive paths. (I shall not spell out the simplistic misunderstandings that were represented in these beliefs.)

The veto they would have in the Security Council of the United Nations—which alone would have enforcement powers—would assure each of the big four powers that the organization could not be used against its vital interests, while the enforcement procedures of Chapter VII of the UN Charter would enable them to halt or to limit wars among the smaller powers which otherwise might, like the Balkan wars that had escalated into World War I, produce major war.

The UN, we believed, had a more realistic rationale than did the failed League of Nations. The presumed realism of the United Nations was reflected in the aforementioned powers of the Security Council and also in the fact that the powers of the new organization were to be more circumscribed than those of the League. For instance, the United Nations was not supposed to have authority to interfere in matters that were partly within the

3

domestic jurisdiction of the member nations. Furthermore, the United Nations Charter would not be tied to the peace treaties and, thus, would permit peaceful change. Although the United States did not intend the General Assembly to be more than a forum for discussion, and although the Soviet Union resisted even this modest authority for the smaller nations in the General Assembly, the United States did believe in a world in which all independent nations would play autonomous and responsible roles.

That the Soviet Union acted in ways that appeared inconsistent with this new image of world politics was attributed to the Soviet Union's historical experience and subsequent fear of external attack. These fears were to be assuaged over time by the conduct of postwar diplomacy.

The Soviet Union did have fears and security interests. Stalin did see the United States as an economic giant whose productive capacity could be used to defeat the Soviet Union. However, Stalin's view of the world differed so much from that of the Western nations that his objectives could not be brought within the same framework. Although Stalin likely did believe that capitalism would lead to disputes, probably even wars, among the Western powers, and also with the Soviet Union, he saw no more need for autonomy in other states than he did for an autonomous Communist Party in the Soviet Union. Rule was secured by power. The more power, the more secure the rule. Foreigners were to be distrusted, and especially foreign Communists.

While Russia was weak, Stalin intended to consolidate Soviet control in as much of Eastern Europe as he could get without provoking war with the United States. He was prepared to recognize an American sphere of interest in Western Europe, at least, as he told the Yugoslav leadership, for the "twenty years" that were necessary for Russia to regain its economic, and hence its military strength. Until then, he was not prepared to challenge the United States in its sphere.

The Russian control of Eastern Europe would be insulated from American influence while Western Europe would be divided politically and, in any event, would not have space for defense. This was part of Stalin's strategy of "divide and conquer." We know from Yugoslav documents that Stalin had even used that phrase. In any event, no student of Stalin's policies could mistake his mastery of the technique. He had applied it inside the Soviet Union to the Communist Party, to the secret police, and to every other segment of Soviet society. In Eastern Europe, he played the Communists who had been in exile in the West against the underground resistance Communists and against the Communists who had spent their exile in Moscow. Stalin's inability to follow this procedure in either Yugoslavia or China was a key factor in explaining their ability to break away from the Soviet bloc. Stalin most likely intended eventually to use similar tactics in Western Europe to achieve Soviet hegemony. He would use politics, including the efforts of indigenous Communist parties, to divide the Western European nations from each other and from the United States.

However, even if one doubts my explanation of Stalin's attitudes and expectations, the situation in Europe mandated an eventual cold war. Perhaps the excessive fears of that period could have been avoided, but not the basic conflict of interests. The fact is that except for Czechoslovakia, where the Communist Party had the support of 38 percent of the electorate until the programs mandated at the first Cominform meeting began to erode its popularity, Communist rule in Eastern Europe would have been fragile if democratic voting had been permitted. Because Stalin was in no position to gain popularity by assisting the economies of Eastern Europe—it was the Cominform decision to increase capital goods production that threatened the Communist position in Czechoslovakia—Eastern Europe might have swung into the American orbit unless Stalin had used the power of the Red Army and Communist control of the Ministries of the Interior to support the imposition of unimpeded Communist Party rule in the satellites. On the other hand, the power of the Communist parties in France and Italy threatened the independence of the Western periphery of Europe. Thus, rather than being allies in keeping down the former fascist powers, Germany and Italy, the United States and the Soviet Union were rivals that had the most to fear from each other.

It was this set of circumstances that mandated the policies of consolidation—by political control in the East and by economic assistance in the West—that put the United States and the Soviet Union at odds and that created the exaggerated fear of immediate war in both camps, for consolidation of power could look like the first step toward the forcible extension of power. These circumstances also mandated the division of Germany and the eventual emergence of two German states. It was also these policies that led first to the Brussels pact and then to NATO on the one side, and first to bilateral military treaties and then to the Warsaw Treaty Organization on the other.

In the United States, we have come to think of this situation, in which two armed blocs confront each other in Europe, as natural, or at least as so obviously necessary as not to need explanation or defense. But we need to recognize that a situation that looks so natural to us is quite uncongenial to those Europeans whose hopes and interests are affected by it.

Strains in the Postwar Settlement

When the French shifted their policy on Germany from one of keeping it repressed to one that even permitted some degree of economic expansion, the French foreign minister, Georges Bidault, told a committee of the French parliament that this unnatural state of affairs would not last forever, that it was produced by the Cold War, which, he said, resulted from the Marshall Plan, and that some day France would be able to revert to its old policies. There was great turmoil in France over the proposed European defense force and the eventual re-establishment of German armed forces. The Germans, on the other hand, were told repeatedly that American policies would lead to the reunification of Germany, a promise that we could not, and probably did not intend to, keep.

In Eastern Europe, Stalin was finding nationalists under every bed. Apart from Czechoslovakia and Bulgaria, Russia was not particularly popular in Eastern Europe. In Poland, for instance, Soviet interests were protected only by the fact that the Poles feared the Germans even more than the Russians, a condition that resulted primarily from the territorial changes of World War II that Stalin wisely, from a Russian standpoint, insisted upon.

There was little recognition of these facts in the United States, even as late as the mid-1950s. This is indicated by the in-house reviewer's response to the initial draft of *United States Foreign Policy: 1945–1955*. The Brookings Institution sent the book to more than twenty reviewers, each of whom said the book was excellent, except for the fact that it made the clearly incorrect claim that great strains were occurring both in NATO and in the Soviet bloc. After I left the project to spend a year at the Center for Advanced Study in the Behavioral Sciences, much of the material emphasizing these strains was later removed, at the insistence of the president of Brookings by my former colleagues. Ironically, the book was published in September, 1956, only a month before the Hungarian uprisings, an event whose massiveness surpassed the original assessment.

By October, 1956, no observer could have missed the strains in the Soviet bloc. The Hungarian revolt could be put down only by a Soviet invasion. Khruschev was forced to accept Gomulka as the Polish Communist Party boss after a coup within the Party, for otherwise, as he was threatened at the airport, Polish divisions would fight the invading Russian forces.

We began to be aware of divisions within NATO after General de Gaulle came to power in France, although we intended to attribute his policies to an overweening pride. We failed to recognize the legitimacy of de Gaulle's complaint that the United States might not use nuclear weapons in defense of France now that the Soviet Union also had nuclear weapons and missile delivery systems. We failed also to recognize the desirability of serious negotiations in response to his demand that there be a directorate for controlling the use of these weapons in Europe. Nor did we really understand the driving motivation behind de Gaulle's desire to build a "Europe from the Atlantic to the Urals." France's policies, we believed, were aberrations that would not survive de Gaulle. Furthermore, Germany had rallied strongly behind the United States, a factor that we believed, not entirely incorrectly, would force future French governments to recant the most extreme versions of de Gaulle's policies. The Berlin blockade was only a decade behind us. Moreover, Khruschev's forays against Berlin and his blunt threat that Germany could be reduced to dust by four fusion weapons rallied the fearful Germans, and also other Europeans, behind the American banner. This was the situation that enabled John Kennedy in Berlin in 1961 to state, "Ich bin ein Berliner."

Political threats to NATO's unity, at least in that period, were still only small ripples on the surface. A period of great economic advance was under way. Even the Italian economy was emerging from backwardness. Domestic political and economic satisfaction, combined with seemingly overt Soviet threat, seemed to presage an indefinite continuation of the existing international order.

Similar phenomena were occurring in the Russian sphere of influence. The Russians were no longer exploiting the Eastern

Europeans and were even assisting them in certain respects. The governments of Eastern Europe at least had a negative consensus behind them because the conditions of life were improving and, in the aftermath of the events of 1956, there was recognition that agitation for change would be dealt with harshly and that the United States would not come to the rescue.

Despite de Gaulle's removal of France from the NATO chain of command, the two blocs were in a period of political consolidation, particularly given the momentum towards a modest European common market. This was going on despite the Berlin crises and the Cuban missile crisis, an illustration of the fact that opinions and beliefs, and sometimes policies, more often follow than precede changes in factual situations.

The world was ripe for detente; and it is no accident that it occurred in this period. At this time there was no opportunity for either bloc to break through the defenses of the other, no situations of turmoil that could be exploited drastically to change the European order. Even the disturbances of 1968 in France were too momentary to permit exploitation. Detente existed because the common interests of the United States and the Soviet Union overwhelmed their differences. Moreover, after his initial adventurism, Khruschev thrived on the naive belief that the Soviet Union would soon surpass the United States in economic production. The Russian economic model was still attractive in much of the world. And the Japanese, Korean, and Taiwan examples had not yet been sufficiently noted, let alone digested.

But little-noticed undercurrents were already in motion. By the 1970s the ground was set for *Ostpolitik* in Germany. This policy was initially opposed by the Christian Democrats, but it appeals so deeply to the sentiments of the Germans that the government of Prime Minister Kohl is still pursuing it vigorously. The effects of the oil shocks of 1973 and the failure of the Russian economic model were soon to have impact. The failure of the United States in Vietnam would cast considerable doubt both on the good judgment of the American government and its political will to carry out its policies. As at least one important Russian scholar put it, "I will never be able to understand why the United States went into Vietnam if it did not intend to win." And we were soon to see Soviet moves into South Yemen and, via Cuban proxies, into Angola, the Caribbean and Central America.

A number of things had been going on simultaneously. The

Soviet Union had become a global military power and was in a position to challenge the United States at great distances from its borders. Of course, some of these challenges were tentative and operated through proxies. But the European theater was being affected by the diversion of the resources of a weakened United States. At the same time, serious inflation occurred after the oil shocks of 1973. This hit hard both in the Western and Soviet spheres. It was one of the factors that helped to produce conditions in Poland during the spring of 1979. It also put enormous internal pressure on the Soviet Union, which, considering its huge military budget, was faced with a shortage of resources. Life expectancy in the Soviet Union was declining and infant mortality was rising rapidly; and drunkenness, industrial sabotage, and corruption were becoming endemic.

In the West, new generations were coming to power that had no memories of World War II or of the significant events that followed. Many Germans remembered the Berlin blockade only as ancient history. The Soviet Union was seen as a satisfied power that would not risk war. And a new nationalism was on the upswing (as was also the case in Japan) that failed to comprehend the need for the postwar European settlement and that blamed it equally (at best) on the United States and the Soviet Union.

The "Greens" in Germany are merely the tip of the iceburg. If overkill exists and nuclear winter threatens, as many intellectuals believe, then what security is provided by Pershing IIs or cruise missiles? These are seen merely as attractive visible targets to a population that feels threatened rather than protected by them. An attitude is spreading that is reminiscent of what Franklin Roosevelt said to business and labor: "A pox upon both your houses."

The rhetoric of Ronald Reagan and of Alexander Haig in the first years of the Reagan administration reinforced these attitudes. They created the appearance of an administration so hostile to the Soviet Union that it was unable to reach any agreements with them, and one so reckless that it might even be attempting to send the Soviet Union into a crisis.

In the Central American and Caribbean campaigns, the United States is seen by many Europeans merely as a big bully that is trying to impose its will in this area, like the Soviet Union in Afghanistan. The public is almost totally ignorant of the documents seized in Grenada demonstrating that even the assassinated Maurice Bishop was a dedicated Marxist-Leninist whose apparent initial pluralism, on Cuban advice, was, in his own words to the Grenadan politburo, merely a fiction designed to avoid a pretext for American intervention while the New Jewel leadership gradually transformed the Grenadan political system into one similar to that of the Soviet Union. The documents reinforce the belief that the Nicaraguan government is on the same path. They show the interest of Cuba, Grenada, and Nicaragua in spreading revolution, a position that elsewhere is candidly and publicly aserted by Tomas Borge, the Nicaraguan Minister of the Interior, a post that in Communist countries puts him at the levers of tremendous physical power. Thus, the captured Grenadan documents strongly support the inference that a campaign is in process designed to produce Communist domination of the Caribbean exits, the chokepoints that control the bulk of American marine traffic with Europe and much of its Atlantic naval capabilities.

This inference is reinforced by testimony from captured and defecting guerrillas concerning Cuban direction of Central American guerrilla campaigns from Cuban and Nicaraguan centers with occasional direct, although secret, participation by Russian generals. Given the low Soviet propensity for risk taking, these activities by the Communists are merely targets of opportunity that will not be strongly defended except by disinformation and political warfare. So far, however, this has been managed with consummate success. The United States is widely regarded, even at home, as obsessed by "the red menace" in tiny and distant countries, foolishly neglectful of opportunities to encourage supposedly more moderate factions among the guerrillas, indifferent to international law and guilty of bullying.

Suggestions that our relations with Latin Leninists might some day parallel those with the Chinese are inapt on several grounds. In the first place, even if true, by then irreversible defeats may have occurred in Europe and Asia. In the second place, China has a long border and severe strategic conflicts with the Soviet Union. Latin radicals see the United States as a threat for historical reasons. They also are frustrated by our economic and cultural dominance. Our role as their "enemy" is not one that our policies can change as long as they have undisturbed control in their countries. For this reason, the Soviet Union will remain their "natural" ally, a fact that has little or nothing to do with improvement in internal standards of life.

Few in Europe, even among the political elite, understand the vital importance to the defense of Western Europe of keeping the Soviets out of the Caribbean, beyond what they already have in Cuba. Indeed, the evidence seems clear that even a majority in the American Congress does not understand this relationship.

Thus, in addition to the serious situation inside Eastern Europe, which threatens Soviet legitimacy and which, for reasons I shall soon discuss, demands increased Soviet external power, natural tendencies to erode the solidarity of NATO are accompanied by suspicion and distrust of the United States in Western Europe.

Furthermore, the recent agreement by the United States to meet with the Soviet Union every six months for nuclear non-proliferation discussions will exacerbate the fissiparous tendencies in NATO. Most Germans (and most Japanese) are aware that Soviet non-proliferation activities are designed primarily, although not exclusively, to prevent Germany (and Japan) from acquiring nuclear weapons. Even those Germans who are thoroughly opposed to Germany's going nuclear will eventually be gravely offended by this, particularly if their noses are rubbed into it every six months.

I remember that when the nuclear non-proliferation treaty was being ratified and while Germany was being pressed by the United States to sign it, a distinguished German physicist, Goethe Prize-winner Carl von Wiezacker, who had been in the forefront of numerous peace campaigns, protested this treaty on the grounds, that as he put it (although surely he knew better), the treaty would interfere with German use of peaceful nuclear power. In the same period, the Netherlands ambassador to the United States, gave a luncheon talk at the University of Chicago in which he vigorously supported the then-pending nuclear non-proliferation treaty. I asked him whether he really believed that the proposed treaty was fully acceptable. His response was that, while he did not, he was saying what he believed Americans wanted to hear. Then he told me about an Indian official who had indignantly asked him what he thought the Americans believed. Did they believe that they could be trusted to handle nuclear weapons but that the Indians could not? We have a tendency to expect people to tell us what we want to hear and not to probe for opinions that lie beneath the surface.

The Soviet Regime and Its Aims

Before discussing what I think ought to be done, I should like to consider what I believe to be the actual nature of the Soviet regime and the character of its aims. I shall then discuss where I believe the danger of war lies.

The Soviet regime, in my opinion, is an ossified bureaucratic imperialist regime dominated by a Party elite that is closely allied to a military elite. That characterization virtually coincides with Joseph Schumpeter's definition of imperialism and is a better example of the genre than were the Egyptian or Assyrian empires to which he made reference.

Unlike Schumpeter, who saw such regimes as inherently expansionistic, I think Soviet expansionism occurs for other reasons. The regime is based upon a Nomenclatura whose members occupy the chief positions in the system, while their children have similar preferential access to education and position. Although the Soviet Union is enormously more powerful than in Stalin's days, a major motivation of its leaders, I believe, is to maintain their privileged positions. In Stalin's days, Russia was weak and also fearful of external attack because Stalin attributed to the West motives that were similar to his. The current Soviet regime is not fearful for those reasons now, although it is for other reasons. It is more willing than the Stalin's regime to risk its prerequsites recklessly. Khruschev was an aberration, and his adventurousness was one of the factors that led to his removal. To this extent, those Europeans who believe that the Soviet Union has no interest in a war in Europe are correct. But they miss important factors in the equation.

Every regime requires some degree of legitimacy to survive. In the Soviet case, the leaders do not claim to have been appointed by God. Nor does anyone believe that elections in the Soviet Union reflect popular choice. For a period of time, the Soviet economic model appeared to be working, and it conferred some legitimacy upon the Soviet regime. The figleaf has been removed and the legitimacy of the regime as the correct interpreter of Marxist-Leninist doctrine is now merely rhetoric, although important rhetoric, for if it were challenged openly and publicly the regime would be in desperate trouble. However, one type of legitimacy remains. The Soviet Union is extremely powerful in a military sense; it is recognized as one of the two most powerful nations in the world. Meager though his lot may be and miserable his life, the Russian peasant takes enormous pride in this, for the ordinary Russian is patriotic. Moreover, the ordinary Russian wants peace, and Soviet strength is viewed as a guarantee of peace.

Is the Postwar Settlement Still Viable?

Buried in the Russian psyche is a constant fear of invasion that stems from a history going back to the Tatars and the Mongols, and coming forward to the Swedes and Napoleon and Hitler. Peace and security are associated with authority and control. Anarchy threatens this, and the Russian citizen expects his government to put down disturbances on the border that might spread into the Soviet Union. He may resent the economic aid that is sent abroad, particularly during these harsh times, but he does not resent the military control exercised by the Soviet Union.

The legitimacy of the Soviet regime, I believe, rests upon the power that it can make manifest to the Russian public. This, I believe, is one reason why the Soviet Union cannot make those prudent border compromises with the Chinese or that prudent cession of the northern islands to Japan that would cost virtually nothing in terms of strategic or economic importance. Although the Russians can understand retreat under pressure during war, such a retreat in peacetime might well be seen as failure of will, particularly given the claims the Soviet Union makes about its military might, and hence a possible stimulus to enemies to rupture peace.

The burden on the Soviet leadership is not one of merely avoiding retreats. It must demonstrate its power by making positive gains that can be appreciated by supporting groups in the Party, and that will convince the masses of the inevitability of continued Communist rule. Periods in which gains are consolidated are well understood by the leadership. Even retreat under enormous external pressure can be understood. But a failure to strive for possible gains, whether by attempting to fragment unity and resolution among adversaries or by extending logistic facilities, bases, and alliances, can be neither understood nor accepted by important Party circles. Contenders for power in Soviet ruling circles must justify a failure to achieve gains and show that they have pressed to the limits, short of a degree of adventurousness that threatens war. This will apply to the negotiation of treaties, to the violation of treaties already signed, to extensions of influence, and also to the extension of physical power.

If the Soviet leadership is seen by ordinary Russians as lacking will, then it will also be seen by them as inviting anarchy. Anarchy would be extremely threatening to the Russian masses, who live in unholy fear of the Chinese on their border despite the lack of effective Chinese offensive power. It is a fear that is also shared by the elite, which may be even more worried by the secret Sufi sects in its Moslem areas.

Even if to a great extent Marxism is merely necessary rhetoric for the Soviets, there are certain elements of Marxism-Leninism that fit in with the mind cast of the Russian leadership and that affect its behavior. The world is seen as a sea of conflict where contending forces struggle ceaselessly. Stability is regarded as a dynamic process and the Western belief in compromising differences is regarded as superficial. Conflict, Russian leaders believe, eventually produces qualitative changes in the world. Policies that do not seek to control this process to advantage risk ultimate defeat.

Hence, although the Russian leadership does not intend to take great risks, it continually tests its opponents to see where temporary equilibria can be achieved that will assist in changing the total correlation of forces and produce a system change. Each American president is tested by the Soviet leadership when he enters office. John Kennedy's test was verbal and occurred at Vienna. Presidents Carter and Reagan were tested by the movement of Soviet submarines and aircraft near sensitive American locations.

But that is only one type of test. Soviet violations of Salt I and II are others. American failure to react strongly only ensures additional violations. Grenada, El Salvador, and Nicaragua constitute still a third type of test. The Russians prefer to work through proxies. And they keep their distance until the waters have been thoroughly tried. Their lines of retreat usually remain open until matters have gone irreversibly in their favor.

The Threat of War

One danger to the United States is that we may fail these tests so thoroughly that the Russians become overcommitted. In that case, our necessary response in defense of vital interests runs the risk of major war. Another threat of war lies in a potential regime or bloc crisis in the Soviet Union during which the Soviet leadership believes that a show of strength or even a minor victory over NATO—for instance, by forcing a change in the status of Berlin, or in the size and disposition of the West German forces, or in the status of Norway or Denmark—will help it to survive the crisis. It may bank so much on a perceived lack of resolution and disarray in NATO that it commits itself irretrievably to a position that we must oppose, with force if necessary, even at risk of war. Or, if war does not occur because NATO shows such irresolution that Western Europe is Finlandized, that also would be a tragic result.

The Threat of Nuclear War

Let us examine the issue of nuclear war in Europe. Contrary to the beliefs of many observers, the threat of nuclear war in Europe is not affected more than marginally by whether there is a SALT agreement or by the nuclear dispositions in Europe itself. If we removed all the nuclear weapons from Europe, except for those at sea or in the Soviet Union, and if a war broke out, there is a likelihood that the losing side would resort to use of nuclear weapons in an attempt to change the course of military events, or at least to force the winning power to prudent compromise. Even a government that did not want to use such weapons might change its mind or might be driven to that resort by public demand. A faction in the government or the armed forces might become so disgusted by apparent defeatism in the political leaders of the nation that nuclear weapons might be seized to commit the government to at least the avoidance of defeat. But after the battle lines had shifted in a major way, it would be much more difficult to arrive at a compromise than if more effective strategies had been applied earlier.

Even if one cannot say with complete assurance that the threat of nuclear war in Europe lies exclusively in the possibility of a conventional war, it surely lies primarily there. Certainly no thoughtful person believes that either the Russians or the Americans would use nuclear weapons over a European issue in the absence of a conventional war or the immediate threat thereof.

Therefore, the threat of nuclear war in Europe lies primarily in the conventional confrontation. If the possibility of that confrontation did not exist, the United States and the Soviet Union could continue to extend their nuclear arsenals, and we would be no more worried about a nuclear war between them than we are about a nuclear war with England or France, or than we would be with Canada if Canada had nuclear weapons. If it is the threat of conventional attack that invokes the possibility of nuclear war, as I believe is the case, then almost everyone from the American bishops who issued the declaration on nuclear war and the American "gang of four," including Robert McNamara and

McGeorge Bundy, down through most editorial writers has approached this mattter back end forwards.

Towards a New Settlement

How can we avoid the danger of a nuclear war in Europe? Let us recognize that it is precisely the World War II settlement that produces the danger of war. Let the United States propose a complete restitution of the postwar settlement. Let us massively reduce both the Russian and American forces. Then let us pull the American forces back in stages to the continental United States, and the Russian forces back behind the Urals, with the exception of modest forces on the Russian frontier that would not be significantly larger than those of its combined immediate neighbors. Major reductions would be made in the forces of all European countries and in the types of weapons available to them. Alliances and bilateral military treaties would be dissolved, although both the United States and the Soviet Union, if they wished, and as I believe we should, could promise to come to the assistance of any European nation under attack or threat of attack.

There would be no external European threat to the Soviet Union if this new settlement were achieved. The Soviet Union would still have nuclear weapons. It is difficult to imagine that Poland or Rumania would use its limited military forces to attack the Soviet Union even if that country did not have nuclear weapons. Furthermore, most of the myths that encouraged previous wars in Europe no longer have any currency. The Japanese, who engaged in their colonial campaigns because in their desire for security they copied the successful European powers, are well aware that they are far more prosperous without external conquests than they ever could be with them. Surely they are not the only major nation to have learned that lesson.

Beyond this, the external obligations of both the Soviet Union and the United States are placing extremely great burdens upon their economies. Indeed, both imperial powers may choke themselves if they do not divest themselves of this burden, the Soviet Union reaching a state of "heat death" first. Without this external burden, the Soviet regime would be capable of maintaining enough legitimacy to avoid a regime crisis through improving the living conditions of a population that has never experienced democratic rule. And the Russian people would be assured that war does not threaten them.

I am aware that many will say that the Russians would never accept this proposal or that, if they accepted it, they would do so with so many qualifications that the plan would be gutted. Many may argue that other nations also would reject it. If the Russian government rejected a plan such as this, it would pay a price with its own population, for to the extent that information gets through, and eventually some does, the Russian people would be aware that it was the position of the Russian government that invoked the danger of war and that they were enduring harsh conditions of life without purpose. The ordinary German would see that this plan, if adopted, would permit, although it would not necessitate, German unification in a manner that would present no threat to any other country. It may true that the French and the English might be a bit scared of the economic competition of a united Germany, but eventually they would see that as a small price to pay for removing the threat of war and the heavy burden of armaments.

Moreover, a settlement of the type that I propose would permit a Europe independent of both the United States and the Soviet Union, and this is something that most Europeans really want. So if the Russians protested, or attempted to gut the plan, they might do so to their heart's content. We should persist with our proposals just as do the Russians with theirs. But let us also test whether the Soviet Union, as it claims, really does adhere to the Litvinov proposals of the 1930s, which are even more radical than my proposal, and whether Mikhail Gorbachev really means what he said to Prime Minister Thatcher in December, 1984: that the Russians are prepared to remove all systems of armaments either in whole or in stages. If they are serious about their proposals, then we may be able to negotiate an end to the threat of war in Europe and to move to an international order that is more just. If they are not, we will demonstrate that it is Soviet policy that is responsible for the division of Europe and the threat of war.

A Backup Proposal

However, we should also have a backup plan if the Russians should not accept this proposal or if they delay acceptance. This plan should be largely independent of what the Russians do. In short, we need not negotiate it with the Soviet Union although of course we would do so with our bloc partners.

In the first place, we should remove the Pershing IIs and the cruise missiles from Europe. It was not wrong to put them in, given our commitment, although I believe the original proposal was a mistake. Now that we have demonstrated that the Soviet Union could not stop us and that their removal is our option and not a result of Russian pressure, we are free to negotiate within NATO a better unilateral Western disposition of forces.

The Pershing IIs and cruise missiles are visible targets that are likely to produce political disturbances in European countries, particularly during crises. We should not misinterpret the present calm on the issue as an indication that things will remain calm in crisis periods. Indeed, we now know that even Sir Winston Churchill was disturbed by the possible attractiveness as targets of American nuclear weapons in Europe. And crises are the worst times for alliance disturbances, for the Soviet Union can then exploit them and that could lead to a serious Soviet miscalculation that might produce a war.

The cruise missiles could be not on surface ships, and other area targeting, to the extent that such targeting is necessary, could be handled through Poseidon and Triton submarines. Now, it is true that the limitations placed on submarine vessels by SALT I, because two-thirds of our nuclear submarines are either in port or under repair, make difficult both strategic and tactical targeting with a fleet of its current size. However, we should not make a fetish of the SALT treaties, as some of our representatives have done. The object is not to sign treaties, but to reduce the danger of war and to increase the solidarity and assurance of NATO. When Neville Chamberlain returned from Munich in 1938 and stepped off his plane, he waved a piece of paper and proclaimed, "peace in our time." That is an illustration of how a treaty can be merely a fetish.

But reordering the dispositions of intermediate range nuclear weapons is not sufficient. The Europeans are right to fear that we might not be willing to use nuclear weapons in their defense. Berlin, or even Paris or London, is not New York or Chicago. De Gaulle did have a case to make and we did not respond to it appropriately, unless the bowdlerizing of my proposal for a joint NATO nuclear force in the subsequent MLF program can be considered a response.

I have a new, and perhaps better, suggestion to make. Let us, with some economic assistance from our European allies, build more nuclear submarines than we are now scheduling for construction. Let us sign treaties with any European ally that so wishes permitting them to place officers and men on a specified number of our nuclear submarines. The treaty would further specify that if any member of the alliance is either attacked or under immediate threat of attack, the officers of our NATO partners, at their government's instance, will take command of these submarines; and our officers and men will have been informed that the treaty has the force of law and they are ordered to obey under these circumstances.

This proposal would provide enormous deterrence. The Russians would know that they could not localize their threats against a particular country as a device for producing either dissension in NATO or immense fear in the target nation. They would not know which countries had taken control of the submarines, for it need not be the country under direct threat of attack. And if the Soviet Union were hit, it would not know whether it was it by the United States, the country under threat, or some other member of NATO.

That would not be a very auspicious situation for the Soviet Union. This surely, would give them an added incentive to consider the proposal for a reconstitution of the postwar settlement.

Other New Organizations

The proposals I have made, I believe, would increase the national security of the democratic nations and also their resolution and cooperation. However, foreign policy, to be effective, requires substantial support from the public and the attentive elite. We must remember that ours is a democratic nation and that if our policies do not have substantial support based on confidence in the goals and competence of the government, the government likely will find itself hamstrung by dissent when the implementation of policy runs into difficulties or imposes substantial costs on the nation. Thus, national security policies, when possible, should be implemented within a framework of goals and ideals that maintains the requisite degree of confidence.

Consider one important task that we face. We cannot permit Marxist-Leninist regimes in the Caribbean or the Central American area; our sea lane communications would be threatened and our attention diverted from the periphery of Eurasia, which is vital to our security but more distant. However, our attempt to control this situation produces widespread misconceptions. I will not argue that we can entirely defeat these misconceptions, but it should be possible at least to produce important marginal changes in public perceptions.

Therefore, I suggest a policy for the Caribbean island nations. In the first place, it should be recognized that it is a myth that all states are equal. As Mr. Dooley said of citizens, "In a dimocracy, all of us is equal but some of us is more equal than ithers." A state with a hundred thousand people and no army is not a state in the same sense as is the United States. Grenada was seized by seventy armed men when the New Jewel Movement took over. I am not suggesting that the people of Grenada should not rule themselves but rather that we should not ignore, or be incapacitated in the face of, the actual conditions that are present.

We should declare that we will permit no foreign bases on these islands and no Leninist regime that can repress competing parties. However, we should not make these conditions completely dependent upon American decisions. With the cooperation of the leaders of the Caribbean nations, we should spell out a set of conditions which a court with members from the United States and Western European democracies can enforce by adjudicating complaints. A common army and police force recruited from islanders with American and European officers and weapons should be put at the disposal of the court to implement its decrees if governments refused to accept decisions of the court. Although many might argue that this would be an imposition upon the autonomy of the inhabitants of the area, this objection is misconceived. This is a system designed to assure the inhabitants of the islands a continuing autonomy in deciding their own fate.

Obviously this same kind of system cannot be applied in Central America because the nations of that area come closer to being states in the full sense than do the Caribbean nations. On the other hand, the United States cannot permit Soviet bases in these states. It also cannot permit an unimpeded Marxist-Leninist regime in these states because such regimes would create the conditions for bases by slow stages. They are smart enough to be sure that no individual stage would appear sufficiently grave to provoke our intervention. Indeed, it is likely that we would be taken in by disinformation and make claims that could be disproved, so that our later claims would be disbelieved. One way of controlling such developments is by supporting insurgencies sufficiently to force these countries into accepting genuinely pluralistic conditions. Another would be some variation of the suggestion I made for the Caribbean island states, but changed sufficiently to accord with the different conditions in Central America.

I should like also to see two organizations established by the OECD nations. One would be designed to coordinate economic policies. By coordinate, I do not mean that the economies would be run the same ways but rather that some agreed-upon limits for unemployment, inflation, and monetary expansion would be adopted to prevent excessive disequilibrium in the world economy.

In addition, I would propose another organization that would have both public and private functions and that would report on the state of democratic development in the world. It would make suggestions for improving the growth of democratic polities. Perhaps such an organization might even be able to provide a framework for nations such as South Africa to enunciate as a goal the kind of multi-racial constitution they are willing to work toward and the conditions under which they would do so. And that is only one possible example of how such an organization might encourage democratic development without attempting to impose its will in a manner that would turn out to be counterproductive.

Although I recognize that one must often cooperate with regimes one does not like—as we did in World War II with the Soviet Union or as almost any group must do in getting its positions adopted in larger organizations—I also think it is important to keep in mind and also in public view the direction in which we are aiming. If it is wrong, as I believe it is, to demand simple-minded consistency in national policies, it is not wrong to so manage our foreign policies that the objectives of superficially inconsistent policies are supportive of national and international goals that Americans of all parties can agree on.

Although I agree with Dean Acheson that it is extremely cumbersome and almost impossible to conduct an effective foreign policy in a democracy, I think he made a mistake in not recognizing that he was Secretary of State in such a democracy. And although I often get angry at members of Congress, who are irresponsible in the sense that they will not have to pay the price for the foreign policy compromises they force on the executive branch of the government—that is, when in the foreign field they indulge in the same practice of bargaining and compromise that is employed in the domestic arena—it is also important to understand that a Congress that does not respect and trust policy (and also a public that does not) makes for ineffective policy.

In short, we need to be serious about what we are doing, and this is true of the President, the Congress, the bureaucrats, and even the lowliest clerk and foot soldier. We need both to talk and to listen. And we need to learn how to formulate policies that appeal to the optimism of our people, that hold out the hope of a better world, that accord with our ideals, and that are effective in ways the public can observe and comprehend. If we don't learn how to do these things, then I am afraid that the existing settlement will not last, nor will it be replaced by one that is consistent with American interests or values.

2

German Unity: Is the Question Still Open?

KLAUS HORNUNG

The question of German unity has again become an important issue in national and international discussions after a long period of silence, particularly during the era of appeasing detente. In this context I remind you of the remarks of Italian Foreign Minister Andreotti in 1984 that there are "two Germanies" today and this should remain so. I also remind you of the debate in the Federal Republic of Germany over the motto for the meeting of the exile Silesians in the summer of 1985: "Silesia remains ours" was changed to "Silesia remains our future in a Europe of free peoples."

The so-called "peace movement" against deployment of United States intermediate-range missiles in West Germany with its nationalistic coloring and neutralistic aims—which can also be found in the Social Democrat (SPD) opposition—has contributed to reopening the discussion of "the German Question." In addition, there has been in West Germany a debate in recent years about the so-called "national identity" or the "identity of the Germans." Within the international discussion, the concern of some allies that the Germans might leave NATO for the sake of restoration of their national unity and walk the path of neutralism has also contributed to this. However, the change of government in the fall of 1982 from Chancellor Helmut Schmidt's to Helmut Kohl's and the fact that the new government insisted on and deployed intermediate-range missiles should have quelled such fears for the time being.

The German Question in Contemporary History

A problem as complicated as the German issue cannot be discussed without looking at least briefly at Germany's background in contemporary history. During World War II, the allies discussed plans for the "dismemberment of Germany" at the conferences of the Big Three in Tehran and Yalta. Germany was to be divided into several states. Certain areas such as the Ruhr were to be placed under international control. There were, however, no binding agreements about this at the end of the war.

Although Stalin at first emphatically supported the Western dismemberment plans, he changed course spectacularly just before the end of the war and proclaimed, "Hitlers come and go, but the German people, the German nation remains" and "The Soviet Union celebrates the victory without, however, intending to destroy or enslave Germany." Stalin of all people now tried to make himself the protector of German unity, although he had already had the Red Army expel more than twelve million Germans from Eastern Germany (Eastern Prussia, Silesia, Pomerania). Even before the war ended and before the Potsdam Conference, in March 1945, Stalin had the German areas east of the rivers Oder and Neiss placed under Polish administration. When he spoke of "German Unity" he therefore can only have meant Potsdam Germany without the Eastern regions. He thus created a *fait accompli,* with which the United States and Great Britain at Potsdam agreed only under the condition "that the final delimitation of the Western frontier of Poland should await the peace settlement." But this condition was questionable, because the two Western powers in the Potsdam Protocol also agreed to the explusion of Germans from Poland, Czechoslovakia, and Hungary "in an orderly and humane manner."

The three victors in Potsdam did agree, however, "to deal with Germany as a single economic unit"[1] and to have this Germany governed by a joint government which was to consist of military governors of the four powers (including France) working in the so-called Control Council (*Kontrollrat*). A German government no longer existed at this time, since the government under Admiral Donitz after Hitler's death was ended by the British, on special pressure by Stalin, on May 23, 1945.

The plan, however, to govern Germany jointly by the four occupation powers could not be realized. They differed too greatly with regard to their concepts of the economic treatment of Germany—for example, food rations for the German population, the question of whether industrial plants should remain or be dismantled (reparations), and denazification. No trade exchange worth mentioning took place across the occupation zones: the

Soviets, for example, did not send any foodstuffs or soft coal from their zone, although the Americans at first delivered industrial goods from their zone.

The Iron Curtain

The Soviet Union increasingly sealed off its zone and began, in the summer of 1945, a far-reaching "social revolution" following the Soviet model. It was a from-above type of "proletarian revolution" by order of the Soviet military administration, which quickly "socialized" industry, banks, and insurance companies, and by the so-called "democratic land reform" seized the property of "war criminals and Nazi activists." In some cases this was legitimized through "referenda," so-called plebiscites.

On April 21, 1946, barely a year after the end of the war, the SED (Socialist Unity Party, East Germany's Communist party) was founded through the forced union of the KPD (Communist Party of Germany) and the SPD (Social Democratic Party). Stalin's remarks to the then Yugoslav Communist leader Milovan Djilas show what led him to form the SED: "This war is not like in the past; whoever occupies an area will also impose his own social system on it. Everyone will import his own system, as far as his army can advance. It cannot be otherwise."[2] Although the wartime dismemberment plans were abandoned and replaced by occupation zones which were to last only for a transitional period, the borders between the Western zones and the Soviet zone became finally the dividing line which persists today.

In March 1946, Winston Churchill in his famous speech in Fulton, Missouri, spoke of the "iron curtain" that had descended between East and West; Stalin created within his zone a *fait accompli* of a new society, and simultaneously expected the Western zones to become totally impoverished in a Germany destroyed by the war and nearly bled to death. The Western powers would then be unwilling to bear the financial burdens for their zones, and German dissatisfaction would grow into a revolutionary situation. (Stalin, after all, had seen that millions of expellees from Eastern Germany were packed into West Germany.) At such a moment, West Germany and the rest of Western Europe, with their then-strong Communist parties, could easily become prey for Soviet Communism.

The Truman Doctrine

In this situation, President Harry S. Truman practiced the strategy of containment against Soviet expansion. The "year of decisions" was 1947. On March 12, Truman announced the doctrine named after himself, economic and military aid for countries threatened by Soviet communism like Turkey and Greece, which at this time were engaged in a civil war with Communists. Truman's conviction was that "the seed of totalitarian rule thrives in misery and deprivation" and that therefore only such aid would create the conditions for a new economic and political stability in Europe. The Marshall Plan put into practice and made concrete this policy of creating stable, free, and democratic conditions and institutions in Europe to help Western Europe back to its feet. This decision was inevitable, and it had decisive consequences for Germany. George Kennan, the architect of the concept of containment described it as follows:

> The idea of a Germany run jointly with the Russians is a chimera. The idea of both the Russians and ourselves withdrawing politely at a given date and a healthy, peaceful, stable, and friendly Germany arising out of the resulting vacuum is also a chimera. We have no choice but to lead our section of Germany—the section of which we and the British have accepted responsibility—to a form of independence so prosperous, so secure, so superior, that the East cannot threaten it. . . . Admittedly, this is dismemberment. But dismemberment is already a fact, by virtue of the Oder-Neisse line. Whether or not the remainder of the Soviet zone is rejoined to Germany is not now important. Better a dismembered Germany in which the West, at least, can act as a buffer to the forces of totalitarianism than a united Germany which again brings these forces to the North Sea.[3]

For the West Germans, this was certainly not an easy sentiment. They could easily be accused of arrogantly ignoring the fate of their fellow men in the Soviet occupation zone. But there was no choice unless we wanted the whole of Germany sooner or later to fall prey to the Soviet Union—united, but not free. There was only one way to go, and that was first to unite the three Western occupation zones into a provisional state, without losing sight of the long-term goal of uniting the whole of Germany in freedom. Unless Germany (and Europe) wanted to become an "appendage of Asia" or a power vacuum through neutralization, only a firm tie to the West could halt Soviet expansionism.[4] In 1947, the

German Social Democrats and their leader Kurt Schumacher decided in favor of the creation of a West German "emergency-roof" state: "We (the SPD) want the democratic German republic, but we do not want the people's republic of SEDistan."[5] Governing Mayor of Berlin Ernst Reuter—whose commitment to the freedom of Berlin during the time of the Berlin airlift remains unforgettable—also saw the economic and political consolidation of West Germany as indispensable for a later "return of the East to the common motherland."[6] The real separatists were in East Berlin. The division they created could, also in Reuter's opinion, only be overcome through a long historical process. A clear congruence of the interests of the Western allies and West Germany was thus noticeable.

While the division was the result of the incompatibility of the plans of the Soviet Union on the one hand and those of the Western nations on the other about the future political-social order in Germany, the creation of a provisional but functioning democratic state in the West was based "on the desire of an overly large majority of the population to construct from the ruins of Hitler's Reich a free democracy of the Western type, and not to become the subjects of a new, this time communist party dictatorship."[7] This was the consensus on which the Federal Republic of Germany was founded.

This sentiment was also firmly expressed in the "Convention on Relations between the Three Powers and the Federal Republic of Germany" (*Deutschlandvertrag*), signed in Paris on October 23, 1954. Its seventh article summarized the goals of the policy of the contract nations as follows:

> (1) The Signatory states are agreed that an essential aim of their common policy is a peace settlement for the whole of Germany, freely negotiated between Germany and her former enemies, which should lay the foundation of a lasting peace. They further agree that the final determination of the boundaries of Germany must await such a settlement.

> (2) Pending the peace settlement, the Signatory states will cooperate to achieve by peaceful means their common aim of a reunified Germany enjoying a liberal-democratic constitution, like that of the Federal Republic, and integrated within the European community.[8]

This commitment, binding by international law, is and has been the basis for the policies of the Federal Republic of Germany.

East-West Detente

Until the end of the 1950s (which could be called "the Dulles-Adenauer era") this joint policy held the premise that a "junctim," or a close connection, existed between the easing of East-West tensions and German unity. That is to say, it was believed that progress concerning detente and progress in reaching the goal of reunification via free elections in the whole of Germany were closely linked. Policy was therefore based on the view that the essential cause for the East-West tension, at least in Europe, was the division of Germany. With the policy of detente (introduced in the United States mostly by President John F. Kennedy) a new premise, another school of thinking, became prevalent: Because German unity through free elections could not for the present be obtained from the Soviet Union, the West would make detente the precondition for a later solution to the German question.

Particularly effective in pushing the United States towards detente were the dangers stemming from the policy of nuclear deterrence, from the burdens of the arms buildup, and from the growing military strength of the Soviet Union. Specifically, the Cuban crisis of October 1962 concretely evidenced the dangers of nuclear deterrence. On the other hand, Soviet interest in detente was to reach at least an international guarantee for postwar boundaries in Europe, and thus for the division of Germany, since at that time German unification could not be obtained by the Soviets according to their conditions either. According to Soviet understanding, the recognition of the status quo in Europe, of course, was only the first step on the way to their *actual* goal, namely to "de-couple" West Germany and Western Europe from the United States and to lull them to a sense of security through the impression of peace on the basis of detente.

This central goal of decoupling Western Europe—including Spain and Great Britain—from the United States would push the United States back into its own hemisphere and make it a secondary power. The evaluation of the policy of detente is thus closely tied to the evaluation of the aims of the Soviet Union: whether it is a defensive, peaceful, saturated power that wishes nothing more than once and for all to secure the "results of World War II," or whether it is still an aggressive, imperialistic power with targets for worldwide revolution. The Soviet Union attempts to compensate for its growing domestic weaknesses with political offensives and the expansion of military power and is ready to use offensively every weakness and every retreat of the Western democracies in order to change the global balance of power in its favor.

It is not my task here to describe the history of the era of detente and its failures. I must point out, however, that the gradual dissolution of East-West detente and hopes for German reunification led to disappointment in Germany with United States politics. Germans increasingly saw the United States as a global power that since the time of President Kennedy increasingly set its own interests above its commitment to the German question. In this light the construction of the Berlin wall in August, 1961 signified an important turn in the German-United States relationship. The then-Governing Mayor of Berlin and later Chancellor Willy Brandt never denied that the beginning of his later "Ostpolitik" and "Germany-Politik" of 1969 was decisively influenced by this experience in the summer of 1961. Although he did not oppose the United States detente policy, Brandt's policies reflected *de facto* recognition of the existence of "two states in Germany" and of the Oder-Neiss line.

Deutschlandpolitik tried to create a *modus vivendi* with "the other German state" as well as with Moscow and the states of the Warsaw Pact. But West Germany still avoided either recognizing East Germany (DDR) or calling it a foreign country; "German-German relations" were always considered those of a "special kind." This policy, however, resulted in an enormous international rise in status for East Germany, including broader diplomatic recognition and acceptance as a member in the United Nations, even though the SED-rulers had at no time since 1949 permitted free elections. The ink had not yet dried on the Helsinki Final Agreement of August 1, 1975 (CSCE)—which internationally and multinationally sealed and gave its blessing to this new Ostpolitik—when the Soviet Union took its next steps to threaten the interests of West Germany and of Western Europe: The Soviets made a political-military expansion in Africa and the Near East and attempted to lure West Germany itself out of its rooting in the Western alliance. In this light, the detente policy of the Brezhnev era was a "continuation of war by other means"; it was an enormous maneuver of deception against the free world in general and against West Germany in particular. It was time to end this game and again to place East-West relations as well as the policy regarding Germany on solid ground and principles.

The Political–Psychological and Moral Climate in West Germany

One cannot meaningfully judge the German question, and especially one cannot discuss it abroad, without considering the political-psychological and moral climate in West Germany. The peace movement, the "Greens," did not suddenly fall from the sky; they have their roots in the intellectual and social development of West Germany since the war.

Dr. Antje Vollmer is a Green party deputy to the Bundestag and was one of the Green's three spokeswomen there until recently. She is a teacher and theologian from the left-wing Protestant group surrounding Gustav Heinemann, who in 1949 was minister of the interior in the first government of Konrad Adenauer. In protest against the German defense contribution, Heinemann separated himself from Adenauer with the argument, "God beat the weapons out of our hands; we must never take them up again." In 1953 Heinemann founded a neutral party, the All-German Popular Party (GVP), which he later integrated into the SPD; and finally he became federal president from 1969 to 1974. Dr. Vollmer a few months ago admitted in the Bundestag that she and her political group altogether rejected the Federal Republic "with rage and with grief."[9] Adenauer is hated by them as a "man of the West, a man of big money, an anti-Communist." An anticapitalist socialism is combined in these groups with a Protestant moral rigidity and a great gesture of self-accusation, as in the statement, "We belong to the daughters and sons of a nation which is mainly responsible for two world wars."

The Greens and similar groups combine national self-hatred with a preaching of political salvation and the belief that they alone have the prescription for a lasting peace. This represents the German apolitical tradition that Biedermaier observed in the first half of the nineteenth century. The people of these groups want to be left out of the conflicts of the superpowers, through neutrality, and are unconditionally ready to "recognize realities as they developed in Germany" (after World War II). Their position thus makes the Soviet Union appear harmless, but they have intense emotion against the United States of President Reagan.

Roots of the Greens

What are the roots and motives of such attitudes among West German students, many of whom are in the social sciences and humanities? There are environmental problems in this highly industrialized and densely populated country. West Germany includes approximately 15 million expellees from the eastern provinces, 3 to 4 million refugees from East Germany, nearly 4 million foreign workers and their families, the allied troops and their families, and recently tens of thousands of asylees from all parts of the world. One can understand the fear of an accumulation of soldiers and weapons in Central Europe, and especially on German soil.

But the real roots of this peace movement are of a spiritual-intellectual nature. It is the protest of a young generation against the priorities of economics, an expression of a search for meaning in life by a people that has lost its history and its tradition, and in which the effectiveness of the Christian faith and of the churches has weakened.

The collapse of 1945 has remained a trauma for Germans and often discredits German history as a whole. Economic reconstruction after the war, the so-called "cultural revolution" under the banner of neo-Marxism, and today a "green" socialism inimical to industry and technology have been attempts to fill the spiritual vacuum created by this lack of a sense of history. The re-education by the Allies after the war has become automatic. It has produced a rather solid guilt-and-repentance complex nurtured by a morally rigid Protestantism. Thus, a bridge over 40 years connects the "Confession of Guilt" by the Protestant Churches of December 1945 to today's Greens and peace movement, which not by chance recruits strongly from Protestant (and to a lesser extent from Catholic) circles.

Here it becomes apparent that Germans may go from one extreme to the other: from the obsession with power under Hitler and National Socialism to the rejection of power today (as Hans-Peter Schwarz put it[10]); or "from the omnipresence of nationalism to the glorification of everything foreign; from the urge to meddle with everything to no commitment whatsoever. . . . They have been conditioned such that they begin to tremble every time someone merely speaks of power—which of couse makes them susceptible to any enfeebling teaching" (as the

Frenchman Alain de Benoist said).[11] *The Economist* called West Germany, even years ago, "an economy in search of a nation." Reference was made to the widespread tendency in Germany to make things non-political; this tendency also makes Germans accept the status quo even in the German question—or even to see the division of Germany as God's judgement. Along with the natural tendency of many Germans to frolic with success and to be contrite in defeat, if possible they tend to exaggerate the model—"to be more papal than the pope," as the Germans say; to be more democratic than old democracies, more Marxist than Soviet Russians; to be the "best" Christians or the "best" environmentalists in the world.

The Current Debate about National Identity

The picture of the political-psychological situation in Germany would be incomplete without reviewing the current public discussion of national and political identity in both German states. In East Germany the issue was consciously introduced by the SED-leadership because the official state ideology of Marxism-Leninism no longer fascinates the population and can hardly serve to legitimize the Communist Party regime. Therefore, the leadership thought of emphasizing the positive traditions of German history and using them to justify its rule. SED-chief Erich Honnecker himself began a rehabilitation of great personalities in German history: Luther, Frederic the Great of Prussia (whose monument was re-erected in East Berlin on the Avenue Unter den Linden in 1980), patriots of the liberation wars against Napoleon (such as the generals Scharnhorst and Gneisenau), and Otto von Bismarck (his several-volume biography is about to be published). With these measures, the SED regime intends to claim the right to a possible German unification under its own leadership and is thus preparing psychologically.

The intention here is not a "third course" into neutrality, but an expansion of East Germany into the territory of West Germany. According to Article 6 of the East German Constitution, East Germany declares itself "forever and irrevocably allied with the Union of Socialist Soviet Republics" and an "inseparable part of the socialist community of states." In the view of the SED leadership, the nucleus of a "socialist German national state" emerged with an East German long-term mission of national re-unification.

In West Germany also a lively debate over national identity and a renewed awareness of history began in approximately 1980 as a reaction to some exaggerations of de-politization, the oblivion of power, and the constantly renewed accusations of collective guilt. The Social Democrat political scientist Iring Fetscher of the University at Frankfurt wrote: "After many decades of maximal distance from Germany which on the one side expressed itself in socialist internationalism, on the other side in cosmopolitan consumer mentality, the need and the desire awoke again 'to be oneself' and also to be something unique as a nation."[12] SPD party manager Peter Glotz said, "Our focussing entirely on the material reconstruction of our destroyed country never left us the time to produce something like a new identity. Therefore, there is this helpless turning away of larger parts of our young generation. . . . In the long run, a well-organized net of goods and services alone cannot keep a society together."[13] Even members of the young generation coming from the far-left "Extraparliamentary Opposition" now oppose the "tradition of self-accusation" among the German leftwingers: "Germany is pictured in the darkest colors: the whole world is better—only Germany is the perfect horror."[14]

Willy Brandt's son, Peter Brandt, who politically stands left of his father and is assistant professor of history in West Berlin, has criticized the German leftists for using leaders such as Mao Zedung or Fidel Castro as substitute identities. Peter Brandt demands that Germans, in a world of convulsively awakening national identities, overcome their deficiency and re-establish their national identity.[15] In addition, democratic conservatives concerned about West Germany's capability for self-assertion *vis-à-vis* the East, strongly criticize the prevalent loss of an historical sense, where the Germans withdrew into the quiet niches of "middle class allotment-garden idyllic mentality."[16] These people also recognize the loss of national identity as a major cause of the rebellion of the academic youth in particular and of the "lonely world record of conscientious objectors."[17] These conservatives oppose obscuring German history during the 12 years of Hitler's dictatorship; they do not believe that a great nation that grew more than a thousand years could be eternally split after division imposed for just a few decades.

Left and right fringe groups criticize the "servility towards the victors" and the "mechanism of the accusation of fascism and of imbalanced selfconsciousness."[18] They criticize the deployment of missiles and the lack of sovereignty in West Germany; they raise neutralistic demands, speak of concepts of a neutral, re-united Germany between the two superpowers, and also suggest the possibility of a confederation of both German states with a "socialist" order of society *à la* a "third way." These demands find much support among the Greens, a party whose members and voters are mostly under 30 years of age. This will not, however, become a majority view in West Germany as long as patriots there are supported by the policy of the West, and of the United States in particular. In light of the global political situation, such Germans consider West Germany's alliance with the Western democracies indispensable, an alliance that is based on ethnic, historical, and political ties of interest; but these are people who also believe that the political and social structure of West Germany cannot be a mere imitation of the United States and that the Federal Republic cannot simply renounce its own history and replace its great figures with, for example, Benjamin Franklin.[19] They believe that the synthesis of democracy and nationhood remains to be accomplished.

What is also necessary is a balanced position between the desire for peace and an instinct for power—which the Germans have not regained since 1945. Professor Hans-Peter Schwarz warns: "A country whose government almost exclusively speaks of peace policies and whose public prefers dreaming of a world without power, would be doomed for destruction in a world full of power politics and full of the misuse of power; it may be even doomed to become the vassal state within the European empire of the Soviet Union."[20] Without a "modification of mentality" the Federal Republic of Germany also cannot be a stable partner in the alliance, because the "moral factors"—according to Clausewitz—are more important than the number of soldiers or weapons.

The Question of German Unity is Open

I conclude this topic by summarizing several theses:

1. Chancellor Helmut Kohl expressed his view of the Federal Republic of Germany in his "State of the Nation" address in the German Bundestag on February 27, 1985:

> We shall not pay the price of freedom for the unity of Germany either. . . . Europe is divided because part of Germany is not free. The German question is naturally first and foremost a matter for

the Germans themselves. However, since Germany lies at the heart of Europe, the German question has always been closely linked with European interests. It has . . . always been a key European question. . . . Europe and Germany alike seek unity in freedom. The key to this lies in self-determination. . . . Anyone who today, in an attitude of resignation and fatalism, draws a final line under the German question is rejecting the right to self-determination and the realization of human rights.[21]

In an interview with the West German weekly *Die Zeit,* Kohl explicitly added, "I deny everyone in our generation the right to deny future generations their right to self-determination."

2. One of the chancellor's close advisors, Horst Teltschik, summarized his position as follows:

Millions of Germans are denied their human rights and the right to self-determination. The island-situation of West Berlin, wall and barbed wire, symbolize most strongly the unnatural nature of the division of Germany. For 40 years they repeatedly led to tensions and conflicts. We can try to ease them, to regulate them. But we can solve them definitively only by overcoming the cause—if not today, then tomorrow, or the day after tomorrow. A divided people is bound repeatedly to ask the question of its identity as long as self–determination is not granted to all of the people; and this especially if a people historically so rich and mentally so vivid is concerned as the Germans in the center of Europe. If our generation does not do it, then the next one will, or the one after the next one.[22]

3. The German question is also clearly open in light of international law. Both the London Protocol of September 12, 1944 (among the United States, Great Britain and the Soviet Union), and the Berlin Declaration of the Four Powers of June 5, 1945, concerning the "Defeat of Germany," assume a Germany having the borders of December 31, 1937.

Germany as a whole is subject to the provision of a future peace treaty; the same is true (according to the Potsdam Protocol) for the final fixing of the German-Polish border. The three Western powers, as mentioned above, have pledged themselves in the German Treaty (*Deutschlandvertrag*) of 1952, Article 7, to the goal of a "re-united Germany which has a free and democratic constitution similar to that of the Federal Republic." Also in this treaty, Germany as a whole and the reunification are subject to the provision of a "peace treaty settlement." Even the Soviet Union in its Declaration of Sovereignty for East Germany in 1954 committed itself to the goal of a "national re-unification of Germany on a democratic basis" (although "democratic" here naturally must be understood in a Marxist-Leninist sense and not in the free Western sense). No treaty by West Germany in the course of the German Ostpolitik (including the Moscow and Warsaw Treaties of 1970) ever changed this legal position. A clause in these treaties says their content does not touch the "formerly agreed bilateral and multilateral treaties and agreements." In the light of international law, therefore, even the annexation of the German Eastern regions by Poland has not taken place.

The Soviet Union would like to interpret the Treaties of 1970 (Moscow and Warsaw Treaties) and the German-German Basic Treaty (1973) as something like pre-peace treaties. But this cannot be the case. Rather, they are treaties committing West Germany to renounce the use of force in order to change the current borders. They do not mean a renunciation of bringing about a change by peaceful means. The German expellees had already solemnly declared this renunciation of force in 1950 in their Stuttgart Charter. And even Soviet Foreign Minister Andrei Gromyko confirmed to West German Foreign Minister Walter Scheel on July 29, 1970, that the Soviet Union renounced using the term "recognition." Reinterpreting the treaties in this direction, which the governments in Moscow and East Berlin repeatedly attempt, and which even the SPD-opposition and Foreign Minister Genscher do (with ambiguous wording), has no legal foundation in the treaties.

4. By international law, and politically, there has been a continuity of the German state since 1871 which could not be eliminated by the defeat of 1945: The Berlin Declaration of the Four Victor Powers of June 5, 1945, "Concerning the Defeat of Germany" did not cause—according to their own words—"the annexation of Germany." The occupation powers with this declaration, merely took on "supreme authority in Germany." However, Germany remained subject to international law, a bearer of rights and duties, even though it was temporarily unable to act and function. (Thus, 63 nations who had been at war with the German Reich one after the other declared the end of the state of war—which would not have been necessary if Germany had been a non-existing state.)

5. The Federal Republic of Germany is the democratically legiti-

mized new order of the German state that did not perish. In this part of Germany—also according to the view of the fathers of the German constitution (Basic Law) of 1949—the Germans' right to self-determination was not eliminated by capitulation and occupation and is exercised (by West Germany) as trustee for the whole German people, as it was wisely formulated in the preamble of the Basic Law:

> Conscious of their responsibility before God and men, animated by the resolve to preserve their national and political unity . . . desiring to give a new order to political life for a transitional period, . . . the German people . . . have enacted, by virtue of their constituent power, this Basic Law for the Federal Republic of Germany. They have also acted on behalf of those Germans to whom participation was denied. The entire German people are called upon to achieve in free self-determination the unity and freedom of Germany.

6. The Federal Constitutional Court stated in a ruling of July 31, 1973, regarding the Basic Treaty between West and East Germany (the ruling had been requested by the Bavarian Government of Franz Josef Strauss), "that the German Reich survived the collapse in 1945 and was not obliterated later either with the capitulation or with the exercising of foreign government power in Germany by the allied occupation powers." The founding of the Federal Republic of Germany did not create a new West-German state; a part of Germany was simply reorganized, the ruling said. "No constitutional authority or institution of the Federal Republic can therefore renounce national unity as a political goal; instead they have to keep this goal alive on the domestic scene and stand up for it unswervingly abroad."

7. The Basic Treaty between the Federal Republic and East Germany in 1973 meant the *de facto* recognition of the "GDR" by the Federal Republic of Germany. However, neither the Allied reserved rights concerning "Germany as a whole," nor the West German Basic Law (*Grundgesetz*), nor consideration of the right of self-determination for the Germans in the Communist-dominated part of the country, allows for a recognition of the "GDR" in terms of international law, by which East Germany would automatically become a foreign country like Poland to the Federal Republic. Therefore the German nationality fixed in the Baltic Law of the Federal Republic, is indivisible, and the Federal Republic supports it legally and politically.

8. Clinging to the goal of political unity of the German nation does not necessarily mean preventing pragmatic politics in the relationship of the present two German states in the interest of the people concerned. But such pragmatic politics must not be confused with the goal of reunification, and it cannot lead to the actual *solution* of the German question. It could at most make it easier. As long as there is a wall in Berlin and the monstrously fortified, so-called "state-frontier West" of East Germany, nobody should speak of "normal" conditions in Germany. "As long as the Brandenburg Gate is closed, the German question remains open," the West Berlin Interior Minister Henrich Lummer recently said. A lasting peace arrangement in Central Europe is not possible on the foundation of a divided Germany. The close connection remains between the solution of the German question and actual detente.

9. The German question in fact seems to be more open today than 10 years ago. It is increasingly clear that the East and Southeast European nations are looking for their own national courses. Within the Soviet military empire there are indications of ferment from the Baltic areas down to the Caucasus, from the Ukraine to Poland, Hungary, and Romania. In June 1982, Alexander Grlickov, a member of the Politburo of the Alliance of Communists in Yugoslavia, predicted at a party congress in Belgrade:

> I do not believe in de-nationalization. Karl Marx and his claim that the national question was the problem of the 19th century and of capitalism, has been contradicted by history. The national question—as we can see everywhere—is a question of the 21st century and it is a problem with which both capitalism and socialism are confronted. And I even believe that the national question is stronger today then the social question.

It is only natural that the reawakening of national awareness in Eastern Europe has consequences for the German question; it cannot leave the Germans untouched.

10. The division of Germany is also the division of Europe. The German question can be solved only in connection with the interests of all European peoples and not by a German nationalistic solo tour or escape into "neutrality." The solution will be possible only within a Europe of free peoples on a continent of free nations which occupies its place in the world through democratic self-determination of its peoples. In such a Europe the German people in the heart of the continent could again find their position. A just

solution also to the German-Polish conflict then will finally be possible. The reconciliation between Germans and Poles (as happened long ago between Germans and the French) requires that the people on both sides can freely move and express themselves. As long as they live west of the rivers Oder and Neiss in Moscow's most westward province, in East Germany, or under the present Communist military dictatorship, this will not be possible. It was Stalin's plan 40 years ago to divide Poles and Germans forever and thus to bind Poland eternally to the Soviet Union. Increasingly, more Poles begin to recognize this today. In a Europe of free peoples, borders would be permeable and of secondary importance (as they are already today in Western Europe). In addition, the question of one million Germans now living east of Oder and Neisse would be solved, for example, by granting them a minority statute within Poland.

11. History is always open towards the future. One cannot even exclude the idea that the Soviet leaders one day might reconsider their German and European policy. They might recognize that the security of the Soviet Union itself cannot always be guaranteed by the expansion of the Soviet empire into the center of Europe, to the gates of Hamburg, the Thuringian Forest or Bohemia; they might recognize that a friendly cooperation of free peoples is more fruitful—even for the Soviet Union—than the current situation.

12. If the Germans wish to solve the German question they must overcome the widespread political and national paralysis; they must overcome the shift from imperialistic power politics to the current national masochism. Without overcoming their present apolitical cast of mind, the Germans will be unable to assume their political role in Central Europe. A new self-confidence is needed. Otherwise the political vacuum in the center of Europe will remain, and this does not serve the cause of peace on the continent and in the world.

The Germans have enough reason not again to blindly accept the so-called "normative power of the facts" and thus succumb to force. Through the passage of time alone, unrighteousness and force do not become international law. The acceptance of force, like the expulsion of Germans from their eastern provinces in 1945 or the massive military presence of the Soviet Union in East Germany, would mean sanctioning force as a means of international relations. It must not be that the weakness of the weak in accepting domination increases the strength of the strong. In the case of Germany this has meant the installation of a satellite system on German soil, the expulsion of more than 12 million people from the eastern territories and the annexation of a third of the territory of the Reich of 1937, and the refusal of the right to self-determination and of human rights for millions of Germans.

But the Germans themselves must first remember the high goal contained in the letter and spirit of the Germany Treaty (*Deutschlandvertrag*) of 1952. The Western alliance must substitute for its strategy of timidly preserving the status quo a new strategy of change, with the goal of a world of more than individual and national freedom—alone through which the East-West confrontation can be solved. Such a strategy of change would conform with history which, always in a state of change, has never known stagnation. According to the deep insight of Heraklit: "There is not genuine peace without freedom and there is not genuine freedom in a state of 'peace' imposed by coercion, which only suppresses rather than eliminating genuine, deeply-rooted cleavages and conflicts."[23] The unsettled German question is among them. But the other insight—of George Kennan, about which he writes at the end of his memoirs—is likewise valid:

> Much depends on health and vigor of our own society. World communism is like a malignant parasite which feeds only on diseased tissue. This is the point at which domestic and foreign policies meet. Every courageous and incisive measure to solve international problems of our own society, to improve self-confidence, discipline, morale and community spirit of our own people, is a diplomatic victory over Moscow worth a thousand diplomatic notes and "joint communiques."[24]

NOTES

1. Potsdamer Abkommen [Potsdam Agreement], August 2, 1945, in Ingo von Munch, ed., *Dokumente des Geteilten Deutschlands* [Documents of a divided Germany], (Stuttgart: Kroners Taschenausgabe, 1968), pp. 32ff. The formula "Germany, within her frontiers as they were on December 31, 1937, will, for the purpose of occupation, be divided into three zones" is to be found in the London Protocol of September 12, 1944.

2. Milovan Djilas, *Gespräche mit Stalin* [Talks with Stalin] (Frankfurt: Europäische Verlagsanstalt, 1962), p. 146.

3. George F. Kennan, *Memoirs 1925–1950* (Boston and Toronto: Little, Brown and Co., 1967), p. 262.

4. Konrad Adenauer, *Erinner ungen 1945–1953* (Stuttgart: Deutsche Verlagsanstalt, 1953); Klaus Gotto, "Adenauer's Deutschland- and Ostopolitik 1954–1963," in Klaus Gotto, ed., *Konrad Adenauer. Seine Deutschland- and Aussenpolitik 1945–1963* Adenauer, his Germany and foreign policy (Munich: Deutscher Taschenbuch-Verlag, 1975), pp. 156ff. See also Hans-Peter Schwarz, *Vom Reich zur Bundesrepublik. Deutschland im Widerstreit der aussenpolitischen Konzeptionen in den Jahren der Besatzungsherrschaft 1945–1949* [From the Reich to the Federal Republic. Germany in the controversies on foreign policy conceptions during the years of occupation] (Neuwied and Berlin: Luchterhand Verlag, 1966), p. 425.

5. Speech of Kurt Schumacher in Berlin, August 14, 1947.

6. Ernst Reuter, Governing Mayor of Berlin, in the debate of the West German Ministerpräsidenten on the Frankfurt Documents of the Allied Military Governors in July 1948.

7. Richard Löwenthal, "Vom Kalten Krieg zur Ostpolitik" [From Cold War to Ostpolitik] in R. Lowenthal and H.-P. Schwarz, *Die zwiete Republik—25 Jahre Bundesrepublik Deutschland* [The Second Republic—25 years Federal Republic of Germany] (Stuttgart: Seewald Verlag, 1974), p. 604.

8. Auswärtiges Amt [Foreign Department], ed., *Verträge der Bundesrepublik Deutschland Bd. 7* [Convention of relations between the Three Powers and the Federal Republic of Germany] (Bonn and Köln: Verlag Wissenschaft und Politik, 1957), pp. 8ff. For the German text of the Convention see Ingo von Münch, ed., *Dokumente des geteilten Deutschland* [Documents of divided Germany], p. 229.

9. Dr. Antje Vollmer in the German Bundestag, September 29, 1984.

10. Hans-Peter Schwarz, *Die gezähmten Deutschen* [The tamed Germans] (Stuttgart: Deutsche Verlagsanstalt, 1985).

11. Alain de Benoist, "In aller Freundschaft" [In all friendship], *Criticon,* No. 60/61, 1980, pp. 199ff.

12. Iring Fetscher, "Die Suche nach der Nationalen Identität" [In search of national identity] in J. Habermas, ed., *Stichworte zur "geistigen Situation der Zeit",* L. Bd. Republik and Nation [Notes on the intellectual situation of our time], (Edition Suhrkamp, Vol, 1000, 1979), p. 123.

13. Peter Glotz, "Über politische Identität" [On political identity], *Merkur,* No. 12, 1980, pp. 1177ff.

14. Thomas Schmid, in Heinz Brüggemann, ed., *Über den Mangel an politisher Kultur in Deutschland* [On the lack of political culture in Germany] (Berlin: Wagenbuch Verlag, 1972), p. 112.

15. Peter Brandt and Herman Ammon, eds., *Die Linke und die nationale Frage* [The left and the national question] (Reinbek: Rowohlt Verlag, 1981), p. 25.

16. Gunter Zehm, "Wie Benjamin Franklin zum Ahnherrn der Bundesrepublik geworden ist" [How Benjamin Franklin became an ancestor of the Federal Republic], *Die Welt,* No. 232, October 4, 1980.

17. Heinz Karst, "Wider die nationale Erniedrigung der Deutschen" [Against national humiliation of the Germans] in G.-K. Kaltenbrunner, *Was ist deutsch? Die Unvermeidlichkeit, eine Nation zu sein* [What is German? The inevitability of being a nation] (Freiburg: Herderbucherei Initiative Bd. 39, 1980), pp. 72ff.

18. Bernard Willms, *Die Deutsche Nation. Theorie, Lage, Zukunft* [The German nation. Theory, situation, future] (Cologne: Hohenheim Verlag, 1982).

19. Zehm, "Wie Benjamin Franklin."

20. Schwarz, *Die gezähmten Deutschen.*

21. Federal Chancellor Helmut Kohl in the German Bundestag, February 27, 1985.

22. Horst Teltschik, "Aspekte der deutschen Aussen- und Sicherheitspolitik" [Aspects of German foreign and security policy] in *Aus Politik und Zeitgeschichte, Beilage zur Wochenzeitung "Das Parlament,"* [Politics and contemporary history, supplement to *Das Parlament*], No. B 7/8, February 16, 1985.

23. Alexander Shtromas, *Political Change and Social Development: The Case of the Soviet Union* (Frankfurt and Bern: Peter Lang Verlag, 1981), p. 140.

24. Kennan, *Memoirs,* p. 559.

3

Unity of Germany and Unity of Europe: Culture-Nation or Nation-State?

HANS-MARTIN SASS

The border between the two German states in Central Europe is not just a German border, it is also the borderline between the Eastern, Soviet-dominated hemisphere and the Western alliance. In fact, the dividing German borderline is identical with the Iron Curtain. The question of German unity is also the question of European unity, the most visible result of the post-war East-West confrontation.

This volume addresses the viability of the forty year-old post-war peace arrangement in Europe. The question of German unity, therefore, has to be discussed as a secondary issue within this wider framework.

It is timely to include the question of German unity in contemporary discussions of future global strategy. It is timely because in recent years a new generation of West German Social-Democrats and East German cadres have rediscovered the issue, which used to be a domain of conservative political forces such as the refugee organizations or of evangelical political forces (Gustav Heinemann and his followers), while the Roman Catholics (led by Konrad Adenauer) and the Social Democrats (with the exception of Kurt Schumacher) were less interested in the national issue. It is also timely to discuss German unity these days in Washington, D.C., where so much attention is focused on the Soviet Union's attempts to establish hegemony in Central America. I feel it is extremely important to look at Soviet expansionism—or colonialism—in a global perspective; Lenin's own perspective was global, as are the facts and challenges of today.

Klaus Hornung, arguing for continued discussion of German reunification, presents a four-step thesis:

1. In reviewing the last 40 years we have to recognize the progressive integration of the dismembered Third Reich into the

great global alliances which have shaped the face of the globe since the middle of this century: East Germany becoming part of the Soviet colonial empire, dominated by Moscow and based on the Brezhnev Doctrine; West Germany joining the Western alliance; and Austria remaining neutral between the two spheres and trying to find a political identity independent of the East-West confrontation. The last 15 years of detente, and the "Ostpolitik" of Brezhnev and Brandt, have not brought anything new to Europe; they have merely consolidated and cemented the dismemberment of Germany (and Europe).

2. The mental and moral situation in West Germany is one of lost national identity teamed with guilt, and of general political discontent. This discontent manifests itself either in an apolitical, purely economic identity combined with profit-oriented work ethics, or in ideological, escapist subcultures of various kinds: intellectual Marxism, Marxism-Leninism, environmentalism, etc.

3. A new discussion on national identity has been initiated by the Social Democrats during the last few years. What had been the domain of conservative or evangelical protestant positions, became a concern of left-wing groups (Peter Brandt, Peter Glotz).

4. These three points lead Dr. Hornung to the conclusion that the question of German unity is still unresolved. He strongly argues that the division of Germany is indissolubly linked to the division of Europe. We cannot forecast the future of East-West competition, nor can we deny future generations the right to self-determination. International and German law also keep the question open. For Dr. Hornung it is crucial, however, that the Germans overcome their apolitical attitude towards coercion by Soviet hegemonical colonialism.

Here is my view:

1. I agree with Dr. Hornung's thesis that external factors—primarily the East-West conflict—are responsible for the continuing lack of a solution to the question of German unity. These factors are merely reinforced by internal factors of challenged national identity as a result of losing two world wars. Insofar as external factors may change, for example, through withdrawal of United States global responsibility or collapse of the Soviet colonial system, they in themselves do not constitute a major obstacle to the political unification of Germany; however, other

forces might surface, both external and internal, German and European, and these could render attempts at unification difficult or counter-productive.

2. I would like to discuss some historical, political, and cultural arguments which make the German Question at the end of this second millennium more complicated than the simple issue of having or not having a German nation-state, or of undoing the Soviet colonization of half of Europe. I will address three issues which are particular and specific to German politics and culture, as demonstrated by the political and cultural history of Central Europe:

(a) the historical lack of a stable German *nation-state* and an established German capital;
(b) the difference between *cultural nation* (Kulturnation) and *nation-state* (Nationalstaat);
(c) the *geopolitical history* of continuous protection and defence of European (Germanic) Western values against Eastern invasions.

3. While Moscow, Athens, Rome, Madrid, Paris, and London served as capitals for many hundreds of years, there was no such stable capital in Central Europe. Kaisers were elected by powerful heads of tribes, dukes, and kings. Aachen, Prague, Berlin, and Vienna served as centers for longer or shorter periods of time. For centuries Kaisers traveled like traveling power brokers from castle to castle, mediating between various forces and maintaining only small personal home bases. When Napoleon conquered German soil, he destroyed hundreds of sovereign entities, some small and unimportant, some strong and powerful. It is my thesis that present-day German political culture is the product of this Germanic tribal heritage. Equality and rivalry among peers; balance of power between leadership groups; cooperation only in situations of life or death, while opposing values of autonomy, liberty, and plurality operate in everyday situations;—these are the major features of such a political culture of plurality rather than unity. Franconian and Salingian Kaisers were always on the road traveling among Sicily, Prague, Worms, Aachen, Augsburg. For centuries the Habsburg dynasty had its capital in Vienna, but they did not govern a nation-state; it was a multinational state (*vielvölkerstaat*), stabilizing the southern flank of Central Europe

45

against the Turks. Berlin was a capital for three-quarters of a century, the product of Bismarck's "small-German" solution, which excluded Austria—very different from the "great-German" solution, that is, a Reich of all German speaking middle-Europeans, which was the goal of the 1848 Frankfurt Parliament, and which would have required the dismemberment of the multinational state of Austria. To focus exclusively on political unity between East and West Germany is to take a very short-sighted view, dominated by the East-West conflict. Even the terminology is misleading. East Germany historically and geographically was Middle Germany, while now widely de-populated East Prussia (today mainly a part of the U.S.S.R.) and Silesia (now part of Poland, which lost its Eastern part to the U.S.S.R.) were traditionally called East Germany. Austria has a population of less than 8 million; East Germany has more than double that, 16 million; West Germany has 4 times that many people with 60 million. Bonn is West Germany's capital because Konrad Adenauer, a native of the Rhineland, did not like Frank-furt; Berlin has seen Kaiser Wilhelm II, Führer Adolf Hitler and Party Chairman Erich Honnecker all within less than 50 years; Vienna served as a capital uninterruptedly for more than 500 years. This is the wider historical context of political unity among the German-speaking peoples and within their traditional political culture. Political unity in the form of what is now called "reunification" (of Bonn and Berlin) would not be an outgrowth of genuine German political culture, but rather a result of resolv-ing the European situation in favor of either West or East. The political liberation of East Germany under Western auspices would probably result in a federation of European states, includ-ing a non-unified East and West Germany, for reasons of power balance within that federation. An expansion of soviet hegemony over Western Europe would indeed most likely result in a reunified Germany serving as a strong Soviet outpost for the rest of Europe. A third, in-between solution would even more prob-ably favor a federalistic solution. It would unite European states without the European parts of the Soviet Union, which might perfer to be part of a Northern Asian confederation. A fourth scenario represents the most viable solution for an extended future, based on European history and shared values: a federation of states from the Atlantic to the Ural, including Baltic and East Central European states together with West European states and the states of the Ukraine and of Bielorussia. Such a federation would contain reasonably balanced states, having its capitol somewhere in the middle of Europe, in the vicinity of Krakow or Prague. It would not re-introduce the German Reich in its 1939 borders, nor the European part of the Soviet Union in its entirety; it would have a Ukrainian state, a Russian state, an Austrian state, West Germany and East Germany. No existing borders would be changed; they would lose most of their relevance, however, as is the case already in Western Europe. According to established cultural and historical differences in Europe, such a federation would be less centralized than the United States or the existing Soviet empire, but would have to be much more centralized than Western Europe is today.

As these four options demonstrate, the question of German unity is still open because the European question is still open, and because hegemonical systems like the Soviet Empire have never lasted forever.

4. There is, however, more to German unity than the political *nation-state;* here we must introduce the concept of the *culture-nation.* We can forget about the various dynasties, principalities and succession wars during the last 1000 years, when speaking about the *culture-nation,* which has existed at least since the times of Martin Luther, 500 years ago and has shaped the German national and cultural identity. The German culture-nation extends far beyond the borders of contemporary East Germany and West Germany. Immanuel Kant in Koenigsberg, Mozart in Salzburg, Zwingli in Zurich, Wagner in Bayreuth, Sigmund Freud and Johann Strauss in Vienna, Goethe in Weimar, and Luther in Wittenberg—these are the representatives of German unity. But here we are speaking of a different unity. It is the unity which one German philosopher, Max Scheler, called "plurality in cultural matters" (as opposed to "unity in political matters"), and which another German philosopher, Hegel, made the "software" of reasoning, of understanding and shaping reality, personally, culturally, and politically: *dialectics,* the combination of thesis and anti-thesis in a synthesis which is again due to be confronted by its opposite. Time is too short to give examples of this particular form of unity in diversity within German culture, the dialectically regulated and self-regulating markets of values, concepts, and ideas, which will forever prevent the formation of any except the

most liberal, the most pluralistic German nation-state. Studying German cultural and intellectual history teaches us more about the capabilities and shortcomings of German politics than studying the dynastic power plays.

A look at the last 40 years of culture history in Germany reveals two different pictures in East and West: in East Germany, external factors, i.e., Soviet tanks, provide a framework within which cultural bureaucrats and intellectuals do their best in what is called "acquisition of the heritage" (*Aneignung des Erbes*): Martin Luther the rebel; Beethoven the genius of working class background. Their reinterpretation of cultural history has two aspects: one is the intent to reinforce and stabilize Marxist-Leninist ideology as state ideology; the other is that, nevertheless, the classic readings have their own strong, powerful, multi-faceted values which cannot be reduced to black-and-white, simplistic ideology; this is a rose with a very dangerous thorn. Western media and television is another thorn in East German society; though decreasingly, so are family relations. In West Germany, on the other hand, there is a neurotic relationship with most of German cultural tradition. They do not reinterpret it but throw it away, partly because of the unhappy Third Reich disaster, and partly due to the fashionable Frankfurt School intellectual movement, which even though it is now dead academically, has had and still has plenty of disciples in the media and among left-wing politicians. Studying the unregulated cultural unity-in-diversity driven by internal factors in West Germany, and the regulated but complex unity in East Germany, proves most beneficial and informative. The dialectical relationship between the two provides an index of various probabilities for future cultural and political developments. Cultural and ideological debates in Central Europe are very precise indicators of political probabilities; the infrequently appearing question regarding political unity is one of the signals, and sometimes a catalyst, of actual and future developments in an ever-changing Germanic world.

5. Let me add to the political and cultural dimensions a third, specifically Germanic type of unity: solidarity and brotherhood under severe stress, and in life-and-death situations. From the Nibelung's faithfulness until death, to the Third Reich's fatal end, there is in Germany a tradition of dialectically intertwined tragedy and heroism. One aspect of German history is the problem of

constantly assessing and identifying the enemy by applying good common sense. Commitment to fight was never a problem for people of Germanic heritage. Misjudgment in identifying the enemy, however, quite often had devastating effects in Central Europe (for example, the Thirty Years' War and the Nazis' poor judgment). But attempts to protect the Germanic world from specific hostile and threatening intruders date back 2000 years to the time of the Roman *Limes Germanicus,* the great wall protecting the southern German provinces against barbarian invaders. The greatest successes in this tradition came with Otto the Great's victory over the Hungarians on the Lech fields near Augsburg in 955, and Savoyard Prince Eugen's triumph over the Turks outside Vienna in 1685, which prevented the Turkish annexation of Polish Europe. Central Europe and East Central Europe during the last 2000 years were a crucial field for defending traditional values and lifestyles which were shared by the Germans, the French, and the Anglo-Saxons, but also by Poles, Czechs, and Russians. Although there were different priorities among the shared values over centuries (for instance, Poland was closer to Western, i.e., French culture than Prussia, while the Prussian nobility shared family ties and more paternalistic values with the Russian nobility). The fight against invaders from the East was successful whenever these diverse forces rallied, with last-minute urgency, around the one goal of defending the values of autonomy, freedom, and non-conformism.

The contemporary resignation and inattention which prevails in East and West Germany toward a situation which so urgently and crucially threatens the viability of the German (and European) heritage admits of two possible explanations: either the Soviet threat is not so great that an emergent crisis would menace survival in Central Europe, or it is one of those tragic situations where an inability to identify the enemy leads to disastrous consequences.

I thought an excursion into the complicated areas of the distinction between unity as a *nation-state* and unity as a *culture-nation,* and the weaknesses and advantages of German political culture, was necessary in order to shed a brighter light on the newly fashionable question of German political unity and the language of "reunification."

Let me come back to my introductory remarks regarding the intertwined problems of German unity and European unity. The

Iron Curtain constitutes the most unusual event to occur in Central Europe in the last thousand years of its history. Less unusual, but more dangerous, is the over-extension of the Soviet colonial empire. It was an ill-advised decision on the part of Stalin to expand the original Czarist colonial empire so far into the West, suppressing Central Eastern nations which, according to their cultural and political heritage, cannot and will not be suppressed forever. Instead of concentrating on patriotic national policy for the Russians, the Ukrainians, and the Baltic natives, the Soviet cadres draw on the resources of these people in favor of the preservation, even extension, of the colonial system they inherited from the Romanoffs. If we consider Russian history since 1918, the Soviet Union emerges as a nation still in a pre-revolutionary stage, not a post-revolutionary one as its government claims. The fate of Europe and of Germany is closely tied to a happy, and hopefully evolutionary, process of emancipating the Russian and other Eastern European nations from an outdated political and economic system.

Examining the long-range developments of history, we see that:

1. In Eastern Europe there has been a repeat of the Holy Alliance of elitist oligarchic systems with increasing internal problems and unmanageable leadership challenges;

2. In Central America and elsewhere, we are faced with a return of colonialism in the form of a non-hemisphere superpower recolonizing;

3. Soviet Leninism exists as a curious combination of a new secular salvation ideology, discredited to all but some Western intellectuals, and old-fashioned colonial expansionism, which hurts everyone, including the Russian people. It is within this framework that German unity must be analyzed and assessed. German unity cannot be separated from the larger issue of European unity. True unity in Germany cannot be achieved by merely merging the two German states into one political entity.

4

The Economic Consequences of European Peace

GORDON C. BJORK

Europe has been at peace for an interval lasting nearly the length of its "Golden Age," from 1870–1914. Like the earlier period, it has been a time of rapid growth in real per capita GNP based, in large part, on rapidly expanding inter-European and intra-continental flows of goods, money, and people.

United States policy towards Europe during the period has gone through three phases: rebuilding under the Marshall Plan to the mid-fifties, partnership arrangements with the Common Market and NATO from 1955 to 1975, and increasing economic and political stress over the last decade. This latter period has been accompanied by a slowdown in world economic growth and high levels of unemployment in both Western Europe and the United States.

The peacemakers learned from the aftermath of World War I.[1] The Treaty of Versailles which ended World War I had further fragmented Europe. The interwar period witnessed the continued division of large areas of Asia and Africa into restricted zones of economic influence for European imperial powers. Japan imposed a "co-prosperity sphere" in the Pacific, and the United States continued to regard Latin America as its own sphere of economic and political influence. The interwar period witnessed slow growth, unstable output, deflation, widespread unemployment, and financial instability. Industrial nations raised tariffs and deval-ued currencies in their struggle to maintain employment and output. The per capita volume of world trade and international flows of labor and capital were greatly reduced from the levels and growth rate preceding World War I.

The establishment of the United Nations in 1945 was an attempt to institutionalize multilateral, international political cooperation. Other significant international agreements following World War II established economic institutions for expanding multilateral trade. Those institutions and the policies of economic multilateralism which they embody have made a most significant contribution to a historically unprecedented rate of growth in the world economy over the past four decades.

The economic aspects of the peace settlement projected at the end of World War II were based on economic multilateralism. Visionaries projected institutions such as the International Monetary Fund (IMF), International Trade Organization, and World Bank as supra-national agencies to stimulate aggregate demand, maintain full employment, and avoid the economic rivalries and instability of the interwar period.

The IMF and the World Bank have played more limited roles in international finance than originally intended because of reluctance by nation states, particularly by the United States, to allow international organizations to "run" the world economy. The International Trade Organization was never formed, but the General Agreement of Tariffs and Trade (GATT) has played a moderate and effective role in reducing and forestalling trade barriers among countries.

The internationalism aspired to in the United Nations charter and its counterpart international economic agencies was not realized. The Iron Curtain cut off most important economic flows between Eastern and Western Europe, and the formation of the Common Market in Western Europe represented a deliberate choice for economic integration rather than more loosely-coordinated international trade.

The two most significant changes in economic organizations over the past quarter-century, unforeseen by postwar planners, have been the growth of multinational corporations controlling the production and distribution of goods and the emergence of international banks which have internationalized money and investment. Both have tied Western Europe and the United States into a world economic system which has been both a source of unprecedented growth and prosperity and a source of economic and financial instability. The United States, Western Europe, Japan, and the newly-industrialized countries cannot prosper without the international economy created by four decades of world peace with only "local" wars. However, they are also hostage to the instability created by "oil shocks," droughts, and destabilizing monetary or fiscal policies initiated by the governments of an interdependent world economy.

This paper has four parts. Part I reviews the changing importance of international flows of goods, men, money, and their implications for economic growth and security. Part II discusses the postwar economic institutions which made possible the growth and stability of the world economy over the past four decades. Part III makes some comparisons between the economic performance of the victors and the vanquished of World War II. Six tables containing statistical evidence on the relative performance of various economic indicators can be found in the Appendix in the final section of this paper.

The International Economy and Economic Growth

Why should a nation participate in the international economy rather than strive for economic independence? A good place to start consideration of that question is Adam Smith's famous dictum, "The division of labor is limited by the extent of the market."[2]

Economic growth occurs from the specialization of production. International trade provides the greatest market size and, consequently, the greatest specialization of output and highest levels of output per unit of labor and capital.

Modern economic growth started in agriculture. Mechanization increases the number of acres which can be worked by a single laborer. Then the application of genetics and biochemistry increases yield per acre. The result is a decrease in the quantity of labor and land needed to feed a growing population. Mechanization, of course, depends on factories to fabricate the tractors and plows, machine-tool producers to build the machines to make the tractors, steel mills to produce the metals for the machine tools and tractors, coal mines to produce the fuel to fire the steel mills, and so on.

The specialization of production requires the concentration of population in towns. Railroads must be built to haul food and fuel to the towns, transport the finished goods from the towns and the people within the towns. Urbanization requires steel for buildings, water systems, sewer systems, and transportation systems. Urban dwellers use rising incomes to purchase clothing, travel, education, and health care. Most of the production and distribution is organized and financed by economic organizations of increasing size, complexity, and geographic extent. This was the basis of nineteenth-century economic development and the emergence of the nineteenth century nation state.

The extent of the market becomes important for economies of scale. The size of the market needed to support a given steel, chemical, textile, or automobile *plant* may not require international trade. The specialization of production within an *industry* to allow for the production of capital goods for that industry, in many cases, will require a market larger than a single nation. This generalization is less true for large nations like the United States and the Soviet Union than for the rest of the world's nations. However, world markets are particularly important to our most technologically-advanced industries. Commercial jet-liners, pharmaceuticals, and mainframe computers all depend on world, rather than national, markets for the volume of sales necessary to finance the research and development necessary for success.

International trade has traditionally been thought of as national firms selling finished manufactures or raw materials to consumers. It is increasingly recognized that the most important current transnational exchanges are among components of multinational corporations. Ford assembles cars for sale in one country with components it produces in many different countries. Union Carbide does not ship chemicals to India; it supplies the technical "know-how" to build the plants which incorporate the processes which are the firm's real capital. Paris fashion designers contract for production in Hong Kong to be marketed by their firms' American subsidiaries. McDonald's franchises operations in Tokyo which depend on the firm's knowledge of marketing and cost and quality-control techniques—even for Japanese foods.

Modern international trade does not primarily consist of national firms in industrial nations trading manufactures to consumers in developing nations for raw materials. International flows of men, goods, and money are increasingly among units of multinational firms and among their suppliers and distributors. Increasingly, lawyers', engineers', and accountants' international activities loom even larger as they do domestically. The international flows from services is large and important.

The traditional economic arguments for international trade have been based on comparative advantage and economies of scale on a *static* basis. By specializing in the production of certain goods, trading nations could increase their overall real income. However, the dynamic effects of specialization are much more important, quantitatively than state gains from comparative advantage.[3]

The dynamic elements of comparative advantage and economies of scale have always cut two ways. A nation can benefit from the increase in the size of its markets resulting from international trade. On the other hand, allowing foreign sales in its own markets may prevent the growth of domestic output to a size where domestic producers can compete effectively in domestic and foreign markets. For dynamic reasons, the "infant industry" argument has been used by advocates of protection from Freiderich List to erstwhile proponents of an "Industrial Policy."[4]

While the specialization of production is the means for obtaining economic growth and high per capita real incomes, it also exposes particular firms and individuals to the insecurities of market fluctuations in the demand for goods they produce. In the 1950s, American textile workers protested their loss of domestic markets to foreign competition. In the 1980s, it has been the automobile and steel workers who have been most damaged by international competition.[5]

There are two elements of international competition which make it particularly hard to reconcile with the demands of the population for income security. The first is the size of the gains from trade. As nations become more similar in their production capabilities as a result of international trade and competition, the perceived advantage of international trade may decline. Americans may be willing to import Japanese cars if there is a 25 percent price advantage. If it is only 5 percent, it may seem preferable to keep American auto workers at work.

Second, large fluctuations in the exchange values of currencies may produce socially unacceptable instability in production levels in export- and import-competing industries. It was wide fluctuations in currency exchange values which contributed to protectionist pressures in the interwar period. During the past decade, wide fluctuations in the exchange values of currencies have once again started to build pressures in various nations for government actions, including tariffs and quotas, to protect national economies from the instability of world markets.

One characteristic of modern economic growth is its reliance on basic scientific research and the expenditure of substantial sums on research and development for highly unpredictable returns.[6] Contemporary American dominance in high-technology electronics depends partially on research funded by such huge firms as AT&T and IBM. Similar considerations apply to jet aircraft and pharmaceuticals. The commercial "payoff" for investment in basic research in some of these industries depends on a world market. But then, when scientific research and technological development have brought breakthroughs, what protection is there against foreign firms (which have not borne the development and research costs) from using the knowledge and technology developed by others to compete away returns from investments in research and development in unprotected markets?

International trade is not something which can be turned on and off as a matter of stabilization policy. Firms do not decide to produce discrete batches of goods for uncertain sale to an unknown buyer. Production in the modern world depends upon investment of large sums of capital for long periods of time. Firms undertake these investments on the basis of expected continuity of markets and specific customers for the output of specialized investments. Equally, employment contracts become long-term and fixed by the mutual understanding of employer and employee about the alternatives of the latter and the former's need for employees with an investment in specialized knowledge.[7]

The modern industrial firm needs both large markets and predictable relationships to justify the long-term investments fixed in specialized physical and human capital. The scope of international markets is necessary to modern economic growth. Yet their unpredictability and the difficulties in transnational enforcement of patents and trade secrets make international trade and investment more risky than they would be in a national market.

Thus, the importance of international trade to economic growth is unmistakable, and yet the threat of international trade to income security and to the important source of economic growth from research and development is also omnipresent. The lack of easy answers to this dilemma poses difficult questions for the continuance of unrestricted international trade.

The Economic Settlements of World War II

The key elements of the international postwar economic system had been drafted during the war and immediately after at Bretton

Woods—primarily by the Americans and the British.[8] The system was to have three key institutions and three concepts: an International Monetary Fund to provide adequate liquidity for the growth of world trade; a World Bank for reconstruction and development to provide long-term loans funded in world capital markets; and an International Trade Organization to guarantee fair and non-discriminatory, of not "free," trade. These institutions were built on the recognition that it had been the lack of such institutions and concepts which had led to the miserable performance of the international economy of the interwar period.

A key element of the International Monetary Fund was to be the responsibility of creditor nations to finance the short-term deficits of countries which resulted from the creditors' trade surpluses. This was to discourage the return of the competitive devaluations and erection of trade barriers which restricted international trade in the interwar period which inadequate liquidity made trade expansion impossible.

The World Bank was to finance European reconstruction and Third World development through long-term loans which would make it possible for nations to finance their development free of the terms and conditions which might be imposed by private investors. The World Bank was a means to avoid the assertion of economic spheres of influence by industrial over-developing nations.

The third element in international trade was to be an International Trade Organization which would negotiate multilateral reductions in tariffs and other trade barriers.

All three institutions and concepts were severely limited in their powers by the U.S. Congress. The drawing rights of nations in the IMF were smaller than needed and non-automatic. The responsibilities of creditor nations for their balance of payments surpluses was not accepted as a principle. It was only because the United States' current account surplus in its balance of payments during the decade after the war was offset by defense expenditures and foreign capital investment that the shortage of dollars did not become a more serious problem.

The capital and borrowing powers of the World Bank were similarly restricted. The United States has always been a brake on the enlargement of the World Bank's capital and borrowing capabilities. The International Trade Organization was turned down by the U.S. Congress although the General Agreement on

Tariffs and Trade which was drafted in its place did turn out to provide an effective vehicle for the reduction of trade barriers in the fifties and sixties.

The United States responded to the end of World War II with some of the same isolationism which followed World War I. The Congress was suspicious of giving any power to international financial organizations which might empower them to lend and borrow American financial resources. The generous wartime Lend Lease program was not extended or replaced to help war-torn Europe recover. What changed that isolationism in 1948 was the Cold War.

The initial economic response to the Cold War was the Marshall Plan in 1948 to assist in rebuilding Western Europe through the provision of long-term American economic assistance. The Marshall Plan was of particular importance to Britain and Germany. Britain emerged from the war economically exhausted. The domestic economy was war-damaged; the merchant marine, an important source of exchange earnings, had been sunk; and foreign assets had been sold or encumbered to pay for the war. Britain could not generate the foreign exchange earnings necessary for the raw materials and food required to rebuild her economy. Germany was in an even worse position. The Marshall Plan credits supplied the financial wherewithal to allow both nations to recover.

United States industry invested heavily in Europe during the fifties and sixties and, in combination with foreign aid and defense expenditures, the dollar shortage was converted into a dollar surplus by 1960. In the middle of the 1960s, American expenditures for the Vietnam conflict increased the negative balance of international payments of the United States. In 1968 France began to convert dollars into gold—a process which led to the accelerating outflow of United States monetary gold, and the suspension of U.S. support of the fixed price of the dollar in international gold markets in 1969, and the suspension of dollar convertibility into gold in 1971.

The Bretton Woods settlement was made in the United States Treasury, rather than in the International Monetary Fund, the world's central banker. The system worked remarkably well between 1945 and 1970 to provide adequate liquidity for a growing volume of world trade. It inevitably broke down because the United States had to provide the increase in liquidity through an increase in dollars without an increase in the stock of monetary gold which served as backing for the dollar as an international reserve currency.

The international economic problems of the 1920s were accompanied by deflation. The problems of the 1970s have resulted in inflation. In both periods, the cause has been a rate of growth of international financial liquidity unequal to the potential growth of world trade. In both cases, the results have been a decline in the growth of world trade and increasing levels of unemployment in the industrial and developing nations dependent on world trade.

Lord Keynes' proposal for international monetary reform in 1945 was for the power of the International Monetary Fund to print "Bancor," the international counterpart of the monetary base in the United States. It is understandable that the world's monetarists would have resisted discretionary control for an international central bank in 1945 when even today national monetarist want to limit the discretionary powers of their own central banks. Nevertheless, in absence of a world central bank or effective alternative arrangements to control the world's money supply, the international economy will continue to experience international financial stress from the fluctuations of currency exchange values dependent on volatile international capital flows and shifts from currency to currency for reserves.

Over the past decade, America and Europe have witnessed first a steep drop and then a steep rise in the value of the dollar against major European currencies. The initiating and dominant factors in these changes of currency exchange values have been short-term capital flows rather than balance of trade changes. The latter have been effect, rather than cause, and the concomitant effects on prices and unemployment have created serious problems for both Europe and the United States. The September 1985 and January 1986 decision by the G-5 financial leaders to realign exchange rates and lower real interest rates are a promising alternative to "benign neglect" by governments to deal with the problems created by fluctuating exchange rates. These governments realize that the alternative is an increase in barriers to international flows which will be deleterious to all.

The second element of the Bretton Woods settlement was the World Bank. Its powers were also limited by economic conservatives who feared that its lending policies would be unsound and possibly deleterious to the political and commercial interests of the

United States and other developed nations. The United States in the fifties and sixties and, increasingly, Europe and Japan in the sixties were successful in financing most of the growth in the developing world on private or bilateral basis. The problems of the private system did not become manifest until the late seventies when the international commercial banks assumed a major role in financing major trade deficits and development programs with the enormous increase of "petrodollars" and Eurocurrencies freed from the discipline of gold and fixed exchange rates.

A combination of the overextension of credit coupled with high interest rates, depressed commodity prices, and the rising exchange value of the U.S. dollar due to the domestic governmental deficit of the United States has led to the present international debt crisis in which many countries cannot pay their debts, or even the interest on them, and the banks cannot afford to allow default. Another result of the debt crisis has been the stagnation of world trade as nations sought to control inflation and their current account trade balances.

Could a more powerful World Bank have avoided the current problems? Present problems were caused by international private banks' competing to loan money to supposedly "risk-free" sovereign borrowers. While there are no easy answers to bad lending processes internationally (just as there are none domestically), one answer might be some kind of agreement among international central banks in their roles as regulators of their own national banks to require both country diversification of loan risk and mandated levels of loan-loss reserves commensurate with risk even to sovereign borrowers. Peace has not created international financial stability.

Victors and Vanquished

One of the ironies of the forty years of peace in Europe is the different economic consequences for victors and vanquished in World War II. The United States, Britain, France, Russia have all had their economic performance adversely affected by the burdens of defense and the costs of fighting small wars in Korea, Vietnam, Afghanistan, and elsewhere. Japan and Germany, prohibited from the building of offensive capabilities and limited in expenditures even on their own national defense, have been able to allocate men and machines to gain competitive superiority in the world's economy rather than military capability.

The most significant element in the Japanese "economic miracle" following World War II may have been the American prohibition on the rearming of Japan. Japan's burden for defense expenditures was assumed by the American conquerors. The five to ten percent of GNP *not* spent on peacetime defense was available for a level of capital investment more than double the American level. Japanese scientists, engineers, and technicians did not get bid away by firms engaging in weapons research and arms production. The compensation levels were lower, in relative terms, and they turned their talents to the development of new technologies in the capital goods- and consumer goods–producing industries.

Before the Japanese acceded to Article 8 of the International Monetary Fund in 1962, opening up its own markets to international trade and capital flows, they had established dominance in their own markets for manufactures. They then found in the countries surrounding the Pacific and, particularly, the United States enormous markets for their technologically advanced consumer goods industries.

Germany was occupied by the armies of four nations: Britain, France, the Soviet Union, and the United States. The three regions occupied by the Western Allies were formally reconstituted into the Federal Republic in 1955 when the division of Germany into East and West was recognized as a *fait accompli* of the Cold War.

As in Japan, the military governments of the occupying powers turned to civilian bureaucracies for assistance in the rebuilding of a shattered economy. A critical element in the German case was the Marshall Plan, which began in 1948. The Marshall Plan mandated cooperative planning for the participating European governments as a condition for receiving American aid. The Organization for Economic Cooperation and Development (OECD) was established in Paris for collaborative planning. The postwar rebuilding of the war-shattered iron and steel industry to provide the capital goods for the postwar reconstruction was carried out by the European Iron and Steel Community. The history of European military and economic rivalry was ended in the signing of the Treaty of Rome in 1958, which established the European Economic Community or "Common Market."

The economic basis of the Common Market was the linking of

German heavy industry with French and Italian agriculture and light industry. Rail and water links were rationalized and increasing portions of the energy needs were supplied by cheap oil from the Middle East. All of the six signatories to the Treaty of Rome had a tradition of central governmental planning and economic control. In Germany, the control was characterized by strong links between the major banks and the powerful state governments in the control and provision of investment. Germany, like Japan, had an "industrial policy" formulated by a partnership between business and government instituted, ironically, by the victorious United States which did *not* have an industrial policy.

As in Japan, one important contributor to the German "economic miracle" was the prohibition on rearming. The cost of German defense was assumed by its conquerors. Funds not spent on defense were available for investment. Expenditures by occupying armies became an important source of foreign exchange earnings, particularly, before 1960.

World War II had another significant effect in both countries in releasing women from traditional roles into wider participation in the labor force. In Germany, the labor force was further increased by the flow of refugees from East Germany and Eastern Europe until the Communist nations sealed their borders. In Japan, the release of additional labor from a shrinking agricultural sector added to the industrial labor force. In both countries, an ample supply of skilled but low-wage labor gave an international competitive advantage. The Germans reasserted their longstanding competitive advantages in chemical and metal-working industries based on the scientific and technological knowledge of their labor force.

The post-World War II economic performance of the victors, in comparison to the vanquished, is one dramatic demonstration of the economic consequence of the peace settlement. Germany grew twice as fast, and Japan grew three times as fast, in per capita output as the United States or the United Kingdom. How does one explain this disparate economic performance?

The first and most obvious explanation is "catch up." Germany and Japan grew more slowly than the rest of the world between 1913 and 1950. Another explanation is the sectoral composition of output. The United States and the United Kingdom had a larger proportion of their output in the government and service sectors of their economies where productivity is not measured and reduces aggregate averages. Further, 10 percent of the growth in output per person was accounted for by intersectoral shifts in Germany and the United States as opposed to 25 percent in Japan. Britain had *no* growth in output from intersectoral shifts.[9]

Taking these factors into account, it is still possible to argue that significant policy decisions affected economic performance in the third quarter of the twentieth century to invert the outcomes for the military winners and losers of World War II. The first area is investment: In 1950, Germany had 50 percent and Japan had 15 percent of the capital stock per employed worker in the United States. By 1978, Germany had *more* capital per worker than the United States, and the level in Japan was two-thirds of the United States level.[10]

This is not the place for an extended analysis of differences in the levels of saving and the patterns of investment among nations. Nevertheless, a few suggestive comments are in order. First, the United States has spent between five and ten percent of GNP over the last quarter century, while Germany and Japan were limited to very small defense establishments by the World War II peace settlements. Second, household and corporate savings rates in Germany and Japan have been stimulated by their tax systems and discouraged in the United States. Third, those countries chose to allocate a smaller proportion of investment to housing while housing construction was stimulated and subsidized in the United States as a matter of national policy. As an explanation of differences in savings rates and investment, differences in government policy rather than cultural differences are a large explanatory variable.[11] The military losers of World War II have become the economic victors in its aftermath.

Conclusion

The German military strategist, Clausewitz, coined the famous dictum that war is the continuation of politics by other means. Total war is no longer a rational solution to any unsolved political problem, and the limited wars in Korea, the Middle East, Indo-China, and Afghanistan over the decades since the end of World War II have illustrated the reticence of the major powers to escalate political conflict into total war. The result has been a continuing Cold War with occasional "hot flashes." The Cold War has had a chilling effect on the international economy.

The early economic result of the Cold War was the prevention of an American return to isolationism after the World War II peace settlement. The longer-term effect of the Cold War has been a high level of military expenditures by the United States, the USSR, Britain, and France which might otherwise have been channeled into their own development. A continuing drag on worldwide economic progress has been the consequence of the failure of the peace settlement to bring real peace and political mechanisms for maintaining it.

It was not Clausewitz but a civilian who jibed that generals were always preparing for the previous war. The comment might be adapted to economists and politicians whose economic doctrine and policies are based on a previous ages' international economy. International trade no longer consists primarily of industrial countries' exchanging manufactures for raw materials with developing countries; most world trade is manufactures trading among industrial countries. This is one reason why the politics of protection are more complex. Some firms and industries are threatened while others are dependent on international trade for both suppliers and customers and their own intra-firm flows.

In the past, if Ford lost domestic market share to GM, the contraction at Ford might be offset by the increase at GM. If Ford loses market share to Toyota, the domestic auto industry contracts employment and purchases from supplies. Ford may avoid losing out to Toyota by producing engine blocks in Mexico and transmissions in Spain. The contractionary results are the same for domestic employees and suppliers but not for the multinational Ford corporation. Firms and workers now have divergent interests in tariffs and quotas.

World peace and world trade promote economic interaction. One domestic consequence will be the erosion of relative incomes of workers whose wages depend on sharing the gains from oligopolistic market power with their employers as in steel and autos. If Ford or IBM use the same technology internationally, the wages of American Ford or IBM workers will be forced toward the levels paid by the companies in other countries by Ford and IBM and their multinational competitors.

There are two ways for workers to avoid this—stop imports and/or foreign "sourcing" or move from production employment to the design of technology and manufacture of capital goods where there is not yet foreign competition. The first strategy would significantly raise the price of cars or computers, while the second would reduce the number but increase the compensation levels of the remaining workers in the American subsidiaries of multinational corporations. This is a viable industrial policy for continued growth. Protectionism is a prescription for job security and economic stagnation.

The internationalization of financial flows makes the old arguments for benign neglect of international capital flows far more risky. The dollar-gold standard and the Bretton Woods fixed exchange rate systems were supposed to stabilize income and price-level adjustments. With floating rates the dollar still serves as a reserve currency, but with adverse consequences for the U.S. economy. Presently, high real-interest rates in the United States resulting primarily from large federal deficits have sucked in foreign investments in the United States. The foreign capital inflows drive up the dollar and erode the competitive position of all American exporters and import-competing industries. There are frightening parallels in the current situation to the 1930s when European capital flight drove up the dollar, contributed to low agricultural prices, rural financial collapse, and simultaneously produced the notorious Smoot-Hawley Tariff in response to protectionist pressure from the manufacturers adversely affected by high exchange rates. In the 1980s, substitute defaults by various developing countries for the 1930s European default on war reparations to complete the analogies.

What can be done? An international economy needs some arrangements to provide adequate international liquidity and appropriate relationships between central bankers and/or international commercial bankers to avoid financial crises. The solution must be multinational. It cannot be unilaterally controlled by the American Treasury or Federal Reserve. Significantly, reflecting the exchange rate between dollars and yen, Japanese commercial banks have just surpassed American banks in their total value of both international assets (loans and bonds to borrowers outside the country) and international liabilities (deposits by foreign holders).

The economic consequences of peace are most certainly preferable to the consequences of war. Yet, they are not an unmixed blessing to the United States when we bear a disproportionate share of the costs of defense. The creation of an increasingly integrated world economy, similarly, has long-run consequences for growth and prosperity and domestic priorities. Absent suitable institutions and policies to stabilize and provide some measure of income security the politically powerful workers in the industrialized nations of the world are unlikely to accept the lower relative wages and increased uncertainties of international competition and interdependence. Like many political issues, the gains are great but diffuse, and the losses are concentrated with small, powerful groups.

History has its ironies. Temporary arrangements become permanent. Political compromises and economic policies have unforeseen consequences. The demilitarization of Japan and Germany have made them economic powers. The economic unification of the Western nations has been accomplished by private multinational corporations and banks. We have international economic interdependence without adequate international governance for the sharing of defense burdens and the protection and reconciliation of conflicting economic interests.

The economic integration of even Western Europe has been slow, painful, halting, and partial. Xenophobia will continue even among neighbors who are inextricably bound together—the economic and political relationships of Canada and the United States over the past several decades attest to that.

If I were to counsel the best policy stance for the economic interests of the United States, Europe, and the world, it would be continuing incremental attempts among governments and private multinational organizations to promote trade, stabilize financial flows, and protect the intangible capital embodied in scientific, technological, and organizational knowledge from unfair competition.

We need to avoid simple ideological platforms like "free trade" and visionary "final solutions" to international economic relationships. Peace does not end economic tensions internationally—just as national governments cannot finally resolve them domestically. The powers of national governments will be inexorably eroded by the transnational flows of goods, money, men, and ideas. That may be our best hope for another four decades of peace—especially if the flows could expand across the Iron Curtain.

═══════NOTES═══════

1. J.M. Keynes, *The Economic Consequences of the Peace* (London: Harcourt Brace and Howe, 1920).

2. For an interesting discussion of the impact of scale economies on an industry, George J. Stigler, "The Division of Labor is Limited by the Extent of the Market," *Journal of Political Economy*, Vol. 59, No. 3, June, 1951.

3. Gordon C. Bjork, "NAFTA: Technology, Trade, and Growth," *Columbia Journal of World Business*, September, 1969.

4. "Industrial Policy" is a term frequently used in modern debates on economic policy to represent a more active federal policy of grants, subsidies, and selective tariff protection to certain industrial sectors to encourage investment and research and development. See, for example, Robert Reich, *The Decline and Rise of the American Economy* (New York: Vintage books, 1982).

5. A recent NBER working paper has estimated that the decline of the American steel industry is more attributable to the decline in the domestic demand for steel than to foreign competition. Further, the study finds that it is the rising exchange value of the dollar rather than declining technological advantage which has hurt the United States steel industry over the past five years. Gene Grossman, "Imports as a Cause of Injury: The Case of the U.S. Steel Industry," *NBER Working Paper, No. 1494* (New York: National Bureau of Economic Research, 1985).

6. Nathan Rosenburg, *Inside the Black Box: Technology and Economics* (New York: Cambridge University Press, 1982).

7. Oliver Williamson, *The Economic Institutions of Capitalism* (New York: The Free Press, 1985.

8. Richard Gardner, *Sterling-Dollar Diplomacy: The Origins and Prospects of Our International Order* (London: Oxford University Press, 1956).

9. Angus Maddison, *Phases of Capitalist Development* (New York: Oxford University Press, 1982), Table 5.12, p. 119.

10. Ibid., Table 3.5, p. 54.

11. For a summary of Japanese policies to encourage saving and investment, see the testimony presented by Leon Hollerman to the Hearings of the Joint Economic Committee of the United States, 98th Congress, Second Session. USGPO: 1985.

Appendix

Table 4.1

Growth in Per Capita Output:
(Annual average compound rates for selected countries)

	1870–1913	1913–1950	1950–1973	1973–1979
France	1.5	1.0	4.1	2.6
Germany	1.6	.7	5.0	2.6
Japan	1.5	.5	8.4	3.0
U.S.	2.0	1.6	2.2	1.9
U.K.	1.0	.9	2.5	1.3
World★	1.4	1.2	3.8	2.0

★Arithmetic mean of 16 countries: Australia, Austria, Belgium, Canada, Denmark, Finland, France, Germany, Italy, Japan, Netherlands, Norway, Sweden, Switzerland, U.S., and U.K. Adapted from various national sources summarized in Angus Maddison, *Phases of Capitalist Development*, New York, Oxford University Press, 1982, Table 3.1.

Table 4.2

Per Capita Gross National Product at
1970 U.S. Prices in U.S. $

	1870	1950	1979
France	627	1693	4981
Germany	535	1374	4946
Japan	251	585	4419
U.K.	972	2094	3981
U.S.	764	3211	6055
World★	671	1834	4647

★Arithmetic average of same countries used in Table 4.1. Adapted from Angus Maddison, *op. cit.*, Table 1.4.

Table 4.3

Amplitude of Changes in Industrial Output
(Maximum peak/trough fall)

	1870–1913	1920–1928	1950–1973	1973–1978
France	−10.6	−25.6	−2.2	−6.5
Germany	−5.7	−40.8	−2.6	−8.3
U.K.	−9.7	−32.4	−2.6	−8.7
U.S.	−16.7	−44.7	−12.9	−8.2

Source: Maddison, *op. cit.*, Table 4.2.

Table 4.4

Unemployment as a Percentage of the Labor Force: Selected Years, 1921–1979

	France	Germany	Japan	U.K.	U.S.
1921	2.7	1.2		11.0	11.4
1926	1.2	8.0		8.6	1.9
1931	2.2	13.9		14.8	15.2
1936	4.5	4.8		9.2	9.8
1950	2.3	8.2	1.9	2.5	5.2
1955	2.4	4.3	2.5	2.1	4.2
1960	1.8	1.0	1.7	2.2	5.4
1965	1.3	.5	1.1	2.5	4.4
1970	2.4	.6	1.1	3.1	4.9
1975	4.1	4.1	1.9	4.1	8.4
1979	5.9	3.3	2.1	5.1	5.8

Source: Adapted from Maddison, op. cit., Table C6.

Table 4.5

Annual Average Rates of Change in Consumer Price Level

	1870–1913	1920–1938	1950–1973	1973–1979
France	.1	3.6	5.0	10.7
Germany	.6	−.1(a)	2.7	4.7
Japan	2.8	−.3	4.1	10.0
U.K.	−.2	−2.6	4.6	15.4
U.S.	−.6	−2.0	2.7	8.2
World	.4	−.7	4.1	9.5

(a) 1924–38
Source: Maddison, op. cit., Table 6.4.

Table 4.6

Volume and Value of Exports: Selected Countries, Selected Years **1870–1979** (1913 = 100)

	Germany	France	Japan	U.K.	U.S.
1870	18	42	3	31	13
1880	22	43	7	41	35
1890	30	53	13	55	40
1900	44	62	29	59	73
1910	77	88	74	88	73
1913	100	100	100	100	100
1920	37	86	145	70	141
1925	65	124	183	75	128
1930	87	132	256	66	130
1935	49	82	525	60	93
1950	35	149	210	100	234
1955	85	203	462	101	299
1960	154	298	924	120	388
1965	224	407	2101	144	497
1970	387	678	4202	192	680
1975	518	970	6765	253	966
1979	678	1318	8794	319	1214
1970 Value (a)	39	18	19	19	43
1970 Value Per Capita (b)	650	360	190	350	210

(a) Total Value of Exports, f.o.b., at Official Exchange Rates (in $ billion)
(b) Value of per capita exports, f.o.b., at Official Exchange Rates (in $)

Sources: Maddison, *op. cit.*, Tables F1, F3, F4, F5, B4.

5

Economic Consequences of Soviet Domination in Poland

ZDZISLAW M. RURARZ

Introduction

This paper concerns certain phenomena in Poland resulting from Soviet-imposed Communism, officially called "socialism"; hence, no detailed effort is undertaken here to present the origins of this domination. Nevertheless, it should be recalled that Soviet armies swept across Poland in the period between June 1944 and April 1945 when marching into Germany. As a result Poland fell under Soviet control. The country's frontiers were drastically changed, with the overall territory of prewar Poland being reduced by roughly one-fifth and the population reduced roughly by one-third, half by death.

Yet the Soviet domination of Poland, like that of the other countries of Central and Eastern Poland and unlike that of the Baltic states, has not taken the form of direct incorporation into the Soviet state. Officially at least, Central and Eastern European countries are sovereign, although tied closely to the USSR by bilateral agreements, the Warsaw Treaty Organization, and the Council for Mutual Economic Assistance. Moreover, even the constitutions of the countries in question, Rumania excepted to some extent, explicitly tie them to the USSR.

Finally, and primarily, that domination is also exercised by close links among the pillars of "people's power" in the countries of Central and Eastern Europe and the USSR—the Communist parties and military and security police. Many within the domestic Communist parties and police agencies are simply Soviet agents. Soviet troops stationed in and around most of the countries of the area, as in the case of Poland, together with unrestricted activities of Soviet intelligence and counter-intelligence services, complete the picture of the situation.

In other words, Soviet domination in Central and Eastern

Europe, including Poland, is a matter of fact. What is only of interest are its multifaceted consequences. In this paper it is the economic consequences of domination which are dealt with. Because of the brevity of the paper only certain salient features are highlighted to this end.

Main Characteristics of Soviet Domination in the Economic Domain

Soviet domination in Poland, as elsewhere in Central and Eastern Europe, is characterized by a Communist system, officially called "socialism." That socialism is basically Soviet-styled, although it is not the exact replica of socialism practiced in the USSR. Its main characteristics, however, are so similar as to sometimes be identical with Soviet socialism.

This very fact has grave economic consequences which are, however, difficult to measure in quantitative terms. Central planning, central management, and arbitrary interference by the Communist Party in daily economic activities mean a tremendous loss of potential and real opportunities and add to wastefulness of an economy which *per se* is uneconomic (Ludwig von Mises said even in 1922 that a "centrally-planned economy is not an economy at all.") Together with built-in autarchic tendencies and exaggerated, or even forced Soviet bloc intra-trade orientation, the loss is further compounded.

All of this takes place in an environment where the private sector, even a genuinely cooperative one, either does not exist or, as in Poland, exists to some extent only and is subjected to all sorts of state interventionism which borders on sheer persecution. The absence of the private sector, the absence of genuine competition and of other incentives favoring enterpreneurship and efficient work, aggravate the wastefulness still further. But as mentioned above, it is hard, even impossible, to measure the exact economic impact of all the factors under consideration. Everybody in the countries in question knows the wastefulness of the system under which he lives, but the people are helpless and do not know precisely how serious the situation is. Frustration and lack of precise knowledge in turn reduce the will to improve the situation, thus adding further to wastefulness.

Apart from all this, the USSR keeps a watchful eye on its satellites in general and their economies in particular. This is because it is well aware of the fact that any serious deviations from the Soviet-type economic model could undermine Soviet control of these countries. Moreover, not only does the USSR watch their behavior carefully but it tries to integrate their economies with its own in all possible ways, bilateral ones first of all.

The latter point is particularly important.   The USSR maintains a wide spectrum of formalized ties with its satellites in the economic domain. The main characteristics of these ties are:

1.   Five-year and long-term (now usually fifteen-year) agreements on "economic and scientific-technical cooperation."

2.   Five-year trade agreements and yearly trade protocols.

3.   Several other yearly, medium-term and long-term branch agreements (for example, those on "specialization" and "cooperation" in production, negotiated also within the CMEA).

4.   Existence of various "committees" and "mixed commissions" which meet regularly or *ad hoc* to supervise and strengthen ties in trade and economic cooperation, as well as to initiate them.

5.   Periodic major initiatives launched by the highest bodies (such as the 15-year economic agreement between Poland and the USSR signed by General Jaruzelski and CPSU General Secretary Chernenko on May 4, 1984, in Moscow).

6.   Permanent locally based trade and other representatives whose task is to control the actual cooperation and trade flows and search for all possible new initiatives.

Although the above list may not look like Soviet domination, the reality is different. Due to the Soviet ideological-political and strategic domination, the framework for the economic domination of the satellites is already solidly established. It is compounded by the inequality of partners. The Soviet economy is dominant in the Soviet bloc, with some 70 percent of the bloc's combined GNP falling to it. The second-largest Soviet bloc economy, at least in the 1970s, the Polish one, was roughly nine times smaller. Moreover, the USSR is the main supplier of important fuels, most notably oil, and raw materials to the satellites, as well as being the main customer for their manufactures. This makes the satellite economies critically dependent on the Soviet market, and this together with the very unequal size of the partners, leads to a virtual Soviet *diktat* in mutual economic relations.

These characteristics of the Soviet domination of the economic domain are only a point of departure for certain specific actions whose consequences have never been truly measured.

Soviet Domination of Poland In Early Postwar Years and its Economic Consequences

Before tackling the issue of the economic consequences of the Soviet domination of Poland in general, certain historical experiences must be understood.

By the end of 1945, Poland despite heavy destruction and loss of population and territory was in a rather favorable economic situation due to the changes in her frontiers. Poland's western and northern territories, once in a German possession, were highly developed. True, they were war-damaged, cut off from the rest of Germany, and hardly integrated with newly emerged Poland, but their economic potential was great. Thus Poland's economic potential by the end of 1945 was some fifty percent higher than that of prewar Poland. On a per capita basis it was still higher. Obviously enough, these conditions created a good chance for a take-off. The only problems were the lack of raw materials, fuels and food, as well as a changing amount of available labor because of the heavy migration of the population following the war and the change in frontiers.

Entrepreneurship was another problem. There were never many entrepreneurs in prewar Poland. Many perished during the war. But those who survived could not demonstrate their talents in a "nationalized" economy which embraced all enterprises employing over fifty people. Many of those with managerial skills did not return to Poland at all, and most who happened to be in the country were not permitted to hold any managerial positions anyway. The few who were allowed such jobs were later removed. Ideological and political criteria counted the most and these did not select for those with managerial skills.

Thus, from the very beginning there was an adverse impact on utilizing the full economic potential of Poland.

But this was not the end of the story.

Soviet domination of Poland, apart from certain transformations in the socio-economic system caused by it, had another very negative influence. This was the looting of Poland and the signing in 1945 of the so-called "special deal" on coal deliveries from Poland to the USSR.

Looting, which was practiced by the Soviet troops on a large scale, in Poland came to take on a new character, one that was by far more damaging than that of the former. This was particularly true of the western and northern parts of Poland, which the Soviets treated at first as German territories, even though formally they were under Polish rule. Many plants and other facilities in those territories were disassembled and their equipment sent to the USSR. This was also true of stocks of raw materials, semi-manufactured products and spare parts. What was not exported was sometimes deliberately destroyed. Several plants, long after the end of war, some of them even as late as 1948, were disassembled even when fully operational.

All the transportation equipment, rolling stock first of all, was taken; and in many places rail tracks were disassembled, with rails and signal equipment shipped to the USSR. The communication system suffered largely the same fate, as did the energy system, especially high-voltage power lines.

Large farms, or even small ones in many places, were also stripped of equipment and tools, and as a rule the livestock was either slaughtered on the spot or run to the USSR (with much of it dying on the way). Many large farms were even run directly by the Soviet troops with hired Polish labor.

The heavy presence itself of Soviet troops in Poland, especially in the west and north, where the resettled population had already once been victims of Soviet occupation (in 1939–1941), was another problem. The tension arising out of this led frequently to bloodshed, which again only delayed the normalization of life in Poland and thus the economic recovery as well.

Poland in general was a busy transit area for the Soviets, sometimes clogging her frail transportation system. Heavy redevelopments of Soviet troops, a problem in itself because of their lawless behavior, was also a pretext for their involvement in a kind of a civil war in Poland, which lasted until 1951 and delayed the country's economic recovery.

It is true that the Soviets made some repairs of bridges and other public works but later they were generously recompensated for those repairs, which, by the way, served their own purposes first of all.

When it comes to the "special arrangement" for coal deliveries by Poland to the USSR, it was a heavy burden imposed on the Polish economy. It requires some explanation.

As is known, Poland was formally a Soviet ally after July 1941, that is, after Germany, with which Poland was at war, attacked the USSR. The Soviet-led 400,000-strong Polish Army, in addition to troops in the West and those in resistance against Germans occupying Poland, was quite a contribution to the Soviet war effort. Hence the Soviets had no formal pretext to impose any war reparations on Poland. In fact, Poland was to receive fifteen percent of the war reparations the USSR was to get from Germany.

Yet the USSR imposed on Poland the "special arrangement" of 1945 by which Poland was to deliver to the USSR 100 million tons of coal at "special prices" (they were then fixed for 4.04 rubels or $1.01, per metric ton, roughly one-tenth of the world price at that time). On the average, Poland exported about 7 million tons of such coal a year during the period 1945–1953, that is until Stalin's death in 1953—a total of about 56 million tons of such coal over the period. It is worth adding that the above "arrangement" was never published, and its terms were known to only a very few people in high positions in Poland.

Apart from the above "special coal," similar quantities of coal were exported by Poland to the USSR on a barter basis. Since Poland's exports in 1946 were more than 90 percent coal, with that share falling to some 60 percent in 1940, it is obvious that by exporting to the USSR the bulk of her coal which was much on demand elsewhere, Poland was deprived of a significant part of potential export earnings. The barter trade also compelled Poland to import many Soviet goods of secondary importance and poor quality (at that time Poland imported only a small quantity of Soviet oil). Export earnings lost because of that "special coal" can be estimated at $600 million at that time, perhaps $2.5–3.0 billion nowadays. For a country whose GNP was by that time barely exceeding $20 billion in today's prices, this was quite a drain on the economy.

There were some other irregularities in Polish–Soviet trade, always in Poland's disfavor. For example, Soviet movies, flooding Poland at that time, were imported for hard currencies, which were hardly in Poland's possession.

Thus the Polish economy suffered a great deal. It is believed that

Central and Eastern Europe were looted by the USSR in the early postwar years to the amount of some $14 billion.[1] Much bigger, richer and less war-damaged, Western Europe received at that time under the Marshall Plan some $12 billion. The USSR forbade Eastern and Central Europe to benefit from the Marshall Plan. Although no firm amount of data exist as to Poland's share in the amount looted, it is believed that it could be some one-third of it, a tremendous hemorrhage for that battered economy.

But this was not all. Poland, helped at first to some extent by the West (mostly the United States under UNRRA), was soon compelled by the USSR to renounce such aid. In addition, Poland was not allowed to join the General Agreement on Tariffs and Trade, something very detrimental to Poland's foreign trade. Nor was it allowed to retain membership in the International Monetary Fund and World Bank, a membership inherited from the Polish Government-in-exile in London.

Obviously, no private capital could be imported by Poland and no public loans from the West could be negotiated. On the contrary, due to the "nationalization" of foreign property in Poland, which resulted from Soviet domination, Poland was compelled to pay indemnification to some Western countries. Though the sums agreed upon were not too impressive, they still deprived Poland of hard currency earnings.

More important were other issues. From the very beginning Poland had a *de facto* (and since 1949 *de jure* as well) state monopoly in foreign trade, as well as inconvertible and non-transferable currency. This automatically complicated Poland's trade with the West and was in itself detrimental to Poland's economic development. The number of economic alternatives and opportunities was shrunk drastically from the beginning, and the situation has worsened with time.

This deplorable state of affairs further deteriorated during the Cold War and the Stalinist period, starting in the second half of 1948. The West was compelled to introduce many trade restrictions, on top of those already existing, *vis à vis* the Communist countries. Poland was no exception. Many Soviet-imposed and self-imposed restrictions in trading with the West had also existed, and these increased in intensity. For example, Poland was compelled to break a 4-million ton coal contract with Sweden, which undermined her reliability as an exporter.

At any rate, the Soviet-inspired Cold War and Soviet-imposed

Stalinism increased the heavy burden on the Polish economy, which, despite all the anomalies, was somehow taking off quite promisingly.

First of all, after 1948 Poland followed a strictly Soviet line, styling her institutions on the Soviet model. Private businesses and even cooperatives were also totally suppressed. Private farming became hard-pressed and the collectivization drive was initiated. Both resulted in the stagnation and even the fall of the agricultural production. The "three sector" concept of running the economy (State, cooperative and private) was abandoned in favor of the "socialist sector," which meant State-owned. The role of a central plan, obligatory and highly bureaucratic, was elevated to sanctity. The State Planning Commission, like the Soviet Gosplan, as well as the newly created and numerous branch ministries and other central agencies, also Soviet-style, in addition to the sharply increased interference by the Party apparatus, transformed Poland into a sort of Soviet replica where the economy became subject to politico-ideological and strategic directives.

Second, the development strategies clearly had a preference for the expansion of heavy and engineering industries. (Expansion in coal extraction was mainly labor-intensive.)

Moreover, after 1950 emphasis was put on the rapid growth of defense industries, something originally not even anticipated in the Six-Year Plan (1950–1955). This unexpected growth seriously disrupted the plan itself and was to a large extent responsible for its failure. Originally the growth in the standard of living was planned to be 40 percent; instead there was economic stagnation.

Third, the men in the armed forces amounted at times to 0.5 million, a drastic increase compared to pre-Cold War and pre-Stalinist periods. This was surely a heavy drain on the economy. The same was true of security forces, Party apparatus and bureaucracy in general, whose expansion was tremendously costly. These rapidly growing outlays together with rapidly growing long-maturing investments, created an inflationary pressure. To neutralize it, the regime effected a currency reform in the fall of 1950 and launched a State loan in June 1951. Rationing of food products also was reintroduced. All these measures reduced the standard of living, adding to the growing malaise and reducing the incentives for higher productivity of labor.

At the same time, various purges and trials of "class enemies" were in vogue and led to the firing of many specialists from the economy's fabric. This, together with an overall deterioration in human relations, was responsible for a very subdued mood in the country, which was not without influence on the economy's performance.

The above was particularly reflected in overblown investments. Soon, nobody was in control of them and nobody really cared for their course. This resulted in their "freezing" and cancellation. Even those which were completed, their cost was by far higher than originally planned. The loss to the economy was exorbitant.

Fourth, economic ties with the West were sharply reduced and those with the USSR and other Soviet bloc countries expanded during the Cold War from less than half of Poland's total trade to two-thirds.[2] This particular shift had especially grave consequences for Poland's economy.

The investment drive was mainly based on Soviet and Soviet bloc know-how and capital goods. Both were obsolete and of poor quality. With Soviet help Poland built dozens of huge plants which are still a drag on her economy. Those projects are ill-located, energy- and material-intensive and, strangely enough, labor-intensive as well, despite great capital intensiveness. The end-products from these facilities find few customers outside the Soviet bloc.

Moreover, the inherent tendency toward autarchy was strengthened, and the GNP in the years 1950–1955 grew even faster than foreign trade, a sharp reversal of the early postwar trend.

Due to such a Soviet-style accelerated industrialization of Poland, a structural disequilibrium in the economy took place which in fact was never totally overcome. In 1954 Poland became a grain importer for the first time (excluding 1947), and on an ever growing scale. By the end of the seventies Poland imported some 10 million tons of grains and their equivalent, which was responsible for almost 40 percent of the country's foreign debt.

After Stalinism and the Cold War period came to an end, the Soviet domination of Poland eased up and, as elsewhere, Poland's development policies became more flexible. Due to the bloody worker's riots in Poznan in June 1956 and the return to power of Wladyslaw Gomulka, there was a certain easing of the situation. This was in fact preceded by Stalin's death. "Special coal" deliveries by Poland ceased, and in December 1956 the USSR agreed to pay the coal price differential by cancelling the two loans extended by the USSR to Poland in the years 1948 and 1950, both amounting to 2.2 billion rubels, or $550 million. Unfortunately, those Soviet credits were in kind, mostly as Soviet know-how and capital goods, something of little use to Poland. They were to be repaid by Poland after 1955. Had this been the case, the economic consequences of Soviet domination in Poland would have been felt still more.

The consequences of the first decade of Soviet domination in Poland, although difficult to quantify, were highly adverse and set the course for even more adversity in the future.

New Forms of Soviet Domination of Poland and their Economic Consequences

Stage Two of Soviet domination in Poland, beginning after 1956 and lasting until the end of the 1970s, was characterized by more subtle forms than was the case in the past.

Nevertheless, the economic consequences of that domination, rather than being milder than during Stage One, have been, in a sense, graver.

After the 1956 events in Poland there was a genuine chance for profound socio-economic reforms, even if Poland was totally freed from Soviet-imposed socialism and tutelage. It was a chance to render the economy less wasteful at least.

This did not occur, however. The Soviet model of running the economy and the state in general was already too strongly entrenched in Poland. Besides, the Soviet intervention in Hungary sent a message, and the Polish Communist leadership, no matter how much it had tried to be disloyal to the USSR, grasped it. Poland, moreover, was strategically important to the USSR and hence the Soviets would not tolerate any serious departure from the constraints it had imposed on Poland.

Thus, no basic reforms occurred, and a few minor ones affected on an *ad hoc* basis were soon reversed. Yet the old rigidity and open Soviet interference in Poland's affairs were not restored either. Still, this was not enough to begin any meaningful overhauling of Poland's situation. Stalemate was rather a typical feature of the "new times." This was surely not enough to make the economy function more efficiently. And, since the economy was approaching the limits of the so-called extensive growth and the so-called intensive growth was to come next, a common feature of maturing economies, the lack of basic reforms was sure to foil the process.

Indeed, the Polish economy, until the bloody events of December 1970 in Baltic port cities, could neither resolve any of its problems nor take advantage of an improved international atmosphere where trade with the booming West and even most of the Third World might have contributed favorably to its growth.

Stalemate especially plagues agriculture. True, the regime did not press now for its collectivization, but neither was it ready to help peasants, still a dominant force in Poland's agriculture. In this way agriculture grew even less efficient, and this, together with pricing policies for agricultural products, created a structural crisis which lasts until this day.

In the meantime, all other facets of Soviet domination in Poland remained in force. In the early sixties, the USSR again took a lively interest in the Polish armed forces in connection with its concept of a *blitzkrieg* in Western Europe. Soviet military doctrine, as officially pronounced, assumes also a "strategic surprise." Among its several options is the strong possibility of a surprise attack in Europe, most likely in Northern Europe with the North German Plain the most likely theater. Soviet, Polish, and East German armored and mechanized troops can probably reach the Rhine river in three to four days.

The offensive-oriented Polish armed forces, insisted upon by the USSR, became very costly. It is believed that the country was burdened with defense spending of close to 10 percent of its GNP.

The Soviet grip on Poland similarly demanded a strong security police. The "police complex" in Poland costs as much as education, science, and health taken together, and after the marital law was imposed it probably cost even more.

The Party's interference in economic affairs, as well as its production of an overblown bureaucracy, both characteristics inherited from the Stalinist period, remained as built-in factors in paralyzing any sound initiative for running the economy.

Thanks to all this, the standard of living, after some improvements in the years 1957–1959, practically stagnated throughout the 1960s. Similar to the situation in the first half of the 1950s, this stagnation reduced incentives for higher productivity of labor or better management. Together with a rather depressed level of imports from the West, and despite some improvements, these conditions made Poland a country with a rather modest growth rate. A highly propitious period for modernization of the Polish economy was almost entirely missed.

By the end of the 1960s, the people's mood was bordering on frustration and despair. This resulted in bloodshed in December 1970 and the toppling of Gomulka. Thus, another period, called the "Gierek era" (from Edward Gierek's becoming head of the Party) commenced, most probably the last chance for Poland in this century to become an economically developed country.

Once again, however, the main pillars of Soviet domination in Poland remain not only as entrenched as ever, but actually strengthened. After the Warsaw Pact invasion of Czechoslovakia in August 1968 and after the "Brezhnev doctrine" was revealed, there was not even a question of Poland's trying to escape Soviet domination, even if Gierek had really wanted anything like that.

The USSR, it must be remembered, was at that time closing the gap in strategic weapons with the United States. In conventional weapons the USSR had had superiority long before. This gave the USSR more self-assurance than ever, especially because the United States was going through Vietnam and Watergate traumas, and the West in general was shattered by the oil crisis following the Ramadan War in the fall of 1973. Soon, detente culminated in the signing of the Helsinki Accords in August 1975. Soviet domination over Central and Eastern Europe was now formally sanctioned.

These events strengthened Soviet control to the extent that the USSR began to quite openly build a "socialist community," under whose guise the Soviet super-state was to be built. Even the constitutions of Central and Easter European countries, as well as of the USSR, were accordingly revised to create a formal basis for such a "community." (Only Rumania should be partly excepted here.)

Such Soviet-controlled organizations like the CMEA and the Warsaw Pact, both tools of domination, were strengthened, thus increasing Soviet control in the area.

In these circumstances, basic reforms, which were never pursued under Gomulka, became even less possible under Gierek. True, Hungary continued the economic reform initiated at the end of the 1960s, but Poland was denied such a possibility. (As Gierek's economic adviser in the period of September 1971 and December 1972, I know this only too well.) The Soviet's uncompromising stand on any meaningful Polish economic reform could be explained by Poland's special importance as a strategic asset to the USSR as part of the so-called Northern Tier.

Besides, any meaningful economic reform in Poland threatened the weakening of central control over a country which was basically hostile to Communist and the USSR, and Soviets could not allow any toying with such a reform.

But the USSR encouraged something else, namely, seeking Western credits and know-how. It sensed rightly that the West was eager to go along, both because of detente and for short-term economic considerations. Moreover, the USSR believed that by such a move it would escape the necessity of proceeding with deep economic reforms in the Eastern bloc. On the other hand, the West saw in the Soviet bloc, which at first had escaped the oil shock, an "island of stability" and in the USSR a newly enriched country since the prices of its oil and gold exports were soaring. Besides, the West, quite strangely indeed, was led to believe that it would ultimately be the USSR which would repay the debts of its satellites. In such a situation, the Soviet bloc, and Poland especially, was flooded with Western credits and know-how.

The first effects of this Western infusion, in Poland at least, were clearly accelerated economic growth, creating a false picture by implying that one could forego deep economic reforms and still enjoy a high growth rate. In this way the necessity to proceed with reforms was circumvented, something the Kremlin desired.

As to agriculture, the weakest spot in the Poland economy, Gierek at first encouraged private farming; the positive results of such a policy were almost instantaneous. But soon he fell under Moscow's pressure, seconded by its "fifth column" in Poland, that Polish agriculture be finally "socialized." Although Gierek did not return to any drive for collectivization, some other measures were adopted discouraging private farming and encouraging the expansion of state-owned farms. This, together with unfavorable weather conditions which had been plaguing Poland for several years, led to the stagnation of agricultural production, and even occasional short falls. Since the elasticity of demand for food, especially meat and dairy products, was high, and the income of the population was on a rapid increase due to accelerated growth, refuge was sought in expanding imports of foods, especially grains. Poland became a net importer of food, from having been a substantial net exporter. Hard currency export earnings were thus reduced, and some 40 percent of newly acquired Western credits had to be spent on food imports.

In other words, with all the tenets of Soviet domination of Poland intact, this time mostly in the form of Soviet-imposed socialism and obligation under the Warsaw Pact, no Western credits and know-how could make the economy function efficiently. On the contrary, with the economy's becoming more mature, despite all the follies of development strategies and managerial methods, it also became more involved in international trade, at least when it came to imports, and with investments overblown beyond any reason. Disaster was sure to follow.

In this connection, another observation should be made. Soviet domination in Poland has certain established patterns such as the "leading role" of the Communist Party in running the country's affairs, aided by a huge state bureaucracy; the preponderant role of the security policy in all walks of life; and the expenditure of large portions of the GNP to support the military. There is also good reason to believe that the Soviet leadership greatly complicated all of this through its "fifth column" in Poland and Gierek's intentions to build a "second Poland." Through such agents as Premier Piotr Jaroszewicz, Vice Premiers Mieczyslaw Jagielski and Tadeusz Wrzaszczyk, both consecutively chief planners in the Gierek era, as well as Jan Szydlak and Stefan Olszowski, Politburo members and consecutively Central Committee Secretaries for Economic Affairs, Polish affairs were deliberately complicated. The chaos soon turned into a deep crisis.

The Kremlin had good reasons for complicating Poland's economic growth.

First, Poland's "economic miracle," as one might initially think of it, could not be allowed to end in success. The country was preponderantly Catholic, with predominant private ownership of agriculture. And, it was basically pro-Western, despite all the formal links with the USSR and official socialism.

Moreover, the Catholic Church believes that Poland can easily feed 70 million people and that the population of Poland should actually reach that level, the best guarantee of the nation's survival between Russia and Germany. Obviously, the USSR is not interested in the success of anything like that.

Second, Gierek was not too eager to increase still more Poland's military expenditures, something the Soviets pressed him to do. Such spending would have meant more imports of military hardware from the USSR and more war-oriented production by Polish industry, which was at that time one-tenth war oriented anyway. Gierek tried to argue with the Kremlin leaders that Poland's deteriorating economic situation could not afford more defense spending. Yet the Kremlin was far from persuaded, and after the Eighth Party Congress held in Warsaw in February 1980, when Gierek ousted Jaroszewicz and Olszowski from the Politburo, it became clear that he was inviting a showdown with Moscow. There are good reasons to believe that the wave of strikes in July and August 1980 was used by Moscow and its men in the Polish Politburo as an occasion to oust Gierek. This, however, only deepened a crisis already in full swing.

In this way Act Two came to its end.

Act Three of the Soviet Domination and its Economic Consequences

Poland's GNP fell by 2.4 percent in 1979, the first drop in the postwar period. This was the result of many factors, most of which have been mentioned above.

What was even still more ominous, however, was the lack of prospect for improvement in the GNP's performance. The crisis was full-blown, but the official position continued to be a "propaganda of success," something typical of Soviet-style socialism, where failures are rarely admitted. Since crises are not admitted, no countermeasures are designed. The year 1980 was additionally bad because of very adverse weather conditions, which led to the 10 percent drop in agricultural production.

In such circumstances Solidarity was born. With the shake-up in the Party and state leadership, a totally new situation was created. It was undoubtedly a severe test for Soviet control and Soviet-imposed socialism in Poland.

Whatever political situation in Poland emerged, it was clear that the country was in deep crisis and continuing to sink still deeper into it. The strikes, as well as the malaise in the Party and State apparatus, hit the level of the overall production and exports. Coal exports suffered especially.

All this came at a time when Poland's hard currency indebtedness already amounted to $23 billion and the servicing of it was beginning in earnest. It became more than evident that the country was insolvent.

But one of the legacies of Soviet-imposed socialism in Poland, as elsewhere, is excessive secretiveness. Because of it, the nation was almost totally unaware of Poland's true economic situation especially its balance of payments situation. The regime did not bother to inform the Solidarity leadership of how grave the economic situation of the country was. Thus, there was no concerted action by the nation to cope with the economic disaster. On the contrary, various tensions, arising mainly from credibility gaps, further aggravated the already bad situation The regime even deliberately tried to create the impression of chaos in order to blame Solidarity.

Obviously, such a situation could not continue without grave economic consequences. Yet the Soviet-imposed socialism and Soviet domination in Poland excluded in advance any pluralism or power-sharing, both of which were badly needed to overcome the crisis.

Soon the nation was to pay an even higher price because of this state of affairs. Before tackling this particular point, however, another more general observation should be made.

Poland, despite heavy investments throughout the postwar period, remained a heavily underinvested country. There was practically no domain where investments were sufficient. But such heavy investment, apart from all the misconceptions and mismanagement, had a serious flaw characteristic of all centrally-planned economies. This was the tendency to create an industrial base capable of producing all possible items and, if possible, without any imported components. Known as the "anti-import policy," this influenced investment policies adversely. Investments thus called for larger sums than would have been the case under conditions of a market economy.

Moreover, by rejecting any foreign private investments in Poland, especially direct and wholly-owned ones, raising funds for such investments, usually with a high import content, demanded either expanded exports, something rather hard to achieve, or foreign credits. The latter were obtainable, but as commercial ones tied to particular items and countries. They were far from cheap, especially after 1977 when the interest rates shot up.

Finally, since no subsidiaries of multinational companies were allowed in Poland, the items produced in newly-commissioned investment projects could hardly enter the world trade network.

There was no foreign marketing of the products, and marketing done by State-run foreign trade enterprises was generally very inept.

This state of affairs, clearly a result of Soviet domination and Soviet-imposed socialism, had grave economic consequences, especially visible when Poland entered the 1980s. Large investment projects were severely delayed and could not turn out the products supposed to boost export earnings. At the same time, the newly built or expanded industries demanded more imports, as they were mostly import-intensive industries. Finally, the servicing of debts was commencing, and without their rescheduling all the export earnings in the West were still far too little to meet such servicing needs.

In this way, from a purely economic point of view, the situation became unsolvable. Only political solutions seemed possible during Solidarity's existence: They might be sacrifices by a nation aware of the gravity of the situation and united in its efforts; or they might be aid programs of the West.

Unfortunately, Soviet control made all such things impossible. The martial law declared on December 13, 1981, created a completely new situation and made solutions less hopeful than ever. The crisis became still deeper and the chances of overcoming it more remote than before.

The West, especially the United States, was more willing than ever to help Poland during the Solidarity period. Debt rescheduling and fresh credits were sympathetically approached. Paradoxically, the USSR also started to help Poland economically, something which was rather a novelty. The democratization of Poland thus became a sound commercial concern. One could hope for still more, as, for example, admitting private foreign capital to overhaul the economy from within.

The mood in the country, where rays of hope for change were strong, could be very helpful. Together, it created a situation which compelled the West, especially the United States, to adopt economic sanctions which continue to affect the Polish economy to the extent that it cannot recover from its crisis. Ironically, the USSR stopped helping Poland formally. The USSR tolerates Poland's trade deficit, but that deficit is largely from increasingly expensive Soviet oil, only now catching up with the world prices of three years ago.

Poland's situation would have been still worse had Poland

started to service her hard currency public debt, some two-thirds of the total, now amounting to $27 billion. This is a hopeless debt if Poland continues to be deprived of fresh credits. Martial law, declared in the name of Soviet domination and Soviet-imposed socialism, has saved them both temporarily. However, the country has been plunged into a structural crisis from which there seems to be no way out. At the time of this writing, Poland's GNP measured on a per capita basis is 20 percent below the level of 1978; it is perhaps even lower. This fall could have been still greater had the weather been less favorable and had public foreign debts been serviced.

The future looks equally grim. With the growing obsolescence of fixed capital and with the impending servicing of some $5 billion in Soviet debt, further fall in the GNP is certain. Only fresh credits from the West, including foreign private investments, as well as the rescheduling of the debt on still more advantageous conditions, can change the bleak picture. A restoration of the 1978 GNP level requires imports from non-Communist countries in the range of some $11 billion. Only half of that is currently received.

The boastful declarations after martial law was declared, that "hard work" and "more trade with socialist countries" would do miracles, have proved to have been totally empty. In the meantime, the pauperization of the country progresses and even the foreign debt grows, although fresh credits are not received. It is believed that hard currency debts will amount to $33 billion before they start to fall.

This grim situation is a direct result of Soviet control of Poland. The economic consequences are hard to measure in dollar terms. The Polish regime claims that Western economic sanctions alone, the outcome of martial law, cost Poland $15 billion. If all costs of domination and socialism in Poland were calculated, they surely would be several times higher.

As to the latter cost, only a fraction of it should be mentioned. Poland's GNP is burdened with defense spending of some 10 to 12 percent. If security police, the Party and the overblown state *apparatus* are added, something like 20 percent of the GNP is surely wasted. Moreover, at the time when Poland's GNP was falling, defense spending was rising, officially by some 12 percent a year.

Another loss to Poland and the economy was a mass exodus of some 150,000 Poles after martial law was declared.

Finally, there is another economic consequence.

The USSR is banking on the desperate situation of the Polish economy. That battered economy has some industries which are modern and are thus of interest to the USSR. Hence, the Soviets seriously think of absorbing such industries. If the Chernenko-Jaruzelski economic agreement of May 4, 1984, is implemented, then by the year 2000 the Polish economy will be very much integrated with the Soviet one. Should this become true, the economic consequences of Soviet domination and Soviet-imposed socialism in Poland would then be graver than anything in the past.

Poland, along with several other Soviet bloc countries, though on a larger scale, participates in "joint investment projects" in the USSR, mostly in the energy sector. Such participation is work "in kind" (e.g., building gas pipelines). The cost of the project is calculated by the USSR at an extremely low level. This leads, in turn, to the subsidizing of the project by a participant. Since such participation takes the form of a credit, repaid later with deliveries of products resulting from the project, like deliveries of natural gas, the creditor is at a great disadvantage.

For example, Poland signed a contract with the USSR, the date and details of which were never reported, by which she is to participate in three major projects in the USSR, including building the gas pipeline.

According to the Polish weekly "Zycie Gospodarce" of March 31, 1985, Poland was to spend 900 billion zlotys in the USSR between 1986 and 2000, mostly on two gas pipelines. This would be an equivalent of more than 10 billion rubles. (At that time the exchange rate was R1 = Z89.)

However, the spokesman of the Polish regime, in response to the journal's article, revealed on July 9, 1985, that actually Poland's credit share in the project is to be R2 billion and not R10 billion. Yet he did not challenge the figure in zlotys (900 billion). That would mean that the exchange rate used in the deal is 1 ruble equal to 450 zlotys instead of 89.

It should be added in this connection, that the Polish underground report, prepared by economists privy to Polish-Soviet relations, maintains that the exchange rate used in "joint investments" varies between 1 ruble = 300 to 600 zlotys. This would mean that Polish credits extended to the USSR in this way are repaid in kind at a highly disadvantageous rate. Or, in other words, such Soviet imported goods are overpriced 3.3 to 6.6 times.

Moreover, the USSR delivers certain raw materials for "further processing" to Poland, with Poland retaining only 15 percent of a given raw material in return. For example, out of one ton of cotton processed in Poland only 0.15 ton of raw cotton is retained by Poland, while the USSR receives cotton made-up goods. It is believed that the ratio should be 50:50 and not 15:85.

What one might expect from the above state of affairs, is a matter of speculation.

Conclusion

The economic consequences in question are thus grave and multi-faceted. As evident from this paper they are both direct and indirect. The latter are especially hard to measure in quantitative terms; they have varied in form and intensity. They have gone through various states and finally culminated in a deep structural crisis from which no way out, especially if everything else remains intact, seems possible.

At the same time, nothing is further from the truth than the view—quite common among many in the West—that Poland, as other countries of Central and Eastern Europe, has become an economy liability to the USSR. Poland, as the other countries in question, continues to be a Soviet asset, even if relatively less so than in the more distant past. The USSR, true enough, provides them with oil, natural gas, and a few other raw materials. But in return, the Soviets also get many primary commodities. More-over, as those products are turned out by factories built on Western knowhow, it receives many valuable finished products of far higher quality than those produced in the USSR.

As to Soviet fuels and other raw materials, which, contrary to some views in the West, are not sold below the level of world prices but well above it (with the exception of oil until very recently), they are tied to imports of Soviet manufactures. By buying oil in barter agreements, countries like Poland have also to buy Soviet capital goods and even industrial consumer goods, both poor in quality and expensive. Recently, imports of Soviet primary commodities became subject to participation in "joint investments" in the USSR in mining and other industries. In other words, the importer must credit the USSR and on terms highly disadvantageous to him.

Economic Consequences of Soviet Domination in Poland

The USSR itself knows best what is an asset and what is not. The very fact that it did not allow Poland to become free and democratic proves that it was not prepared to be deprived of its asset. To be an asset for the USSR is to be a liability to oneself. Poland is the best example here. Simplifying the issue, one could have the impression that by running a deficit in trade with the USSR, Poland is a liability to it. But as this paper has tried to prove, the situation is extremely complex and there can be no doubt that the opposite is very much the case.

Soviet domination and Soviet-imposed socialism in Poland, more than forty years old, have led to the situation that after many "successes" in development, food rationing, something unheard-of in modern Europe, had to be introduced. This perhaps best illustrates what the cost of domination is to Poland.

NOTES

1. This amount is mentioned privately by some Eastern European economists. When it comes to Western estimates they vary. See Peter Summersdale, *The East European Predicament* (New York: St. Martin's Press, 1982), p. 19; and J. Wszelaki, *Communist Economic Strategy: The Role of East Central Europe* (Washington: The National Planning Association, 1959), pp. 68–77.

   It must be added that no reliable data exist to this end as nobody in Soviet-dominated Eastern Europe kept any precise record of the Soviet exploitation. It is especially difficult to estimate the value of scrapped factories relocated in the USSR or to estimate other looting, including the operation of "joint stock companies."

2. Zdzislaw Rurarz, *Handel Zagraniczny—Problemy—Perspektywy* (PWE Warszawa, 1971), pp. 100 and 104. In 1949 the share of centrally-planned economies in Poland's external trade was 44 percent; in 1955 it increased to 65 percent.

6

U.S. Nuclear Arms and the Future of West European Security

ARMAND CLESSE

The North Atlantic Treaty Organization is characterized above all by the multifarious imbalances that appear in the relationship between the United States and Western Europe: imbalance in actual political responsibilities, in actual financial efforts, in the actual implementation of defense tasks inside and even more outside the treaty area, in actual influence upon strategic planning, and in the actual control of certain weapon systems. The imbalances may be even stronger with regard to the potential benefits and losses the different members can expect from their participation in the Alliance.

Article V of the North Atlantic Treaty, which says that an armed attack against one or more of the member states shall be considered an attack against them all, distributes responsibilities equally among the allies. In reality, however, the Alliance is grounded on a unilateral pledge of the United States to defend the integrity of its European allies with all means available, including strategic nuclear weapons.[1]

The willingness of the United States to declare itself prepared to pay such a high price for the security of its European allies can be explained by such factors as the strong historical ties across the Atlantic, the allies' political and ideological affinities, but also the overarching superpower contest which some people perceive as a zero sum game where the losses of one player, however indirect they might be, are considered to be the direct gains of the other.

U.S. Defense Posture in Europe: Constraints and Opportunities

American critics of the Alliance—but not only them—cite the following among the costs to the United States from its participation in NATO:

U.S. Nuclear Arms and the Future of West European Security

1.   The United States is forced, since its resources are not unlimited, to neglect other areas in the world which might also be considered of great strategic interest.

2.   It has to pay a high economic price to implement its security guarantee, especially if it wants to emphasize this guarantee by a strong physical presence in Europe itself.

3.   It risks becoming involved in a major war, even in a general nuclear war, by honoring its pledge.

At the same time these critics point to the European unwillingness to assume a fair share of the common defense burden, above all in the realm of conventional armaments.[2]

Because of financial constraints the United States has tried to minimize the economic cost of its transatlantic commitment: The cheapest way to stick to it has appeared to be a simple, abstract promise that the United States would be prepared, in case Europe were attacked, to use its nuclear potential against the aggressor. The problem with such a form of commitment is that it leaves, should the deterrence produced by the threat fail, no choice between unilateral capitulation and mutual annihilation.

The logical alternative to such a solution and its implied risks is a very strong non-nuclear posture in Western Europe intended to show any potential aggressor that there is no meaningful objective for an attack in Europe. Since there would be no possible physical conquest and since a use of nuclear means by the attacker would above all be self-defeating, the aggressor would lose far more than he could reasonably hope to gain by pursuing his attack.

In fact, American commitment has vacillated between these two theoretical extremes with the emphasis sometimes stronger on deterrence and sometimes on defense.[3] This has produced varying force postures and varying doctrinal schemes. The doctrine of Massive Retaliation of the fifties emphasized the will of the United States to deal with any Soviet encroachment by retaliating instantly and massively with nuclear weapons. Flexible Response, which officially replaced Massive Retaliation as a NATO doctrine in 1967 (but in reality at the beginning of the sixties), provided for a graduated reply: The attacker was to be engaged if possible at the level of violence he chose, but if NATO were not able to stop the aggression at that level it should be prepared to escalate deliberately, if necessary up to a general nuclear response. Beyond all doctrinal changes the United States has always acknowledged the importance of a strong conventional posture, even in the heydays of Massive Retaliation,[4] when Admiral Radford proposed his plan for drastic cutbacks in conventional strength.[5] Secretary of State John Foster Dulles stressed the role of strong local defenses according to the scheme introduced by Truman and Acheson in August 1949 of "balanced collective forces." This said that the United States would provide primarily the strategic airpower, the European allies the bulk of land forces and tactical airpower. Even if the goals fixed by the NATO Council in Lisbon in February 1952—asking for 96 divisions and 9,000 aircraft in 1954, with about 35 to 40 divisions to be ready for combat at all times and the rest to be capable of mobilization within a month—could never be reached, strong efforts were made so that NATO a few years later had 25 nominally combat-ready standing divisions and some 25 reserve divisions in various states of readiness available for the defense of the central region of Western Europe.

In recent years new concepts for the defense of the central front in Europe such as FOFA (Follow-on-Forces Attack) and Airland Battle stress the importance of conventional armaments. Based on new technologies, these concepts provide for deep interdiction strikes against second echelon forces of the Warsaw Pact. The purpose of FOFA, which has been developed on the initiative of SACEUR Rogers, is to avoid NATO's having to use nuclear weapons early in a conflict, and therefore to raise the so-called nuclear threshold.

The debate on new conventional technologies and concepts has highlighted once again the ambivalent character of tactical nuclear weapons: Does their role consist primarily in reinforcing conventional defense or should they, above all, assure a deterrence continuum?

Tactical nuclear weapons were introduced by the United States into Western Europe in the early fifties. The first Army nuclear system to arrive on European soil was the 280-millimeter Long Tom atomic cannon in October 1953; it was followed by Honest John and Nike missiles. In December 1954 the NATO Council announced that it was basing all of its future planning on the assumption that atomic weapons would be used in any war. Between 1957 and 1963 the United States negotiated bilateral agreements with Canada, France, Greece, Italy, Turkey, the United Kingdom, West Germany, Belgium, and the Netherlands for cooperation in the operation of atomic weapons systems for mutual defense purposes.

The some 6,000 U.S. nuclear systems in Europe, about half of which are under dual-key control, consist of nuclear mines which are intended to destroy bridges and tunnels; nuclear rounds for 155-millimeter and 8-inch howitzers; tactical missiles such as Lance and Honest John; naval theater nuclear systems based on nuclear torpedoes and antisubmarine rockets as well as aircraft aboard American carriers; air defense forces such as Nike Hercules; nuclear-capable aircraft such as F-4, FB-111,and F-104, which would be used for gaining air superiority over the battlefield, close support of ground forces, deep strike of enemy air bases, and battlefield interdiction; and, of course, since 1983 Pershing II and GLCM (ground-launched cruise missiles).[6]

These nuclear systems have drawn recurrent criticism from both sides of the Atlantic. Critics have invoked the absence of an agreed-upon and coherent doctrine, extra-vagant yields which would lead to excessive collateral damage, a lack of accuracy, vulnerability in storage and in the field, risks of unauthorized use and of seizure by terrorists, and so on.[7]

NATO has responded in recent years to these criticisms by reducing its stockpile, eliminating some of those systems which are particularly vulnerable to preventive strikes or which have a strong escalatory potential and replacing them with longer-range systems which are less frail.[8] But most systems are still vulnerable in their peace-time locations, the special ammunition sites which are not hardened in any military sense of the term. One of the main problems affecting the combat as well as the deterrent quality of U.S. theater systems in Europe is the cumbersome release procedure; moreover, a coordinated use of these weapons, once released, might prove extremely difficult.

The force posture and doctrine changes the United States has operated were determined by factors such as:

1.   The nature of the strategic risk, that is, the risk for the national survival incurred by the United States. The risk was non-existent before 1950, minimal during the fifties, low at the beginning of the sixties but becoming strong even before the mid-sixties and overwhelming before the end of that decade. The United States as well as its antagonist now risked perishing in any conflict where the "weapons of mass destruction" would be used.

2.   The availability or non-availability of certain weapons technologies: The United States deployed intermediate-range missiles (Thor and Jupiter) on European territory in the late fifties because its intercontinental systems were not yet fully developed.

3.   Financial considerations: The Eisenhower administration brought tactical nuclear missiles on a massive scale to Europe because these weapons were far cheaper than conventional arms and therefore fitted better the "New Look," which provided for massive budgetary cuts.

4.   The state of transatlantic relations: The Flexible Response was adopted after de Gaulle publicly challenged the credibility of the American commitment; the double track decision on the modernization of theater nuclear forces was taken after NATO was shaken by another crisis of confidence due to new American vulnerabilities (in the wake of massive Soviet progress in the MIRV technology) and the development of new Soviet intermediate-range systems (SS-20 missiles, Backfire bombers).

Of decisive importance was not the effect of one single factor, but, rather of a combination of factors: It was, for example, the strategic invulnerability of the United States, plus the scarcity of strategic systems (only bombers with sometimes dubious strategic capabilities against Soviet air defenses), plus the financial choices of the Eisenhower administration, plus the political thoughtlessness of West Europeans at that time which fostered or at least made possible the massive introduction of nuclear battlefield systems on European soil in the second half of the fifties.

Despite the attempts to adapt NATO nuclear posture and doctrine to changing challenges and requirements, the Alliance is still confronted with a number of thorny problems. Some of the problems stem from the fact that it is very hard to unite behind a common strategy two geographically distinct areas with different geopolitical problems, different power assets, different historical experiences, different sensitivities, and partially different world outlooks. These difficulties are further compounded by the fact that the European side of the power grouping is politically fragmented.

The political choices which have been made by the different Alliance members with regard to the functioning of the Alliance add to the basic objective predicament. The force posture and the doctrines guiding the use of force have been forged by Americans largely according to American needs and concerns. Europeans have at best been consulted but often simply informed of a decision taken by the United States.[9]

Among the central issues which the Atlantic Alliance has had to struggle with since its creation are the questions of how the security of the United States can be coupled with the security of Western Europe, how the decisive weapon systems of the Alliance should be controlled, and how the Alliance should respond to threats against the territorial and political integrity of its members.

The Coupling of American and European Security

Since the possession of nuclear weapons seemed during the first years of the Alliance enough to guarantee the security not only of the homeland of the owner of these weapons but also of its allies, Europeans came to rely on the nuclear commitment of the United States. Knowing, however, that it may, in the long term, take more credibility to keep an ally than to deter an adversary,[10] the United States maintained a considerable presence of troops in Europe. In the view of Europeans and also of many Americans, this served as a trip-wire in case of a Soviet attack against the European allies: Its purpose was to trigger an American nuclear retaliation against the vital centers of the aggressor.

The desire to show how intimately the fate of the United States was linked to the fate of Western Europe was also apparent in the American decision to commit five Polaris submarines to NATO, each armed with 16 missiles,[11] and in the deployment in the late fifties of 60 Thor intermediate-range missiles in Britain and 45 Jupiter intermediate-range missiles in Italy and Turkey,[12] and finally in the deployment of 572 long-range theater nuclear forces (Pershing II and ground based cruise missiles) in different West European countries in the eighties.

These deployments of troops and weapons were to counter the European fears of decoupling, fears which were engendered by the growing American vulnerability to Soviet strategic strikes which became visible in the late fifties. These fears became pervasive when the United States lost even its nuclear superiority over the Soviet Union in the late sixties. Indeed, to make extended deterrence work, the United States would have to be able, many observers thought, to initiate strategic counterforce strikes against the Soviet Union. It would only be through such a capability that the United States could deter that opponent from any aggressive endeavor against Western Europe, and respectively, terminate any aggressive venture through its escalation dominance. To possess that capability, however, the United States would have to be guaranteed a certain military and even societal invulnerability.[13] Some believe that to provide nuclear protection to its allies the United States would not only need a high degree of invulnerability but must also possess a notable margin of strategic superiority over the Soviet Union.

For those who think that invulnerability and/or superiority are necessary conditions for extended deterrence, the United States has lost its capability to guarantee the security of its European allies since the development of the first Soviet ICBMs and the attainment of a situation of nuclear parity by the Soviet Union.[14] To such critics, the logical choice for the United States is between an effort to regain invulnerability (for example through strategic defense) and/or superiority, coupled with counterforce options (through a continuous rearmament program), or retirement to a "Fortress America" leaving Western Europe to its own destiny.

Whereas some Americans question above all the efficiency of the nuclear commitment, others are afraid that the United States might be involved in a process of escalation in the European theater, a war the United States would not want, could not control, and could not win. Parallel to these fears of entrapment one can find European fears of abandonment[15] and also of limited nuclear war: In an age of nuclear parity and mutual vulnerability, they ask, might not the United States and the Soviet Union be tempted to tacitly agree to limit any conflict over Europe to the European theater?

Some observers of the nuclear scene have expressed the view that the protection of allies in the nuclear age is questionable not because of specific conditions but because alliances are no longer viable. The most radical formulation of this view has come from French analysts like Beaufre and especially Gallois and is at the core of the gaullist challenge to NATO.

Whose Finger is on the Trigger?

In the context of the coupling/decoupling debate the question has been raised of who should control the nuclear deterrent which has been deployed to guarantee the security of the North Atlantic

Treaty area. More than anything else this issue has illustrated how difficult it is to reconcile the interests of the United States and its European allies when decisions about peace and war are at stake. Since the United States provides almost the totality of NATO nuclear capability—France being outside the integrated system and Great Britain possessing only a relatively small sea-based deterrent—it wants also to retain the exclusive control of the systems, be they of a strategic or theater character. The only exception has been the few Polaris/Poseiden submarines committed to NATO and those theater nuclear or longer-range systems which have been under a dual-key arrangement.

This system of dual control, however, is not quite equitable in the view of some early critics such as Henry Kissinger:

> Thus our allies can prevent us from retaliating. They cannot compel us to do so. Nor is the double-veto system symmetrical. While we can veto retaliation from Europe by the simple device of withholding warheads, our allies cannot veto retaliation from the United States.[16]

The American desire for centralized control of nuclear weapons has been an almost constant source of friction and tension in the Alliance. For the United States it would not only be incompatible with its Constitution to let other powers control American nuclear weapons and thereby possibly determine the American decision to go to war, but such release of authority would also engender all kinds of instabilities, weaken the credibility of deterrence, increase the likelihood of war, make difficult the control of the evolution of a conflict, and strengthen the longing of allies for independent nuclear forces.[17] "Failure to achieve central control of NATO nuclear forces would mean running a risk of bringing down on us the catastrophe which we most urgently wish to avoid," McNamara told the allies in Athens in 1962.[18] Some West Europeans have a right of co-decision in those matters which might decide their survival, but others have rejected such a right because it would confront them with responsibilities they felt themselves unable to assume.

Doubts about the wisdom of exclusive U.S. central control of nuclear systems were voiced particularly in the late fifties and at the beginning of the sixties when the transatlantic partners became aware of the new American vulnerabilities and when the crises over Berlin and Cuba seemed to demonstrate the frailty of the nuclear peace. To quiet the fears and frustrations of the European allies the United States invented a scheme for a Multilateral Force (MLF). After the rejection of an initiative in 1959 by SACEUR Norstad proposing the installation of a mobile land–based version of the Polaris missile in Europe under the double-veto system, a State Department study group proposed to put Polaris missiles on ships which were to be jointly owned, operated, and financed by the participants and were to remain under SACEURs's control at all times. Each ship was to be manned by crews of mixed nationality; each participant was to have a veto.

The MLF scheme was strongly pushed by the United States despite French opposition. In its latest version, in October 1964, it provided for 25 surface ships, each carrying eight A-3 Polaris missiles with a range of 2,500 kilometers. Each ship was to be manned by crews drawn from at least three nationalities; no nation was to contribute more than 40 percent of the total, and the command of each ship was to be in proportion to the final contribution.[19]

In view of the difficulties met by the MLF scheme—Belgium and Turkey also withdrew from it—Great Britain proposed as an alternative an Atlantic Nuclear Force (ANF), which was to consist of a small mixed–manned element including German participation on a non-national basis, together with a large force made up of national contingents assigned to the Atlantic force.[20] Finally both of these schemes were quietly dropped.

The implementation of the MLF scheme would have created three different kinds of nuclear forces—the independent national forces, the Polaris force assigned to NATO, and MLF—so that it would probably have complicated the existing problems instead of solving them. Moreover, the European allies would have had a veto over only some three percent of the U.S. nuclear forces, so that this control would not have changed the essence of the predicament.[21]

After the demise of the MLF, McNamara, who had never been enthusiastic about that initiative, proposed at a meeting of NATO defense ministers in May 1965 to give substance to the so-called Athens Guidelines. At the Athens NATO Council meeting of May 1962 the United States and the United Kingdom had agreed to consult their allies, time and circumstances permitting, before initiating the use of nuclear weapons. McNamara proposed setting up a "select committee" of Alliance members at ministerial level to improve collective participation in nuclear policy and planning and to develop more effective consultation machinery. A "Special Committee on Nuclear Consultation" was created which set up three working groups, to deal with, respectively, crisis management, communications, and nuclear planning. This third group was to consist of five members. However, in December 1966 the Defense Planning Committee was changed into a complex two-tier structure consisting of a Nuclear Defense Affairs Committee (NDAC) open to all interested members of the Alliance and the Nuclear Planning Group (NPG) comprising the United States, West Germany, Great Britain, Italy, and three other members of the NDAC in rotation. Since April 1967 the NPG has met on a ministerial level twice a year dealing with subjects such as guidelines for the use of tactical nuclear weapons in Europe, SALT, and ABM systems for Europe.[22] In fact, the NPG did not give the European allies a notable say in nuclear planning. Perhaps it is useful as a discussion forum; the crucial decisions, however, are taken elsewhere.[23]

In October 1977 the NPG created, at American instigation, the so-called High Level Group (HLG) of allied foreign and defense ministry representatives to study problems with regard to the improvement of nuclear weapons. The HLG proposed at the beginning of 1978 that NATO should make a modest improvement in long-range theater nuclear weapons including the capability to strike targets in the Soviet Union. A Special Group (SG) created in April 1979 at German and Dutch insistence and composed of national government officials at the same level as the HLG studied arms control initiatives parallel to the deployment of longer-range theater nuclear forces.[24]

The United States is said to have been prepared to accept a dual-key arrangement for the new theater nuclear systems under which the host country would have bought the missiles and manned the bases while the United States would have retained control over the nuclear warheads. But it seems that to West Germany such a solution appeared politically provocative; to Great Britain and Italy, too expensive.[25]

The dilemmas involved in the control of nuclear weapons are bound to stay with NATO as long as the Alliance maintains its present structure. The "inconsistency between the technical requirements of strategy and the political imperatives of the nation-state" which Kissinger noted twenty years ago probably will even increase.[26]

The Use of Nuclear Weapons
for Deterrence and Defense:
Massive Retaliation Versus Flexible Response

Linked to the questions of American nuclear guarantee and of the control of nuclear forces has been the debate about the respective roles of nuclear and non-nuclear weapons in NATO planning. The doctrinal concepts of the 1950s provided for a massive use of nuclear weapons in retaliation for any Soviet encroachment. While it seems that in the NATO document MC 14/1 of 1952 as well as in MC 14/2 of 1957, which integrated tactical nuclear weapons, the main purpose of conventional weapons was to serve as a trip-wire or as a kind of plate glass window, more sophisticated conceptions saw the function of conventional weapons as consisting of raising the stakes of the conflict and thereby contributing to a form of intra-war deterrence.[27] In any case, the conventional shield now had to be strong enough to assure the enemy that any attack powerful enough to break through would bring about nuclear retaliation.[28]

As the Soviet Union acquired the means to retaliate with nuclear weapons not only against Western Europe but also against the United States, this deterrence concept lost its credibility in the view of many observers. The new strategic facts materialized in the U.S. war plan called SIOP (Single Integrated Operations Plan), which was modified to emphasize the distinction between military and non-military targets. "Principal military objectives," McNamara announced in June 1962, "in the event of a nuclear war stemming from a major attack on the Alliance, should be the destruction of the enemy's military forces, not of his civilian population." Nuclear conflicts should from now on be approached "in much the same way that more conventional military operations have been regarded in the past."[29]

It is probable that through such counterforce options the United States tried to enhance the credibility of its nuclear commitments, decrease the motivations for independent nuclear forces, and incite its allies to expand their conventional forces.[30] Later, McNamara weakened the emphasis on counterforce options by declaring that, in the event of nuclear war, attacks might be directed "against military targets only, against cities only, or against both types of target, either simultaneously or with a delay" and that they might be selective or general.[31] But despite the declaratory doctrinal shift to Assured Destruction, counterforce options were never removed from the war plan. Later, this concept was refined in the limited nuclear options of Secretary of Defense Schlesinger (NSDM-242) and in the countervailing strategy of the Carter administration (PD-59 of July 1980).[32]

The criteria of selectivity and flexibility introduced by McNamara had a lasting impact not only on American strategic planning but also on Alliance doctrine, even if it took a few more years before NATO adopted officially the new policy of Flexible Response (MC 14/3 of December 1967). Schlesinger himself perceived in a strong conventional posture based on new technologies an important complement of the new American concept of deterrence[33] which was to end the paralysis of the American strategic striking force, to make it again politically and militarily operational.

The European allies were by no means enthusiastic about the new American doctrinal habit. They feared that an overall weakening of the deterrence might ensue from the "flexibilization" of the U.S. threat. Indeed, they wanted neither to fight a large-scale conventional war nor to use massively tactical nuclear weapons on West European territory. If at all, tactical nuclear systems should be used only at a very early moment of a conflict, if possible on enemy territory, and to restore deterrence by demonstrating to the opponent that such use was the immediate precursory step to a massive strategic strike.[34]

The United States, on the other hand, wanted to avoid by all means becoming engulfed in an escalatory process which it would be unable to control; from the American point of view it was of vital importance to rely on some kind of tacit firebreaks which would facilitate the restoration of deterrence.[35]

In light of these American fears, Flexible Response appears as an almost desperate attempt to save the nuclear commitment of the United States and perhaps the only possibility of making the Alliance survive strategically. It offered a way out of the strategic deadlock created by Massive Retaliation. If Flexible Response seemed to be an intellectual tour de force to some observers because it tried to give maximum protection at minimal cost, it served at least to veil and even neutralize to a certain degree the fundamental and perhaps even largely inescapable inconsistencies of the NATO strategic situation.

Alternative Nuclear Forces for Western Europe

To correct some of the major deficiencies of the present NATO nuclear posture and at the same time to improve the overall standing of the Alliance, a number of more or less radical proposals have been advanced by scholars, as well as by political leaders. Among the most discussed alternative solutions for the transatlantic predicament have been a NATO nuclear force, an independent European deterrent, a Franco-British nuclear deterrent, and a Franco-German nuclear deterrent.

The solution which might allow the smoothest transition from the present state of affairs would be a *NATO nuclear force*[36] because it would require relatively undramatic and even largely incremental measures consisting in changing some institutional structures, strengthening certain mechanisms, and improving certain procedures. The aim of such change would be an overall rebalancing of the Alliance, a redistribution of certain tasks, and a modified conception of the political and military responsibilities of the different members.

This model could draw inspiration from the precedent of the MLF and even from mechanisms such as the dual-key arrangements and the assignment of nuclear forces to NATO, but the problems facing the construction of such a force might be the same as those which beset MLF: How can one reconcile the imperatives of national autonomy of action with the requirements of deterrence?[37] How could the United States maintain a strong national deterrent for its bilateral superpower contest and at the same time assure a sufficient Alliance contribution? How destabilizing are ten or fifteen fingers on a nuclear trigger, how paralyzing the same number of fingers on a safety-catch?

It seems difficult at present, when the general mood is rather one of muddling through, to realize such a NATO nuclear force. This was not even possible in the sixties, when the pressures towards change were far stronger and when a multitude of proposals by academics and politicians were advanced and ardently debated.[38]

A more radical alternative for the nuclear defense of Western Europe would be an *independent West European deterrent*.[39] The implementation of such a solution would require the achievement of a high level of political integration, the creation of a West European federation, a kind of amalgamated security community. Attempts in the early fifties to realize a European Defense Community (EDC) and a European Political Community (EPC) failed and have never been seriously considered. [40]

A West European deterrent could evolve from existing French and British nuclear forces, but to achieve a credible deterrence capability the forces would have to be increased considerably. The political control of this deterrent would have to rest with "a popularly elected President of Europe, with powers analogous to those of the President of the United States, with undivided authority in a nuclear crisis" who would be able to "wield a strategic system with full credibility."[41]

It would be very difficult to predict the consequences that the creation of such an independent European nuclear force would have. How would it affect transatlantic relations? Would it mean a total American disengagement from Europe and perhaps the end of NATO?[42] Or would the United States be prepared to cooperate with such a European grouping not only on a political level, but also in the realm of strategic planning? How would the Soviets react? Would they welcome the possible divisive effect of such a force on transatlantic relations or would they be worried above all about a modified power balance on the European continent? What would be the impact of the formation of a third superpower on world political structures?

An independent West European nuclear force appears attractive from a theoretical or political point of view to many people on both sides of the Atlantic because it could solve some of the problems which lie at the core of the present transatlantic malaise. However, an independent force would be very difficult to implement in the foreseeable future in view of the lack of political will of the Europeans.

As a variant of the independent European deterrent model, as a preliminary step to such a European solution, or only as a device to reinforce the NATO nuclear posture, a *Franco-British deterrent* could be considered.[43] In view of the evolution of the two national potentials in recent years and of their programs for the future, such a deterrent would probably consist above all of sea-based capabilities with marginal air-borne and almost negligible land-based components. This structure, which would be different from the triadic organization of the strategic forces of superpowers, might constitute a liability: A breakthrough in Soviet anti-submarine warfare might render it vulnerable; moreover, the reassurance effect of a sea-based force for the other European countries might be weaker than the one produced by a land-based deterrent.

If it seems obvious to most Europeans that an attack against any part of Western Europe would affect the vital interests of France and Great Britain more than those of the United States—this despite the presence of several hundred thousand U.S. troops on European soil—the extended deterrence created by a Franco-British force would also not appear to be totally reliable to some Europeans. Might France and Great Britain not prefer the occupation of a part of European territory, for example West Germany, to risking national suicide? Difficult problems might also arise with regard to the political and military control of such a force.

These problems might even be more serious in the case of a *Franco-German nuclear deterrent*, above all because of the particular international status of the Federal Republic, its commitment not to produce nuclear arms, its specific interest in detente in view of the existence of a second German state, and the anxieties of the Soviet Union due to its historical experiences with German aggression. But the Soviets would probably not be alone in reacting with anger to German participation in such a nuclear force. The other West European countries, especially the smaller ones, and even the United States, would probably have serious reservations about such a development which they would perceive as a fundamental questioning and potential disruption of the delicate political and strategic balance established in Europe after the Second World War.

If the deterrent potential of a Franco-German force for continental Western Europe would probably be somewhat greater than that of a Franco-British deterrent, the problems concerning control would even be worse. Would the Federal Republic also have a finger on the trigger? And where would the nuclear system be deployed, if there were a long-based element? In France only? Or in France and West Germany?[44]

All the alternative schemes for the future nuclear posture of West European defense are characterized by serious drawbacks which question even their theoretical desirability. Since the chances seem very small that these schemes could be realized in the political and strategic environment of the coming years and perhaps decades, the most logical and sensible course to choose for West Europeans and Americans alike is to alter the political and military structures of NATO.

The Need for a New Transatlantic Bargain

Transatlantic relations in the field of security police have been characterized by the fact that most members of the Alliance were usually not prepared openly to face the political consequences of the changing strategic situation. New weapons technology, the increasing military strength of the Soviet Union, the growing vulnerability of the United States, and the new assertiveness of the West Europeans have not been reflected in the overall strategic concept of NATO. Measures to strengthen the participation of Europeans in nuclear planning and decision-making have been of a purely symbolic nature and therefore could not touch the substance of the predicament.[45] The United States has never disclosed the real purpose of its nuclear weapons in Europe: Were they to have a deterrence or a war-fighting role? Were they to make possible escalation to the central level or to avoid such a process? If such ambiguity has contributed perhaps to the strengthening of deterrence, it certainly has had a negative influence upon relations with the allies.

It seems obvious that if the United States wants to maintain its security guarantee for Western Europe it must also maintain a nuclear commitment. Without a nuclear component such a commitment would lose much of its deterrence power; the likelihood of a Soviet attack would be increased. Also increased would be the probability that in such a configuration the Soviet Union would use battlefield and even longer-range nuclear weapons to damage airfields, command and control center, logistical key points, and so on, since it would not have to reckon with a direct Western counter-deterrent. The Soviet Union might indeed expect that the United States would hesitate to employ its central strategic forces in such a contingency. But even if no nuclear weapons were used by the Soviet Union there would be great risk that any conflict would escalate into a large-scale conventional battle, whereas nuclear weapons by their simple presence or through a purely demonstrative use might induce a rapid termination of the conflict.

Two general criteria should guide the formation of the future nuclear posture in Europe: deterrence, that is the avoidance of war through a visible and unequivocal capability to deny the opponent any sensible war objectives; and reassurance that means that the deterrence capability should not only permit but foster the internal stability of the Alliance. To reconcile these criteria[46] NATO should strengthen its conventional forces and perhaps adopt a strategy of "no early first use."[47]

To satisfy these general criteria NATO should possess sufficient survivable forces with a high flexibility in terms of rapid targeting and the control of collateral damage. As one observer has put it:

> What is needed is a mix of strategic theater war-fighting capabilities for limited nuclear conflict which will deter the USSR at all levels of theater conflict and which will provide as seamless a continuum of nuclear options as possible so as to limit any conflict that does occur as much as possible.[48]

The actual and projected deployment of U.S. longer-range nuclear systems in Europe may not be sufficient to fulfill these requirements; but it seems politically impossible at the moment to add further Pershing II and GLCM, which in any case are beset by certain vulnerability in peace-time locations, doubtful reliability, and so forth. One way to correct these deficiencies would consist in the creation of a sea-based element comprising longer-range theater nuclear systems.

A correction of the material aspects of the present nuclear posture alone would not be sufficient to solve the problems of the Alliance. What is needed is a change of attitude. West Europeans must give up their intellectual and political passivity. In the past they have accepted American protection. Some have criticized the modalities of the security relationship or even its essence; they were, however, not prepared to involve themselves actively in a process of change to improve the working of the Alliance. The Americans, on their part, have stuck jealously to their nuclear exclusivity and not given much thought to the concerns of their allies.

It is time for the Atlantic partners to undertake a sober assessment of their security interests.[49] To gain strategic clarity they should examine what the Alliance can offer each of them and what they have to contribute to make the Alliance work. They should consider the strategic rationale of a given nuclear posture:

Who needs or wants how much for doing what? Certain mechanisms could be improved, certain tasks redistributed (Henry Kissinger has, for example, proposed that a European should become SACEUR and an American secretary-general of NATO), and certain organisms strengthened (the Nuclear Planning Group, for example, could be transformed into a body of genuine nuclear planning).

A product of the Cold War, shaped by the feeling of unlimited American power, shaken by the experience of American vulnerability, NATO has never taken up the fundamental challenge raised by the existence of nuclear weapons in the hands of several partially anatagonistic powers.[50] Since the prospect is more than remote that the Alliance will develop into a political community, the countries of the North Atlantic area should not hesitate to try to develop at last a grand strategy which could better cope with the hybrid character of the grouping and the resulting dilemmas which will continue to plague it and, hopefully, keep it alive.

NOTES

1. See Michael Mandelbaum, *The Nuclear Revolution: International Politics before and after Hiroshima* (Cambridge: Cambridge University Press, 1981), p. 153.

2. See, for example, Jeffrey Record, *Beyond NATO: New Military Directions for the United States* in Jefferey Record and Robert J. Hanks, *U.S. Strategy at the Crossroads: Two Views* (Cambridge: Institute for Foreign Policy Analysis, 1982), pp. 1–36.

3. In categories of deterrence the emphasis has been sometimes stronger on punishment and sometimes stronger on denial. See Glenn H. Snyder, *Deterrence and Defense: Toward a Theory of National Security* (Westport, Connecticut: Greenwood Press, 1961), pp. 14–16.

4. Henry Kissinger has argued that the large size of NATO forces during the period of Massive Retaliation was inconsistent with the prevailing strategic doctrine. Henry Kissinger, *The Troubled Partnership* (New York: McGraw-Hill, 1965), p. 107.

5. See Samuel P. Huntington, *The Common Defense* (New York: Columbia University Press, 1961), p. 99.

6. See Paul Bracken, *The Command and Control of Nuclear Forces* (New Haven: Yale University Press, 1983), pp. 129–178.

7. See, for example, Jeffrey Record, *US Nuclear Weapons in Europe. Issues and Alternatives* (Washington, D.C.: The Brookings Institution, 1974), pp. 50–54.

8. In the context of the double-track decision of 1979, NATO decided to reduce its nuclear stockpile by 1,000 warheads. In Montebello in October 1983, NATO decided to withdraw another 1,400 warheads. See Julian Cartwright and Julian Critchley (co-rapporteurs), *Nuclear Weapons in Europe* (North Atlantic Assembly, November 1984, pp. 7–17, 40–44.

9. " . . . NATO strategy has always been based on more or less unilateral American conceptions. The consultative role of our European Allies has been confined in effect to the technical implementation of American views." Kissinger, pp. 94–95.

10. See Earl C. Ravenal, "Europe without America: The Erosion of NATO," *Foreign Affairs*, Summer 1985, p. 1023.

11. These submarines were proposed by U.S. Secretary of State Herter at the NATO Council meeting of December 16–18, 1960. At the NATO Council meeting in Athens on May 4–6, 1962, Secretary of Defense McNamara announced that these submarines had already been committed. See Michael J. Legge, *Theater Nuclear Weapons and the NATO Strategy of Flexible Response* (Santa Monica: Rand, April 1983, R-2964-FF), pp. 11–12.

12. The Thor were manned by the Royal Air Force, whereas the warheads were in United States custody; the Jupiter were all U.S.-manned and controlled. See Gregory Treverton, *Nuclear Weapons in Europe*, Adelphi Paper 168 (London: International Institute for Strategic Studies, Summer 1981), p. 5.

13. "Extended deterrence . . . requires the practical invulnerability of American society itself to Soviet attack." Earl C. Ravenal, "Counterforce and Alliance: The Ultimate Connection," *International Security*, Spring 1982, p. 32.

14. The increasing vulnerability and the lack of counterforce options for the United States led Kissinger to say in 1979 that "our European allies should not keep asking us to multiply strategic assurances that we cannot possibly mean or if we do mean we should not want to execute because if we execute, we risk the destruction of our civilization." Henry Kissinger, "The Future of NATO," in *NATO: The Next Thirty Years—The Changing Political, Economic, and Military Setting*, K.A. Myers, ed., (Boulder, Colorado: Westview Press, 1980), p. 8.

15. On the fears of entrapment and abandonment, see Mandelbaum, pp. 153–159.

16. Henry A. Kissinger, *The Necessity for Choice* (London: Chatto and Windus, 1960), p. 120.

17. See, for example, Robert E. Osgood, *NATO: The Entangling Alliance* (Chicago: The University of Chicago Press, 1962), p. 276.

18. "Remarks by Secretary McNamara, NATO Ministerial Meeting, 5 May 1962, Restricted Session." The speech was declassified on August 17, 1979, excerpts in David N. Schwartz, *NATO's Nuclear Dilemmas* (Washington: The Brookings Institution, 1983), pp. 156–165.

19. See Alastair Buchan, *The Multilateral Force: An Historical Perspective*, Adelphi Paper 13 (London: International Institute for Strategic Studies, October 1964).

20. See Andrew J. Pierre, *Nuclear Politics* (London: Oxford University Press, 1972), pp. 276–283.

21. For critical views of the MLF see Harold van B. Cleveland, *The Atlantic Idea and its European Rivals* (New York: McGraw-Hill, 1966), pp. 54–64; Kissinger, *The Troubled Partnership*, pp. 127–159.

22. See Legge, pp. 15ff; Schwartz, p. 185.

23. Schwartz, pp. 217–219, 231–232.

24. Uwe Nerlich writes about the NPG: "Its output is either provisional or procedural or just unfinished business that in any case rarely gets translated into military planning." Uwe Nerlick, "Theatre Nuclear Forces in Europe," in *NATO: The Next Thirty Years*, p. 65.

25. Ibid., pp. 242–243.

26. Kissinger, *The Troubled Partnership*, p. 117. Kissinger criticized the United States for its "unwillingness to face the political implications of its strategic views: Central command and control over all the nuclear weapons of the Alliance is incompatible with undiluted sovereignty. The United States cannot insist on integration of strategy while jealously guarding its complete freedom of political decision." Ibid., p. 125.

27. The function of conventional weapons was, as General Norstad explained, not "to fight, not even to defend, but to complete the deterrent." House Committee on Appropriations, "Mutual Security Appropriations for 1959," Hearings, 85th Congress, 2nd Session, p. 564.

28. See Snyder, op. cit. Snyder writes that the debate of those years reflects what he calls the central dilemma of the nuclear missile age: "How to pose credibly the greatest possible prospect of cost for the enemy, thus reducing the chances of war, while at the same time minimizing one's own prospective costs should war nevertheless occur." Ibid., p. 160.

29. Robert S. McNamara, "Defense Arrangements of the North Atlantic Community," Address given at the University of Michigan, June 16, 1962, Department of State Bulletin (vol. 49, July 9, 1962), p. 67.

30. Jerome H. Kahan, *Security in the Nuclear Age* (Washington D.C.: The Brookings Institution, 1975), p. 92.

31. Statement by Robert S. McNamara on Department of Defense Appropriations, on the Fiscal Year 1966–1970 Defense Program and 1966 Defense Budget, in U.S. Congress, Senate Committee on Armed Services, Military Procurement Authorization, Fiscal Year 1966, Hearings, 89th Congress, 1st session (1965), p. 42.

32. Secretary of Defense Harold Brown himself called PD-59 "a refinement, a codification of previous statements of our strategic policy." See Anthony H. Cordesman, *Deterrence in the 1980's: Part I. American Strategic Forces and Extended Deterrence*, Adelphi Paper 175 (London: International Institute for Strategic Studies, 1982), p. 22.

33. See Lawrence Freedman, *The Evolution of Nuclear Strategy* (London: Macmillan, 1981), p. 384.

34. "By Americans tactical nuclear weapons are viewed as an adjunct to the defense of Western Europe, and their use is seen as a way of putting off and

hopefully forestalling the employment of strategic nuclear weapons. But by West Europeans, who have no interest in inhabiting a nuclear battlefield, tactical nuclear weapons are seen as an adjunct to deterrence, and the early use of such weapons against the Soviet Union is seen as a way of insuring escalation to the use of strategic weapons and thereby preventing war in the first place." Warner R. Schilling, William T.R. Fox, Catherine M. Kelleher and Donald J. Puchala, *American Arms and a Changing Europe* (New York: Columbia University Press, 1973), p. 60.

35. Ravenal writes: "Coupling is the essence of alliance protection in a nuclear age, and firebreaks are an imperative of American security. But coupling and firebreaks are inversely related." *Europe without America: The Erosion of NATO*, p. 1024.

36. For a discussion of this model see Osgood, pp. 295–307; Snyder, pp. 182–190.

37. "How could the command and control of nuclear weapons be shared among fifteen nations in such a way as to permit effective political direction and, at the same time, smooth, decisive operation?" Osgood, p. 296.

38. Alastair Buchan proposed a NATO deterrent to which the United States would make only a limited contribution; NATO would have two commanders: SACEUR and SACDET (Supreme Allied Commander, Deterrent). The latter was to be a European senior officer. See Alastair Buchan, *NATO in the 1960s* (London: Weidenfeld and Nicholson, 1960), p. 76. The French general P.M. Gallois proposed a NATO force under which the decision to fire the weapons would be subject to a double veto in normal peacetime conditions, whereas control would pass to the host country when that country was attacked or under serious threat of attack. Pierre M. Gallois, "New Teeth for NATO," *Foreign Affairs*, October 1960, pp. 67–81. Kissinger proposed for the political command of a NATO force a defense steering committee of four permanent and three rotating members elected by the Council. Henry A. Kissinger, "For an Atlantic Confederacy," *Reporter*, XXIV, February 2, 1961.

39. On the possibilities of such a European deterrent see Osgood, pp. 285–295; Snyder, pp. 175–182; Schilling, Fox, Kelleher, and Puchala, pp. 175–182; Alastair Buchan, ed., *Europe's Futures, Europe's Choices. Models of Western Europe in the 1970's* (London: Chatto and Windus, 1969), pp. 124–148.

40. EDC was a scheme invented by France to prevent the reconstitution of a national German army. EPC was devised by politicians of federalist inspiration to integrate all the other European institutions (Council of Europe, European Coal and Steel Community). After the failure of EDC the West European Union (WEU) was created whose integrationist potential has proved to be very low.

41. Buchan, p. 137.

42. Cleveland mentions the military risk involved for Europe in the transition from reliance on the American guarantee to self-reliance. Cleveland, pp. 30–31.

43. See Ian Smart, *Future Conditional. The Prospect for Anglo-French Nuclear Cooperation*, Adelphi Paper 78 (London: International Institute for Strategic Studies, August 1971).

44. In recent years there has been some talk on both sides of the Atlantic about an extension of France's nuclear protection to West Germany. The German State Secretary Lothar Ruhl has expressed the view that Bonn would welcome it "if the French nuclear forces were to extend their protection to include the Federal Republic, in addition to the protection offered by the American nuclear forces and NATO's own nuclear weapons in Europe. However, only as an addition, not as an alternative." Defense Minister Manfred Worner has noted that France's nuclear capability is insufficient to protect the Federal Republic, which would have to continue to rely on the American nuclear umbrella. See David S. Yost, "Radical Change in French Defence Policy?" *Survival*, January/February 1986, p. 65.

45. "Western European efforts to base the rationale of nuclear deterrence on agreed risk sharing and shared control failed completely." Nerlich, p. 70.

46. On reconciling deterrence and reassurance, see Michael Howard, "Deterrence, Consensus and Reassurance in the Defence of Europe," in *Defence and Consensus: The Democratic Aspects of Western Security, Part III*, Adelphi Paper 184 (London: International Institute for Strategic Studies, Summer 1983), pp. 23–24.

47. See Johan Jorgen Holst, *Domestic Concerns and Nuclear Doctrine: How should the Nuclear Posture by shaped? Defence and Consensus: The Domestic Aspects of Western Security, Part II*, Adelphi Paper 183, (London: International Institute for Strategic Studies, Summer 1983), p. 37.

48. Cordesman, p. 44. Cordesman adds to these two criteria that the United States nuclear potential must not entail an overwhelming risk of unacceptable damage. Ibid., p. 40. See also James A. Thomson, "Nuclear Weapons in Europe. Planning for NATO's Nuclear Deterrent in the 1980s and 1990s," *Survival*, May/June 1983, pp. 101–102. Thomson proposes similar criteria adding, however, a "hedge against the possibility that the outcome of military action might take time to develop, rather than occur after a single massive nuclear spasm."

49. Stanley Sloan proposes that the European allies should begin to produce a European security assessment, that is, an independent European appreciation of the security environment, and to identify European responses to that environment. Stanley R. Sloan, "European Co-operation and the Future of NATO. In Search of a New Transatlantic Bargain," *Survival*, November/December 1984, p. 249.

50. Nerlich (p. 67) writes that the introduction of nuclear weapons into NATO plans has changed the nature of the Alliance in the sense that "what was set up as a coalition army became essentially subject to unilateral American control."

7

The Nuclear Debate: Lessons Which the Western Governments Should Draw From It

PETER VAN DEN DUNGEN

Introduction

In 1986 Europe entered its fifth decade of peace. This fact, coupled with the recent fortieth anniversary of the end of World War II in Europe, provides an occasion to celebrate: The evils of Nazism and Fascism were defeated, and the peace which ensued in that particular part of the world, which had a blood-stained past second to none, has persisted for an unusually long period. These are achievements which younger generations have perhaps too readily taken for granted. They have been living in peace and freedom and, at least until recently (and for the vast majority of them), in prosperity and material affluence. This is an appropriate time for the younger generation to count its blessings, and also to feel and express its gratitude.

The sacrifices which made victory in war possible and the determination which enabled the building of a new world on the ruins of the old (not least the formation of NATO and of the European Community), were made by their elders. They can derive satisfaction from these successes, although for many joy will be tempered by the pains and traumas of the past. In addition, there is the realization that the victory was, for something like half of the population of Europe, in the nature of a Pyrrhic victory: A tyranny was defeated, but another one took its place. If the outcome of the war was not fully perceived at the time, subsequent events—not excluding the rolling of tanks and the marching of soldiers—cannot have failed to bring home the tragedy of this situation.

Living on this side of the Iron Curtain, I try to remind myself constantly that 1948, the year of my birth, was also the year Jan Palach was born. The flame with which he set himself ablaze when tanks ruthlessly crushed the Prague Spring should continue to illuminate those who were touched by his sacrifice. The expression "Iron Curtain" seems to have gone out of fashion somewhat, at least until fairly recently, but for no good reason. At least for as long as there is the Berlin Wall it will be perfectly legitimate to use the phrase. Churchill first referred to it in his telegram of May 12, 1945, to Truman.[1] Prescient though he was, it is highly doubtful whether even Churchill realized at the time that sixteen years later, in 1961, his figure of speech would be turned into stark reality. The Chinese Wall was built to keep barbarians out; the Berlin Wall, built well over two thousand years later, was and is meant to prevent *escape* from barbarity. It is rather ironic that astronauts tell us that the only human artifact on earth visible from the moon is the older rather than the newer structure. Whereas the former today is of only antiquarian interest, the latter symbolizes like nothing else the essential division of our present world.

In addition to those which have been mentioned, two more factors must inevitably temper any celebratory mood. First, whereas a certain peace and prosperity have characterised our societies since the war, violence and poverty still afflict the overwhelming majority of mankind. As we are reminded only too vividly these days, for millions upon millions starvation is an imminent prospect, and the acuteness and urgency of this problem is almost permanent. We cannot remain indifferent.

Second, mankind, rich and poor, old and young, are united by a common threat which faces us all, namely that of a nuclear holocaust. The end of the Second World War also coincided with the beginning of the nuclear era. Nobody summed up better the significance of this new era than Henry L. Stimson (Roosevelt's and Truman's Secretary of War) some months before Hiroshima. On May 8, 1945, in his opening address to the first meeting of the Interim Committee (set up to advise the new President, in Stimson's words, "On the various questions raised by our apparently imminent success in developing an atomic weapon"), Stimson said that this development "really represented a new relationship between man and the universe."[2] A few weeks before, on April 13, the day following Truman's assumption of the presidency, James F. Byrnes, then the Director of War Mobilization, had informed the new President that the United States was "perfecting an explosive great enough to destroy the whole world." Whereas this was a wholly understandable and pardonable exaggeration, it would not be far into the new era before a stage of "overkill" was reached and Byrnes's claim vindicated with a vengeance. Among the many tragic legacies of World War II none is more poignant than the atomic bomb and the era which it inaugurated. It is to the nuclear debate that I now turn.

Three Levels of Debate

There are many facets of this debate. The question of what the Western governments can learn from it can be considered on three distinct but related levels, according to the locus of the debate and the participants involved in it. On the most elevated and sensitive plane the debate is one which concerns the two superpowers. Next, the debate is conducted within both superpower alliances, but openly (and at times, acrimoniously) only within NATO, especially between the United States and its European allies. Third, the debate is also taking place in individual countries in the West in which, to simplify, the sparring partners are the national governments on the one hand and what may loosely be described as the peace or protest movements on the other hand. The debate we are interested in is thus to be considered as between East and West, and within the Western alliance, and within each member state of the alliance.

Lessons which can conceivably be drawn from an analysis of these various levels of debate will have relevance for the future conduct of superpower diplomacy, intra-NATO policy, and domestic politics. That these debates interact and interlock is obvious. Dr. Henry Kissinger has recently reminded European critics of American policy "that the wider the gulf between Europe and the U.S., the more difficult an East-West dialogue becomes."[3] But, to give another illustration, it is precisely the wish to be dissociated from certain American policies or pronouncements (and the perception of divergent, even opposing, interests) on the part of substantial segments of the West European public which fuel much of the current domestic debate. The undoubtedly strong anti-American aspect of the peace movement can, at least to some considerable extent, be accounted for by its perception of American domination of the alliance and intransigence in dealing with the Soviet Union.

The Internal Dimension of the Challenge to NATO

In considering the various actors in the nuclear debate and the planes on which the debate is taking place, I would like to start with, and concentrate on, the domestic scene. In particular, I intend to highlight some aspects of the European peace movements and of the general politics adopted by various governments in dealing with them. There is a good reason for wishing to do so: NATO is an alliance among democratic peoples and depends for its survival on broad popular support. It is possible to interpret the various public opinion surveys which have been undertaken in the past few years to establish whether this support is still there, in such a way that they confirm one's prejudices, whatever they may be. One can also derive consolation from the fact that strains and differences in the Western alliance are nothing new and that NATO (which celebrated its 35th anniversary in 1984) does not seem to have suffered in the process. However, several leading commentators on both sides of the Atlantic have warned, to my mind rightly, of the dangers of taking a complacent attitude. They have suggested that there *is* a difference today.

Former U.S. Secretary of Defense James R. Schlesinger, for instance, has said: "If we are wise, we shall pay attention. For this difference is qualitative: beneath the historic pattern of tempestuous irruptions, there is now a spreading and mutual disenchantment. . . . This attitude is widespread in the rising generation, but it is by no means confined to youth."[4] Henri Simonet, the former Belgian foreign minister, in commenting on the internal dimension to the political challenge which is facing NATO today, has likewise observed that "since this dimension is incomparably broader than it was ten years ago, it deserves the utmost attention."[5]

One vital change which has occurred, and which makes the growth of this internal dimension so significant, is the fact that the nuclear debate has deeply affected some of the major political parties in Europe. This has resulted, for the first time since the end of the War, in the breaking down of the consensus concerning the fundamental aspects of national defense and security policy in a number of countries. It is no coincidence that a much-respected British commentator has drawn attention to the possible implications of this particular development since it is in his country that the nuclear issue has torn apart the Labour Party and has, in the process, managed dramatically to transform the entire political scene through the emergence of the Social Democratic Party (whose leader, Dr. David Owen, was foreign secretary in a Labour government). As Professor Lawrence Freedman has written:

> The fact that the opposition does not represent a majority view and is generally out of power within NATO, with the exception of Greece, has allowed established policies to continue undisturbed. However, the influence of the anti-nuclear movement on centre-left parties in Europe (here with the dramatic exception of France) promises trouble for the future. In three or four years time, perhaps for reasons more to do with economies than defence, there could be substantial change in the policies of key member states.[6]

Observations such as those just quoted can easily be multiplied. They agree that the current debate is without precedent and that the peace movement, as the main manifestation of dissent has to be taken as a serious political force. That this debate and dissent are not confined to Europe is shown by such phenomena as the widespread support (even at the congressional level) for the freeze movement in the United States, by the emergence of America's own "gang of four" (consisting of George F. Kennan, Robert S. McNamara, McGeorge Bundy and Gerard Smith), and by the support which the critics of current strategy are receiving from a growing number of retired American generals and admirals. They are, for instance, well represented in a recent book which is critical of the West's nuclear policy.[7] Apart from McGeorge Bundy and George Kennan, the following are some of the retired military officers among the contributors: Rear Admiral Eugene J. Carroll, formerly director of military operations of all United States forces in Europe and the Middle East, and assistant deputy chief of naval operations at the Pentagon before his retirement; Admiral Noel Gayler, formerly deputy director of the Joint Strategic Target Planning Staff, director of the National Security Agency, and commander-in-chief of all United States forces in the Pacific; Lieutenant General A.S. Collins, until his retirement deputy commander-in-chief of the U.S. Army in Europe. In Europe, the "Generals for Peace" group now comprises more than sixty adherents.

Three comments can be offered here. First, these indications show that the debate is not confined to Europe but is transatlantic—even though it is more visible and more massive in Europe.

Second, not only are many prominent statesmen and military officers drawing attention to the spread and seriousness of dissent, but others have themselves joined the ranks of the critics. Never before has the peace movement been able to count among its membership and leadership so many distinguished figures from the military and political worlds. Third, it is legitimate to point out (as their critics do) that it is not uncommon for those who are no longer burdened with the responsibilities of high office to voice opinions and propose policies which are more daring and imaginative (or "dangerous and utopian") than those they held while they were still in office. As one reviewer has commented on those who contributed to the book referred to above: "Those in opposition can frame grander and simpler solutions to the nuclear dilemma than those in power . . . former officials are generally in a position to sound more sage and magnanimous on this topic than those who still have responsibility for the day–to–day conduct of the West's affairs."[8]

It would be mistaken to imply, however, that the views of such critics are invalidated simply because they are no longer in office or because their views diverge from those they expressed when still in government service. It is well known that in every bureaucratic structure a whole series of constraints exist, of formal and informal character, which inhibits free and frank discussion. This is *a fortiori* the case in such a sensitive and secretive area as that of military defense and security. To refuse to engage in serious debate with such critics and brand them instead turncoats, traitors, or worse, is disreputable. It is also ineffective and counterproductive as the public will not believe that the vast majority of such critics are suddenly no longer the same intelligent, well–informed, decent, law–abiding patriots which they were before.

I hope I do not sound unduly alarmist when I say that we must be careful not to start adopting the same techniques as those practiced by the Communists, whose heroes of today can be turned into the enemies of the people tomorrow. It is most unlikely that we will ever adopt the barbaric practices which the Communists use in implementing this policy, but we should also guard against the spirit and attitude which makes this possible. Tolerance, reasoned debate, compromise, consensus—these are the values which characterise the democracies and which render them resilient and strong.

President Reagan rightly said in his address to the British

Parliament on June 8, 1982, that "the ultimate determinant in the struggle that is now going on in the world will not be bombs and rockets, but a test of wills and ideas" and the West's "spiritual resolve" to uphold the democratic values, beliefs, and ideals that it cherishes. Bulent Ecevit, the former Turkish prime minister, approvingly quoting these words, has argued that it is time that a NATO strategy reflecting this "spiritual resolve" gains ascendancy over strategies stressing "bombs and rockets."[9] One could add that such a "spiritual" strategy should be pursued not only by NATO, *vis-à-vis* the rest of the world, but also, and first and foremost, at home.

The Peace Movement

Attempts to ignore the peace movement, to belittle it, to adopt a patronizing attitude toward it, or to discredit and slander it are short-sighted and ineffective ways of dealing with it. Such attitudes are unfortunately all too common. The sheer size of the movement and the widespread support it derives from all sectors of society—including such traditional pillars of the establishment as the medical, scientific, and theological professions (we have already referred to the military)—require an appropriate response, in two respects. In the first place, ill will could be prevented, good will gained, and misunderstandings avoided if governments would adopt a less antagonistic and more conciliatory approach in dealing with this domestic opposition. This much is simply a matter of style and good public relations. The various derogatory attitudes should be discarded, including the knee-jerk reactions of labelling the peace movement a Communist creation.

The question of the Communist connection is an important and complex one which deserves careful and constant attention. Although it would be unwise to discount the influence of the Soviet Union in the peace movement, it would be equally unwise to let all response depend on this single factor. I agree with Brigadier General Shelford Bidwell when he writes:

> It is both insensitive and politically naive to write off the peace movements in the Western world as Lenin's "useful fools," or to suggest that they are simply tools manipulated by Soviet agents disposing of "a billion dollars in hard currency." To acknowledge their sincerity and their strength is not necessarily to agree with them.[10]

This is not only an honest and accurate way of analyzing and answering the peace movement, but also one that is constructive and fruitful. It contrasts sharply with the attitude of Franz Josef Strauss, whose views on the matter may be regarded as representative of the polemical, even provocative, approach, when he writes:

> The huge propaganda marches and actions of the so-called peace movement by and large petered out once Moscow recognised, after the NATO decision was ratified and rapidly implemented by the government of the Federal German Republic, that there remained little point in continuing to provide large-scale financial and organizational support to the anti-NATO campaigners.[11]

Incidentally, the attempt to counter peace movements by alleging that they are financially backed by a country's foreign opponent is an old and largely discredited ploy. In the First World War, for instance, Scotland Yard seized the accounts of the leading British anti-war organizations and scrutinized them for evidence of German money or influence, but nothing was found.[12] Critics of the peace movement who stress this element are, on the whole, barking up the wrong tree. This is not to deny that Nazi Germany and Soviet Russia have pioneered methods which may lend substance to the allegation, and some well-documented cases exist. It is also even more important not to ignore or deny the fact that the peace movement may, "objectively," be an unwitting tool of Soviet policy. In order to be able to bring home this essential message to the peace movement's mass following it is in the first instance, and as a preliminary condition, imperative that a more sophisticated approach by officialdom be adopted. To explain the rise (and decline) of the present peace movement exclusively (or even largely) in terms of the Soviet factor is both erroneous and harmful. As Lawrence Freedman has written: "The suggestion that the protestors are merely dupes of Kremlin propaganda is unhelpful, inaccurate and does slight justice to the real concerns that animate the protest."[13]

Peace & Propaganda

Professor Freedman is absolutely right in drawing attention to the *substance* of the protest and the need for governments to take this seriously. This is the second level on which governments' responses to the challenge posed by the peace movement has to be considered. In this confrontation most Western governments can be faulted not only for the manner of their response (an issue we have briefly considered above) but also for its substance. In this respect it seems to me that they have committed sins of both omission and commission—omission, because they have failed to recognise the extent of the ignorance which exists in their own populace (especially the young) concerning the nature of the threat facing the West. In other words, political education is an urgent task.

In their dealings with the peace movement Western governments have also been unwise in not sufficiently recognizing the strong appeal exerted by any movement which rallies behind the banner of "peace." There is great propaganda value in the use of this term, and this factor should be considered more fully by Western governments than they have done so far.[14] This inability to recognize the importance of the propaganda battle and the unwillingness to engage in it is encountered also in a related area: The peace movement has been accompanied by a steady growth in peace studies and peace education. Interest in this subject is spreading among school teachers and college lecturers, pupils and students. To argue that demands for the introduction of this subject are inspired by ulterior motives, or that it is too sensitive politically and leads too easily to political indoctrination, amounts to proffering largely fatuous reasons in order not to have to face up to what are, intinsically, perfectly reasonable and understandable requests. Governments, by putting themselves thus once again on the defensive, are leaving the opposition with the trump cards. Our governments should, instead, take their cues from the Communists, who, as is well-known, always exploit to the full the propaganda value of "peace." (Various "peace" appeals and "peace meetings" of the post-World War II period were engineered by Moscow, and this memory undoubtedly contributes to the suspicion or conviction that today's peace movement is similarly Moscow-made.)

In recent years the Communists have extended their peace propaganda activity specifically to the educational field. When such subjects as peace research and peace and disarmament education were introduced in the West, it was not long before we were told that these subjects were also widely taught in the Communist education system (in fact, so we were informed, more widely and seriously than in the West).[15] But because our concepts of peace and of peace-related terms are so radically different from the meanings which they acquire in Communist phraseology, should we refuse to use them—and thereby leave the field clear to our opponents? I do not think so, but this is what is happening all too often. As someone who is professionally involved in peace studies I am the first to admit that much which goes under the name of peace (in peace studies and peace education) is naive or biased, but this should be no reason to flee in horror whenever the word "peace" appears in front of us. The correct answer is to have a proper discussion and correct and improve what is found wanting. We should not allow peace studies, or anything else to do with peace, to become the prerogative of the appeasers, the unilateralists, or the Soviet apologists (nor should we concede to them that a multilateralist, pro-NATO, pro-deterrence approach is perhaps better referred to as "War Studies.")

Political Education

It is not enough simply to assert that many of the peace movement's demands are ill-conceived and dangerous, and that the object of its scorn, NATO, is the real peace-preserving factor. Many Western political and military leaders echo Strauss, who recently wrote: "I am firmly convinced that the existence of NATO and the effect it has had is the greatest peace movement in the history of mankind."[16] This may well be true, but many in the peace movement will be unfamiliar with the reasoning underlying this assertion, and hence the claim cannot convince.

This brings us to the wider issue of political education. One of its ultimate goals should be the maintenance and strengthening of Western unity since the peace of Europe and of the world is dependent on it. To demonstrate the reality of this connection in the fullest possible way is to indicate the content of political education—and of peace studies. Such an education will also ensure that neutralist and "equidistant" sentiments in Western Europe do not grow more popular than they are already. Norman Podhoretz has forcefully and succinctly described what he would like Europeans to know:

> . . . that the free world is a reality and not a counterfeit construct,
> to be referred to sardonically in inverted commas; that its institu-
> tions represent an immense human achievement not easily dupli-
> cated; that its survival is threatened by an imperialism fully

comparable in political, moral, and military terms to Nazi Germany in the late 1930's; and that the future of liberty and democracy depends on the power and resolve of the U.S., not in Europe alone but in such other vital areas as the Middle East and Central America.[17]

What are some of the more recent factors which have contributed to an erosion of these vital insights?

A perceptive essay by Richard Lowenthal on the deeper causes of the growth of the antinuclear peace movement in the Federal Republic of Germany is most useful for our search.[18] The rise of nuclear pacifism and neutralism are, in his analysis, linked with two changes which have taken place in public opinion—each of these changes referring to one of the two superpowers. The first change which has occurred in the young generation is a decline of interest in, and concern about, the human rights situation in the Soviet Union and Eastern Europe. Whereas for a previous generation the East-West conflict was very visible and acute in such crises as over Berlin, Hungary, and Cuba, successor generations have, at least to some extent, discounted the significance of the Soviet invasions of Czechoslovakia in 1968 and of Afghanistan more recently (and of the troubles in Poland), by drawing comparisons with American involvement in Vietnam and in Latin America. At the same time, the policy of detente (in the German case specifically "Ostpolitik") and the accompanying "normalization" of relations between East and West have greatly contributed to lessening the sense of danger and of difference.

What Lowenthal says about Germany applies in good measure to other countries in Western Europe also: The change in public opinion outlined above can be regarded as a negative consequence of the successes of detente and Ostpolitik. But he goes on to say:

> This negative result of normalization was by no means inevitable: it could have been avoided by an accompanying major effort in the political education of the young West Germans. . . . Yet the leaders of the social-liberal coalition of 1969–82, who were fully aware that *Ostpolitik* could not bring about an end to the larger East-West conflict and actually increased West German military expenditures by 30 percent in real terms during the decade when detente was at its height . . . must be charged with having neglected the equally necessary parallel task of political education.[19]

This failure of political education has resulted, he concludes, in the widespread indifference of the young "to the importance of the conflict of systems between the Western world and the Soviet bloc, as distinct from a mere conflict between two superpowers."[20]

It interesting to point out the anomalous position of France in this connection. This can be explained not only by the Gaullist characteristics of her foreign and military policies but also by certain specific developments in French political culture. Michel Tatu, a leading French commentator on the staff of *Le Monde* has drawn attention to the fact that at a time when previously anti-communist intellectuals in other parts of Western Europe were looking with a much greater indulgence on the Soviet Union, the French left intelligentsia broke its sentimental ties with Soviet socialism, which it now regards as the main enemy instead of the model. "This startling change," he continues, "began with the Soviet invasion of Czechoslovakia in 1968, and was consolidated with the very strong impact of Alexander Solzhenitzyn's *The Gulag Archipelago* some years later."[21] Criticism of the Soviet Union by the French Communist Party leadership and the adoption of an anti-Soviet position by 1968 radicals with Maoist leanings, further contributed to this remarkable evolution. It has resulted in the rather paradoxical and ironical fact that France now appears at times Washington's staunchest ally.

Anti-Americanism & Nuclear War Fighting

The decrease in critical attitude *vis-à-vis* the Soviet Union in large sections of the West European population is paralleled by an increase in criticism of the United States. This anti-American aspect of the current peace movement constitutes a second fundamental change which has occurred in the last few years. Such feelings are, of course, not without precedent and were quite prominent during the Vietnam War years. But they have recently surfaced again under the impact of a number of distinct but nevertheless related events. The peace movement in various European countries (as well as the wider criticism of Western military policy of which it is an expression), although apparently directed at specific new weapons systems and aimed at preventing their deployment, has been motivated by a deeper concern, and one which perceives an insidious link between these various new systems. This is the belief, held by an increasing number of citizens, that a fundamental and dangerous shift has occurred in the West's—mainly America's—basic military posture. The historical background can be briefly sketched in as follows.

For most of the post-World War II period these words by Bernard Brodie, the author of what can be considered the first book about nuclear war and nuclear weapons, have applied: "Thus far the chief purpose of our military estabishment has been to win wars. From now on its chief purpose must be to avert them. It can have almost no other useful purpose."[22] As students of military force and of the international system have pointed out, this constituted, in the history of relations among states and in the thinking about war and peace, a revolutionary doctrine indeed.[23] Deterrence is the essence of the military posture in the nuclear era, and its break-down is likely to be catastrophic.

Before the onset of World War I some had already argued that Clausewitzian war, that is, the use of war as an instrument of rational policy, had become an impossibility because of the scale of weapons development and the increasingly fragile nature of the fabric of industrial society. The most famous "peace" book of the pre-World War I period was Norman Angell's *The Great Illusion* (1910), in which he argued the irrationality and fruitlessness of modern war. Angell experienced the bitter satisfaction of being proven right: Virtually all histories of the Great War concur that "illusion" is the best and most widely used epithet to describe the results of that war.

The arrival (and use) of nuclear weapons has given renewed credibility to the pre-World War I view concerning the nature of war and the use of force. But whereas this was a minority view then (proclaimed by the peace movement of the day) it has become in the nuclear age not merely a majority view but one held with virtual unanimity. Seldom, if ever, can such a profound change of opinion have taken place in such a short space of time as that which characterised the thinking about war in the pre-1914 and post-1945 periods. Although within this overall new consensus notions of limited war, including nuclear war, have been discussed by strategists who have dared to think the unthinkable, that is, the break-down of deterrence, these notions and discussions did not really undermine the consensus about deterrence. Since the late 1970s, however, the idea of not only fighting a nuclear war but, particularly, of prevailing in it and winning it, has emerged, and thereby broken a taboo. Public opinion has been disturbed not so much by the mere fact of the emergency of these atavistic concepts

126

in the arcane, almost theological speculations of some strategists, but by the apparent willingness (not to say eagerness) of high-level policy makers, especially in the United States, to embrace these ideas.

In combination with the introduction of certain weapons systems which are regarded as giving expression to and implementing this change in doctrine, it is clear to see why many believe that deterrence is being eroded by dangerous, destabilizing "nuclear war fighting" doctrines and postures. The consensus which has reigned supreme for much of the post-1945 period (even though some believe that this consensus never extended to the political and military leadership of the Soviet Union) namely, that nuclear war was unfightable and unwinnable, has broken down (if not in reality, at least in the perception of many). These disturbing views have come to be identified with a number of strategic thinkers, most notably Colin Gray, whose articles, "Nuclear Strategy: the Case for a Theory of Victory" and "Victory is Possible," have achieved notoriety. Michael Howard has taken issue with the views of Gray who, he says, "has had the courage to make explicit certain views that are now circulating widely in some circles in the U.S. and which, unless publicly and firmly countered, might become influential, with catastrophic consequences."[24] Michael Howard has gone so far as to blame the Committee on the Present Danger in the United States for the emergence of the European peace movement by describing the latter as "the *doppelgänger* it has conjured up on this side of the Atlantic."[25]

A leading analyst of the concept of limited nuclear war has recently pointed out that it cannot be doubted that the strategic philosophies espoused by the Carter and Reagan administrations show a basic continuity. Pressures for the United States strategic posture to move in the direction of limited nuclear war attitudes are part of that continuity. He finds the explanation for the dramatic increase in public concern on this issue and the perception of a greatly more dangerous situation in a different sphere: "It is said (by many) that the only significant difference between the two Administrations has been that the Carter people did not really believe in their own nuclear strategy whereas the Reagan men do."[26]

The paradoxical nature of deterrence, inherent in the fact that the more credible the threat is, the greater the deterrent effect will be (the more one is able and willing to engage in nuclear war the less likely will it be that such a war will come about), is becoming increasingly more evident in such weapons developments as the neutron bomb, the MX missile, Trident II, BMD, and the concern over C3I (Command, Control, Communication and Intelligence). But for the general public no other issue has succeeded in conveying so vividly the contradictions inherent in deterrence (and in arousing anxiety) than civil defense. To quote Clark:

> Here again . . . there is ambiguity in what a programme of civil defence tells us about the wider strategic philosophy of the government which pursues it. At the one end of the spectrum, a concern with civil defence preparedness can be depicted as no more than a prudent intention to alleviate, even if only at the margins, the horrendous impact of nuclear war; at the other end, civil defence programmes, especially if found in the Soviet Union, are regarded as *prima facie* evidence of an intent to initiate and win nuclear wars. If the critics take the heightened profile of civil defence issues in the U.S. in recent years . . . as signifying gradual Administration acceptance of the idea of nuclear war then the blame lies at least in part with various U.S. Government agencies which have fostered this association of ideas in their repeated attacks on Soviet civil-defence efforts.[27]

For this as well as other reasons (of an emotional-psychological nature) civil defense is one of the most sensitive, two-edged instruments of deterrence. In consequence, the public handling and presentation of civil defense issues require the utmost care. Incredibly, and unfortunately, the opposite seems to have taken place. As Clark has said:

> Civil defense officials have aggravated the situation by their frequently callous and flippant remarks on the impact of nuclear war. The philosophy of Undersecretary of Defense, T.K. Jones, that "everybody's going to make it if there are enough shovels to go around and that the U.S., with civil defense, would recover from a nuclear war in two to four years, may not be representative of official thinking generally but it certainly caused even well-disposed observers of the U.S. strategic scene to think twice about the desirability of present trends.[28]

Similar crude notions about the survivability of nuclear war, and a minimizing of its effects, were evident in the British Government's civil defense leaflet *Protect and Survive* (May 1980). There can be little doubt about the harm this has done, not only to the case for civil defense but, more widely and significantly, to the government's overall nuclear strategy. A credibility crisis developed and the peace movement saw a tremendous surge in support.[29]

Ian Clark concludes his analysis of limited nuclear war discussions and weapons developments by recognizing that it is very difficult to make definite statements concerning the ultimate intentions of both superpowers but that it is nevertheless possible to draw a lesser (but still important) conclusion:

> Even if we accept at face value the various statements that governments today are no more disposed to the idea of nuclear war than they were 30 years ago and that their principal interest resides in maintaining a deterrent-based peace, it is yet possible to distinguish between that end and the means of achieving it. In many subtle and pervasive ways, limited nuclear war ideas have suffused the intellectual framework of deterrence theory. The end, it is claimed, is to secure more effectively the nuclear peace. In the process, however, there is room for legitimate questioning as to whether this end may not be undermined by the means themselves. The more we plan for the execution of nuclear wars and the more that the operational details of nuclear war become a part of the normal, albeit rarified, discourse, the greater is the danger that we lose touch with reality.[30]

It is thus not merely a question of allaying fears and suspicions and of the need to restore trust in (and consensus on) the fundamental object of nuclear strategy which necessitates the halting of the process described above, but also because of the dangers inherent in it.

A simple but most valuable lesson should be learned from the nuclear debate which has raged in the last few years in the West— a lesson which the French have apparently understood all along and which accounts for the at least tacit support of the French people for the nuclear deterrent, namely, "that there is not too much debate about its use."[31] If the opposite has happened in most of the West, it is largely because of the developments described in the previous paragraph. On this occasion it may also be appropriate to offer another reflection, related to the one above: Anyone who reads the somber and sober language in which the nuclear issue was invariably discussed at the dawn of the nuclear era cannot but be disturbed by the crudeness with which our generation talks about nuclear weapons and nuclear war. This is no doubt an example of the maxim that familiarity breeds contempt.

But in this case familiarity should really inspire greater caution and humility, starting with the language we are using.

I hope that I do not appear ungrateful when, on an occasion like the present, I wish to conclude my brief survey of lessons which the Western governments can learn from the nuclear debate of the last few years by simply stating one more sin committed by their leader. It is a lesson which refers to the way the United States has been conducting its relations with its main adversary and which has had a negative impact on relations within NATO. I am encouraged to make this point because in doing so I find myself in excellent Atlanticist company. Lawrence Freedman, for example, has written:

> Before NATO can improve on its communication with the public, it needs to sort out exactly what is to be communicated. One source of the current difficulty is that the prevailing sense of international crisis is not solely the responsibility of the Soviet Union. . . . European governments might find it easier to counter criticisms of the U.S. if they did not, themselves, agree with many of them.[32]

This sentiment is echoed by Lowenthal:

> The more recent rise of criticism and distrust of American leadership among many West Germans, by no means confined to the young generation, must in my judgment be ascribed largely, though of course not exclusively, to the conduct and presentation of American policy by that leadership itself since the crisis of detente became obvious in 1979.[33]

This is not the place to discuss the various doubtful and debatable aspects of American foreign policy but one may be mentioned, namely, "the rhetoric of describing the Soviet political system not only as totally alien to Western concepts of freedom and human rights, which it certainly is, but as the embodiment of "evil" on this earth" (Lowenthal), thereby leaving little scope for negotiation with its leaders. Not long before his death at the end of 1984, Edward Crankshaw, one of England's most respected writers on the Soviet Union, published an anthology of his writing stretching back to the end of the last war. To his surprise and dismay he had found that they had suddenly become relevant again:

> I find myself being asked questions by younger generations which I imagined had been settled forever; more particularly . . . we, and especially Washington, seem quite suddenly to have forgotten what we have learnt. There are disconcerting signs of a drift back to the

old panic fear of the Communist menace, an ideological crusade and the more absurd attitudes of the cold war. There is a general loss of a sense of proportion. Nuclear overkill runs wild. . . . Many years ago I wrote that the Kremlin's one great achievement was turning itself into a bogy to give us an excuse to stop thinking. Is this to happen all over again.[34]

Dr. Kissinger has observed that there is no tradition in America for conducting relationships "simultaneously co-operative and adversary. But that is precisely the challenge before our leaders."[35] It is to be hoped that the nuclear debate and the havoc it has caused in the West, and the lessons which will be drawn from the experience, will contribute to meeting that challenge successfully.

NOTES

1. "What is to happen about Russia? . . . An iron curtain is drawn upon their front. We do not know what is going on behind." See Andre Fontaine, *History of the Cold War* (London: Secker & Warburg, 1968), p. 243. The expression received prominence in Churchill's March 5, 1946, speech at Fulton, Missouri. Goebbels had referred to "ein eiserner Vorhang" in the Nazi propaganda weekly, *Das Reich*, of February 23, 1945.

2. Herbert Feis, *The Atomic Bomb and the End of World War II* (Princeton University Press, 1968), pp. 38–40.

3. Henry A. Kissinger, "Basic Steps to Strengthen the Alliance" in Joseph Godson, ed., *Challenges to the Western Alliance* (London: Times Books Ltd. & Washington, D.C.: Center for Strategic and International Studies, Georgetown University, 1984), p. 13. This is an excellent collection of articles analyzing the state of NATO 35 years after its establishment.

4. James R. Schlesinger, "Problems Facing the Alliance" in Godson, p. 40.

5. Henri Simonet, "NATO's Challenge" in Godson, pp. 30–31.

6. Lawrence Freedman, "Tell and Trust the People" in Godson, p. 110.

7. Gwyn Prins, ed., *The Choice: Nuclear Weapons Versus Security* (London: Chatto & Windus, 1984).

8. Patrick Glynn, "Trying Not to Provoke" in *Times Literary Supplement* (London), January 4, 1985, p. 4.

9. Bulent Ecevit, "From Confrontation to Co-operation" in Godson, p. 73.

10. Shelford Bidwell, "Fighting Talk" (a review of General Sir John Hackett's *The Third World War*) in *Times Literary Supplement*, September 3, 1982, p. 948.

11. Franz Josef Strauss, "Peace and Pacificism" in Godson, pp. 33–34.

12. Keith Robbins, *The Abolition of War: The "Peace Movement" in Britain, 1914–1919* (Cardiff: University of Wales Press, 1976), p. 147.

13. Freedman, p. 111. It is interesting to observe that the most eminent students of war and peace, now and in the past, are often also the most balanced in their assessment of the critics of established policies. According to Sir Basil Liddell Hart: "We learn from history that the critics of authority have always been rebuked in self-righteous tones—if no worse fate has befallen them—yet have repeatedly been justified by history. To be 'agin the Government' may be a more philosophic attitude than it appears." *Why Don't We Learn from History?* (London: George Allen & Unwin, 1944), p. 17. Liddell Hart goes on to relate this to the nature of governments which have an inherent tendency "to infringe the standards of decency and truth." He, and others, have shown that this adage applies with particular force to a country's defense establishment. His student and successor as Britain's leading military historian of today, Professor Michael Howard, has more recently written that:

> It would be morally disreputable as well as politically foolish to treat (those in the peace movement) simply as a nuisance, far less as enemies. More often than not, the questions they raise and the criticisms they make about Western defense postures are entirely legitimate. They furnish our societies not only with a conscience but also with a critical intelligence. If sometimes they deal with society not as it is but as we would all wish it to be, at least they save us from the cynical *immobilisme* that is the besetting sin of bureaucrats and the academics who tend to associate with them. They are the "philosophers" whose freedom of expression Kant modestly claimed to be a condition of Perpetual Peace, and with whom a dialogue is the essential prerequisite of a free society.

Michael Howard, *The Causes of War and other Essays* (London: Temple Smith, 1983), p. 72.

14. For a detailed discussion of this topic see Alexander Shtromas, "The Soviet Union and the Politics of Peace" in Peter van den Dungen, ed., *West European Pacifism and the Strategy for Peace* (London: Macmillan, 1985), pp. 129–157.

15. See, for instance, the various Soviet contributions to the *UNESCO Yearbook on Peace and Conflict Studies 1981* (Paris: UNESCO & Westport, Conn.: Greenwood Press, 1982). I have critically reviewed these contributions in "Peace Research and the Search for Peace" in *International Journal on World Peace* (New York: Professors World Peace Academy), vol. 2, no. 3, Jul.–Sept. 1985, pp. 35–52.

16. Strauss, p. 34.

17. Norman Podhoretz, "NATO and American Public Opinion" in Godson, p. 108.

18. Richard Lowenthal, *Social Change and Cultural Crisis* (New York: Columbia University Press, 1984), pp. 226–238.

19. Ibid., p. 232.

20. Ibid., p. 232–233.

21. Michel Tatu, "French Support for the Alliance" in Godson, p. 116.

22. Bernard Brodie, ed., *The Absolute Weapon* (New York: Harcourt Brace, 1946) p. 76, as quoted in Howard, *Causes of War*, p. 133.

23. See, e.g., F.H. Hinsley, "Reflections on the Debate about the Nuclear Weapons" in David Martin & Peter Mullen, eds., *Unholy Warfare* (Oxford: Basil Blackwell, 1983), pp. 52–61.

24. *Causes of War*, p. 147.

25. Michael Howard, "Peace: The Vital Factors" in Godson, p. 65.

26. Ian Clark, "Limited Nuclear War?" in George W. Keeton & George Schwarzenberger, eds., *The Yearbook of World Affairs 1984* (London: Stevens & Sons for The London Institute of World Affairs, 1984), pp. 243–257 (quotation at p. 248).

27. Clark, pp. 255–256.

28. Ibid.

29. I have argued this at greater length elsewhere, e.g., in "'Protestiere und uberlebe.' Die Friedensberwegung in Grossbritannien." In Armand Clesse & Waldemar Molinski, eds., *Proteste fur den Frieden. Sorgen um die Sicherheit* (Munich: Universitas Verlag/Reine PWPA, 1984), pp. 75–85.

30. Clark, p. 257.

31. Tatu, p. 115.

32. Freedman, p. 111.

33. Lowenthal, p. 233.

34. Edward Crankshaw, *Putting up with the Russians, 1947–1984* (London: Macmillan, 1984), p. XII.

35. Kissinger, p. 11.

8

Nuclear Weapons, Democratic Statesmanship, and the Security of Europe

P. EDWARD HALEY

When the last great war in Europe ended, an American diplomat, George F. Kennan, was chargé d'affaires at the United States Embassy in Moscow. In his memoirs Kennan described an outpouring of joy and relief as the citizens of Moscow spontaneously began celebrating the end of the war in public demonstrations that lasted all day, May 9, 1945.

The street in front of the embassy offices was packed with happy people. As they moved slowly past, Kennan recalled, "they discovered the Stars and Stripes, reacted with what appeared to be in most instances surprised delight, stopped their march, and settled down to demonstrate before the embassy building feelings that were obviously ones of almost delirious friendship."[1] Similar scenes were repeated throughout Europe and North America. For many men and women still under arms there remained months of combat against imperial Japan. But the war was over in Europe, and the end of the struggle to undo the aggressions of Germany, Italy, and Japan was finally at hand.

In the years since 1945, there have again been crowds of demonstrators in the streets of Europe and the United States. However, their purposes and their behavior are often quite unlike those of the deliriously happy multitudes of five decades ago. In the East, in those parts of Central Europe dominated by the Soviet Union, regular outpourings of frustrated nationalism and demands for economic and political reform have threatened to overturn the entire structure of Soviet military and political control: in Hungary, East Germany, and Poland in the 1950s; in Czechoslovakia in the 1960s; in Poland again in the 1970s and 1980s.

Massive demonstrations in Western Europe in the 1950s, and again in the 1980s, have expressed a widespread and deeply felt wish to abolish NATO's dependence on and even possession of nuclear weapons for its defense against the Soviet Union. The Western European anti-nuclear movement spread to the United States in the 1980s on a much smaller, but nonetheless impressive, scale.

The protests in East and West differ in most ways. Those in the East seek the self-determination and basic freedoms that are taken for granted in the West. Those in the West reveal above all a freedom of political expression and organization whose achievement was one of the main objectives of the war against Hitler on the part of the Western Allies. However, the demonstrations are similar in one sense. They arise from the tyranny of circumstances surrounding the defeat of Nazi Germany and the imperfect peace in Europe that followed victory.

Because they had squandered their chances to defeat Hitler in the 1930s, the Western democracies had no choice but to join forces with the Soviet Union against Germany in the 1940s. The opportunities lost in pursuit of appeasement and isolationism could not be recovered. As George Kennan, on another occasion, observed:

Before the war began the overwhelming portion of the world's armed strength in land forces and air forces had accumulated in the hands of three political entities—Nazi Germany, Soviet Russia, and Imperial Japan. All these entities were deeply and dangerously hostile to the Western democracies. . . . In Europe and Asia, Western democracy had become militarily outclassed. The world balance of power had turned decisively against it. . . . Of the three totalitarian powers, Japan was the only one which could conceivably be defeated by the democracies without invoking for this purpose the aid of one of the other totalitarian powers. In the case of Germany and Russia, circumstances were bitter. Together they could not be defeated at all. Individually, either of them could be defeated only if the democracies had the collaboration of the other.

But such collaboration, if permitted to proceed to the point of complete victory, would mean the relative strengthening of the collaborating power and its eventual appearance as a greedy and implacable claimant at the peace table. Not only that: any war in which one of these two powers was fighting on the side of the democracies could scarcely be fought to a complete and successful finish without placing the collaborating totalitarian power in occupation of large parts of eastern Europe simply by virtue of the sweep of military operations.[2]

The two-front war against Hitler brought Soviet power far into Central Europe, engulfing not only Poland and Czechoslovakia, but a large part of Germany and Austria, as well. Five decades later, Soviet control has receded from Austria alone.

Fear of Soviet aggression beyond Central Europe sparked the North Atlantic Treaty of 1949. In response to a Western European request, the United States joined the nations of that region and Canada (Greece, Turkey, and West Germany were to join later) in a defensive alliance to halt Soviet political as well as military expansion. The Communist attack against South Korea in 1950 convinced the North Atlantic Treaty allies of the need to build an integrated defense, to add the "O" in NATO, and significant steps were taken to mount an effective military defense, including the rearmament of West Germany and the permanent stationing of large numbers of American combat troops on the European continent. Inevitably, this brought American nuclear weapons to European soil as part of NATO's defense arrangements, and these shorter-range nuclear weapons were deployed and plans developed for their use, according to ideas and strategies then held by NATO's leading military power, the United States.

The sequence is important. Soviet power entered Europe as a result of the collapse of the European balance and the destruction of German power. The enduring hostility of the Soviet Union toward the West brought NATO to life and American military power to a European continent at peace, for the first time in history.

For the Western Europeans, reliance on the conventional and, particularly, nuclear power of the United States is the only way of balancing Soviet military power. "The real case for U.S. nuclear weapons in Europe," in Lawrence Freedman's words, "is that they provide the best available, though by no means perfect, answer to the problems posed to Western Europe by sharing a continent with a nuclear superpower."[3] For the United States, NATO is an essential element in its entire approach to world affairs. As William Hyland observed: "The only conceivable long-term resolution of the East-West struggle is Soviet accommodation with a permanently adverse balance of power. The essential ingredient of that balance is the European-American alliance."[4]

In considering the role of nuclear strategy in United States relations with its NATO allies, there would be little point in repeating the same coverage of history, strategy, arms control, allied consultation, and recommendations for force improvement that has been provided so often so well in a large and growing number of thoughtful books and articles.[5] Instead, the following is a discussion of the effects on the defense of NATO of the changes in the nuclear strategy and force levels of the Soviet Union and the United States that have occurred since United States nuclear weapons were first introduced in Europe in 1953. Particular attention is paid to the effects of two changes: the loss of American nuclear superiority and the sustained and remarkable Soviet nuclear buildup of the 1970s.

Albert Wohlstetter has argued persuasively that it is militarily logical for all Western European nations to depend completely on the United States for nuclear defense. In an intriguing article in *Foreign Affairs* in 1961 he suggested that there are four nuclear options for NATO: reject nuclear weapons altogether, develop national nuclear forces, construct a jointly controlled force, or depend entirely on the United States. To Wohlstetter, dependence was the most logical choice. The coincidence of interest between the United States and Western Europe is so strong that it is highly probable that the United States would defend Europe against any Soviet attack. Credibility is sustained, Wohlstetter maintained, not by the certainty of response but by its likelihood, and a United States response to a Soviet attack in Europe is more than likely enough to sustain deterrence.[6]

Wohlstetter's logic has been persuasive to most but not all European members of NATO. The United States and the Soviet Union are not the only nuclear powers in Europe. Great Britain and France deploy sizable and increasingly potent and sophisticated national nuclear forces of bombers and submarine-launched ballistic missiles (SLBM). (See Table 8–7.) French and British nuclear weapons express deep-seated feelings of national sovereignty and a desire for international influence that outweigh strict military logic. While the analysis that follows concentrates on the Soviet Union and the United States, the French and British nuclear forces must not be forgotten. They are not and cannot be overlooked by Soviet strategists and military commanders.

United States nuclear weapons were introduced into Europe and their numbers greatly multiplied there in the 1950s and 1960s, a time of United States nuclear superiority over the Soviet Union. By superiority it is meant the ability of the United States to deliver a devastating nuclear attack against the Soviet Union without suffering a comparable attack in reprisal. So great was the margin of American nuclear power at this time that the Eisenhower administration felt it could adopt a strategy of "massive retaliation" and threaten to attack Moscow and Beijing as a means of deterring Communist expansion anywhere in the world. The loss of superiority in the 1960s because of growing Soviet intercontinental ballistic missile capabilities forces the abandonment of massive retaliation. A strategy of "flexible response" was adopted instead, which while sanctioning huge increases in United States silo-based intercontinental ballistic missiles (ICBMs) and SLBMs, nonetheless sought to accord less importance to nuclear weapons and to foster stronger conventional military options for NATO and the United States outside Europe.

The logic of flexible response could have led the United States and its European allies to reduce their reliance on battlefield and short-range nuclear forces in favor, at least, of the more easily protected and commanded intermediate range forces based at sea and on land. In fact, during the 1960s the number of nuclear weapons in NATO Europe tripled to some 7,200 warheads (later to be reduced by 1,000) with much of the growth coming precisely in the most vulnerable, battlefield weapons. (See Table 8–1.) This was a strange development, because nuclear war games in the United States and Europe as early as the mid–1950s (Operation Sage Brush and an exercise called "Carte Blanche") had revealed the enormous collateral destruction and death that would be caused even by the use of a fraction of the "theater" nuclear weapons at their disposal in Europe. Carte Blanche showed, for example, that in two days Germany could suffer more than five times as many civilian casualties (dead and wounded) as in all of World War II, and this with only NATO setting off nuclear explosions. These findings dampened the hopes of NATO, and particularly the Eisenhower administration, to save money and manpower with nuclear weapons ("more bang for the buck"). United States strategic superiority over the Soviet Union cushioned the impact of Sage Brush and Carte Blanche. However, as the Soviet Union acquired the ability to deliver a devastating attack against the United States, it became impossible to avoid a profound shift in United States and NATO nuclear strategy.

Most of the problems associated with the nuclear defense of Western Europe are the same as those of the strategic nuclear defense of the United States against Soviet attack. Once the Soviet Union gained the capability to carry out a major nuclear attack, the conditions of deterrence were forever changed. From that time forward United States planners had to find new ways to counter Soviet capabilities in peace and war. The easy deterrence based on strategic monopoly had to be replaced by a new deterrence that was as potent as its predecessor and far more robust, for it faced much more severe trials. This has not proven to be an easy task, either technically or politically. There is no simple technical answer, for example, to the growth in Soviet capabilities to attack and destroy United States ICBMs. At the same time, the efforts of a succession of United States presidents to carry out nuclear modernization has met severe political resistance in the Congress.

Many of the same problems have been encountered by NATO in its efforts to respond to the loss of United States nuclear superiority. However, the loss of superiority and the massive Soviet nuclear buildup of strategic and intermediate-range weapons that began in the 1970s (see Table 8–2) also presented a unique problem for the United States and the European members of NATO. For a time, the Soviets were able to hang NATO on the horns of a dilemma, the strategist's ideal. If NATO responded with a nuclear buildup of its own, it risked triggering a rending and embittered anti-nuclear controversy, which in fact developed following the decision in 1979 to deploy a new generation of intermediate nuclear forces unless negotiations between the United States and Soviet Union led to significant reductions in the burgeoning Soviet "theater" nuclear forces. If NATO declined to respond, the Soviets would have undermined the confidence of the Europeans in the strength of NATO and the willingness of the United States to defend its allies. In the latter case, the world might have witnessed a parade to Moscow of European leaders seeking the best bilateral terms for their countries in a series of highly unequal negotiations with the new masters of Europe.

NATO's response to the loss of superiority was to embrace "flexible response" and, through a prolonged process of inter-allied consultation, study, and planning, to change the character of its nuclear strategy. Under the new guidelines, developed mostly in the 1970s, NATO would treat nuclear weapons initially as an instrument to force the aggressor to stop his invasion and to withdraw by raising the prospect of the resort to general nuclear war. Presumably, a few targets in Poland, East Germany, or

Czechoslovakia would be attacked in a carefully controlled manner. Although it is misleading to separate the terms, this would be a "political" rather than a military use of nuclear weapons. Of course, the point is not to explode a weapon in this "political" manner, but to deter Soviet aggression by maintaining the capability to act in this way.[7]

The approach is an intelligent and interesting one. However, it failed to persuade a large part of the Western European public, particularly in West Germany, Britain, Denmark, Belgium, and the Netherlands, of its wisdom, and it had no discernible effect on the Soviet appetite to deploy new intermediate-range nuclear weapons, particularly the triple-warheaded SS–20, which by United States count had grown to more than 400 launchers (1200 warheads) by early 1985.

The present NATO nuclear strategy and the widespread public resistance to it offer clear lessons to NATO leaders. These lessons concern the narrow military force improvements that should be made in carrying out the agreed nuclear strategy. More importantly, the lessons address larger issues. The first concerns the future that the NATO allies seek in their relations with one another and with the Soviet Union, and the proper place of such a vision in democratic statesmanship. The second concerns the relation between coercion and persuasion—deterrence and negotiation in current terminology—in national security policy.

A consensus is gathering about what improvements in NATO conventional and nuclear forces would be appropriate to the "political" deterrence on which NATO's nuclear role now rests. These call for the removal of as many of the vulnerable battlefield weapons as possible and increased reliance on longer-range and more secure systems, enhanced arrangements for command and control of these, and further increases in conventional strength.[8]

But these are not bold measures. They have little appeal beyond a narrow expert community. Alone, they will not ease the fears that have fueled the anti-nuclear movement of the last three years and now form part of the political posture of major Western European political parties, notably in Germany and Britain. If they are allowed to become the sole or even the principal public measures taken by the NATO governments, the alliance will undo the public support it must have in order to function. The steps that must be taken to avoid such an outcome combine practicality and vision: on the practical side, the wisdom and prudence needed to manage an alliance of prosperous, stable democratic societies in the late twentieth century; on the side of vision, the ability to bring hope and inspiration to new generations of Americans and Europeans who have, mercifully, escaped the lessons of world war.

In discussing the practical side of "alliance management," it has become commonplace to observe that the growth in wealth and influence of the allies of the United States means that the United States is relatively less wealthy and influential than it was in the first years of NATO. It is also tried but true to observe that these alterations must always be reflected in the procedures and sometimes in the policies of the United States in its dealings with its allies. But these admonitions are easy to forget.

One of the chief problems that arises when they are forgotten is what might be called "getting too far out in front." In recent years, the United States has sometimes taken strong positions in and outside Europe (the Soviet pipeline, Libyan sponsorship of terrorism) only to find that none of its allies were willing to follow its lead. In Europe's view the United States has repeatedly isolated itself by misunderstanding the nature of the threat and the interests of its allies, and then trying to bully them or shout them into compliance. To some Americans, the European reluctance bespeaks parochialism, short-sightedness, and even complicity with Soviet expansion.

It is true that Western European opinion is subjected to massive Soviet propaganda campaigns. The large Communist parties in France and Italy are not neutral bystanders. But the lesson of the last five decades is surely that Western European opinion will rally to protect the vital interests of the alliance. In most situations, in other words, there is ample reason to wait for Western European opinion to "mature" about specific controversises. In the bargain, the United States must be certain that the demands it would impose on its allies are not generated primarily by internal domestic political requirements. The antidote to "getting too far out in front" is to remember that the geopolitical reality of sharing a continent with a superpower fosters different perspectives in Bonn, Paris, Rome, and London than in more distant Washington. In addition, differences in judgments about economic advantage are always important and can be subordinated to the requirements of security only with difficulty, and, perversely, with the greatest of difficulty precisely in times of prosperity and peace such as the alliance now knows.

In addition to the wisdom and prudence needed to manage an alliance of free nations, all concerned must accept that each generation must rediscover the vision of NATO's founders, without benefit, one hopes, of the lessons of war. Defiance and resistance are the appropriate responses to a power such as the Soviet Union—militarily strong; swollen with the domination of other peoples; hostile to much that is cherished by the NATO allies, to their pluralism, defense of individual rights and freedoms, and limited responsible governments. But if the posture of the West is a shallow, strident defiance, the allies will soon lose the allegiance of their own peoples and could even stumble into a nuclear war that could, like World War I, cause destruction and loss out of all proportion to the value of any conceivable gains. It is the task of far-sighted democratic statesmanship to temper defiance with vision, to offer hope that the sacrifices and risks endured in the resistance and defeat of tyranny can lead to a better, safer future. That is the principal challenge for the future nuclear defense of Europe.

As they meet this challenge, allied statesmen should recall the basic difference between activists and ordinary citizens. It is a basic difference of fundamental importance to democratic statesmanship, one that has been revealed in the sudden collapse of mass support for the anti-nuclear movement after the decision of the Reagan administration to undertake serious initiatives in arms control negotiations with the Soviet Union.

Activists approach questions of war and peace in ways that differ sharply from those followed by ordinary citizens. To an activist, the only valid aims of foreign policy must be to "eliminate" all the potentially tragic elements of international life such as war or the competitive accumulation of armaments. The "moral perfectionism" of the activists is revealed in the absolutist slogans of their movement: "*Ban* the Bomb!" "*End* the Arms Race!"[9] The implicit view of activists is that misguided rulers or "representatives of an oppressive regime" and ignorant citizens are the only barriers to the "solution" of war and the arms race. If enough education is conveyed to the public and the corrupted rulers are forced out of office, the world can be made safe and pure.

However, activists are not likely to be satisfied with education and advertising. Their vision of international politics is akin to a prophetic or revolutionary view of life and human possibility. The goals of activists, as Henry Kissinger observed, are based on moral claims, and these "involve a quest for absolutes, a denial of nuance, a rejection of history." The claims of a prophet, as Kissinger put it, are "a counsel of perfection," a call to Utopia that cannot be achieved without the same extreme levelling and dislocation that would be visited on society by foreign conquest. The activist is legitimized by his cause—an end to the arms race, the avoidance of nuclear holocaust—and means are unimportant. The aim of activists is an "exaltation, which dissolves technical limitation."[10]

The approach of ordinary citizens is not that of the activists. Drawing on common sense and an awareness of the tragic flaws of human nature, ordinary citizens intuitively grasp the critical dilemma of the nuclear age: the imperative need to avoid nuclear holocaust without sacrificing fundamental values. Accordingly, their normal demand is not for their governments to do away with war but instead that they conscientiously and seriously seek to avoid war and to reduce armaments. Their views are cautious and prudent, and are normally marked by a distrust of exaltation and absolutes and by a preference for mutual restraint and the gradual reconciliation of differences through persuasion.

Because of these fundamental differences in outlook, expectations, and temperament, activists are usually unable to draw many ordinary citizens to their cause. However, a combination of circumstances can recruit ordinary citizens to their side. Major economic upheavals—the Great Depression—and unpopular and seemingly uncontrollable wars—Vietnam—are the familiar recruiters. Apparently, in the nuclear age, a growing belief that Western governments, and particuarly the United States, are not seriously engaged in an effort to reduce armaments may bring thousands of ordinary citizens into the streets behind the activists. This would appear to have happened after President Reagan's first year in office.

One should state the lesson precisely. Ordinary citizens will not usually ask that their governments "Ban the Bomb" or "End the Arms Race." They will ask that a serious effort be made to avoid war and reduce armaments. They will join the activists in large numbers only if they conclude that such an effort has not been and will not be made by their governments.

The significance of the Atlantic Charter under which the United

States entered World War II was its embodiment of such a vision of the future, one that could not reduce the costs of defeating aggression but might justify them and assuage the grief of those who bore them. After a false start in which large numbers of Europeans and Americans showed signs of abandoning their leaders and taking to the streets because of the lack of such a vision, the Reagan administration has shown that it has learned some of these lessons of democratic statesmanship. By tempering defiance with a willingness to negotiate about strategic and intermediate nuclear arms reductions, NATO holds out the prospect of a better, safer future. It is that vision, as much as the perfection of military systems and consultation procedures about their use, that will assure the defense of Europe and the United States for the next five decades.

NOTES

1. George F. Kennan, *Memoirs: 1900–1950* (Boston: Little, Brown, and Company, 1967), pp. 240–241.

2. George F. Kennan, *American Diplomacy: 1900–1950* (New York: New American Library, 1952), pp. 66–67.

3. Lawrence D. Freedman, "U.S. Nuclear Weapons in Europe: Symbols, Strategy and Force Structure," in Andrew W. Pierre, ed. *Nuclear Weapons in Europe* (New York: The Council on Foreign Relations, 1984), p. 51.

4. William G. Hyland, "The Struggle for Europe: An American View," in Pierre, *Nuclear Weapons in Europe*, p. 29.

5. Among the most helpful works, in addition to the Hyland and Freeman articles already mentioned, are: John J. Mearsheimer, "Nuclear Weapons and Deterrence in Europe," *International Security* (Winter 1984–85), 19–46; David N. Schwartz, *NATO's Nuclear Dilemmas* (Washington, D.C.: The Brookings Institution, 1983); John D. Steinbruner and Leon V. Sigal), eds., *Alliance Security: NATO and the No-First Use Question* (Washington: The Brookings Institution, 1983).

6. Albert Wohlstetter, "Nuclear Sharing: NATO and the N + 1 Country," *Foreign Affairs* 34 (April 1961), p. 3.

7. See, in particular, J. Michael Legge, *Theater Nuclear Weapons and the NATO Strategy of Flexible Response,* R–2964–FF (Santa Monica, California: The Rand Corporation, 1983).

8. See especially, John D. Steinbruner, "Alliance Security," in Steinbruner and Sigal, eds., *Alliance Security*, pp. 197–207; and Legge, *Theater Nuclear Weapons*, pp. 73–76.

9. The term "moral perfectionist" belongs to Arnold Wolfers. See his wonderful essay in *Discord and Collaboration: Essays on International Politics* (Baltimore, Md.: Johns Hopkins University Press, 1962), ch. 4, "Statesmanship and Moral Choice," pp. 47–65.

10. The quotations are from Henry A. Kissinger, *A World Restored: The Politics of Convservatism in a Revolutionary Age* (New York: Grosset & Dunlap, 1964), pp. 316, 330.

Table 8.1

Long- and Medium-Range Nuclear Systems for the European Theatre

Category and type	Range/ combat radius(km)[a]	First deploy- ment[b]	Inven- tory	Warheads per system	Factors Utiliza- tion[c]	Service- ability	Warheads available (approx.)[d]	Indices Surviv- ability[e]	Reli- ability[f]	Pene- tration[g]	Arriving warheads (approx.)[h]	Operating countries and notes
WARSAW PACT												All types listed are in Soviet inventory: USSR holds all warheads
IRBM												
SS-20	5,600	1977	315[i]	3	0.66[j]	0.9	561	0.9	0.8	1.0	404	MIRV(? 1 reload per system)
SS-5 *Skean*	4,100	1961	16[i]	1	1.0	0.75	12	0.6	0.7	1.0	5	
MRBM												
SS-4 *Sandal*	1,900	1959	275[i]	1	1.0	0.7	193	0.5	0.65	1.0	63	
SRBM												
SS-12 *Scaleboard*	900	1969	70	1	1.0	0.8	56	0.7	0.75	1.0	29	
Scud A/B	300	1965	450	1	1.0	0.8	360	0.7	0.75	1.0	189	
Scud B/C	300	1965	143	1	1.0	0.8	114	0.7	0.75	1.0	60	All Pact
SS-22	1,000	1978	(100)[i]	1	1.0	0.8	80	0.8	0.8	1.0	51	
SS-23	350	1980	(10)[i]	1	1.0	0.8	8	0.8	0.8	1.0	5	
SLBM												
SS-N-5 *Serb*	1,400	1964	57[l]	1	1.0[k]	0.45[l]	26	0.8	0.6	1.0	12	On 13 G-II, 6 H-II subs
Ballistic missile sub-totals			1,436				1,410				818	
Aircraft												
Tu-22M/-26 *Backfire* B	4,025	1974	100[m]	4[no]	0.4	0.8	128	0.7	0.85	0.7	53	
Tu-16 *Badger*	2,800	1955	310	2[o]	0.4	0.7	174	0.7	0.75	0.5	46	
Tu-22 *Blinder*	3,100	1962	125	2[o]	0.4	0.7	70	0.7	0.8	0.55	22	
Su-24 (Su-19) *Fencer*	1,600	1974	550	2	0.2	0.8	176	0.55	0.8	0.65	50	

MiG-27 *Flogger* D	720	1971	1	550^m	0.8	176	0.6	0.8	0.65	55	Poland
Su-17 *Fitter* C/D	600	1974	1	688	0.8	110	0.55	0.8	0.65	31	
Su-7 *Fitter* A	400	1959	1	265^m	0.7	37	0.5	0.7	0.5	6	Czechoslovakia, Poland
MiG-21 *Fishbed* J-N	400	1970	1	100^m	0.8	16	0.5	0.8	0.6	4	
Air-delivered weapon sub-totals				2,688		887				267	
Warsaw Pact totals				4,124		2,297				1,085	

NATO

IRBM
SSBS S-3	3,000	1971–80	1	18	0.9	16	0.6	0.8	1.0	8	France

SRBM
Pershing 1A	720	1962	1	180	0.9	162	0.7	0.8	1.0	91	US, FRG

SLBM
Polaris A-3	4,600	1967	1^p	64	0.45^m	29	0.9	0.8	1.0	21	Britain MRV, MARV *Chevaline*, in service shortly
MSBS M-20	3,000	1977	1	80	0.45^m	36	0.9	0.8	1.0	26	France
Ballistic missile sub-totals				342		243				146	

Land-based aircraft
Vulcan B-2	2,800	1960	2	48	0.7	67	0.6	0.8	0.5	16	Britain, Incl. 9 OCL ac
F-111E/F	1,900	1967	2	156^q	0.8	125	0.6	0.8	0.75	45	USac in Europe
Mirage IVA	1,600	1964	1	34	0.7	24	0.6	0.8	0.5	6	France
Buccaneer	950	1962	2	50	0.7	35	0.6	0.8	0.5	8	Britain, *Tornado* to replace
F-104	800	1958	1	290	0.7	61	0.4	0.8	0.3	6	Belgium, FRG, Greece, Italy, Netherlands, Turkey
F-4	750	1962	1	172	0.8	41	0.4	0.8	0.55	7	FRG, Greece, Turkey
F-4	750	1962	1	252	0.8	60	0.4	0.8	0.55	11	US Europe- dual-based ac
F-16	900	1979	1	48	0.8	12	0.5	0.8	0.75	4	US ac in Europe
F-16	900	1982	1	20	0.8	5	0.5	0.8	0.75	2	Belgium
Jaguar	720	1974	1	117^r	0.8	47	0.4	0.8	0.6	9	Britain, France
Mirage IIIE	600	1964	1	30	0.8	12	0.4	0.8	0.45	2	France

Table 8.1 (continued)

Long- and Medium-Range Nuclear Systems for the European Theatre

Category and type	Range/combat radius(km)[a]	First deployment[b]	Warheads per system	Inventory	Factors		Warheads available (approx.)[d]	Indices			Arriving warheads (approx.)[h]	Operating countries and notes
					Utilization[c]	Serviceability		Survivability[e]	Reliability[f]	Penetration[g]		
Carrier-based aircraft												
A-6E	1,000	1963	2	20[s]	0.5	0.8	16	0.5	0.8	0.6	4	US, B-13 bombs
A-7E	900	1966	2	48[s]	0.5	0.8	38	0.5	0.8	0.4	6	US, B-13 bombs
Super Etendard	560	1980	2	16[t]	0.5	0.8	13	0.5	0.8	0.5	3	France, AN-52 bombs
Air-delivered weapon sub-totals				1,301			556				129	
NATO totals (excluding *Poseidon/Trident*)				**1,643**			**799**				**275**	
US CENTRAL SLBM												
Poseidon C–3 or *Trident* C–4	4,600 or 7,400	1971 1980					400[u]	0.9	0.8	1.0	288	
NATO totals (including *Poseidon Trident*)							**1,199**				**563**	

[a] *Range* for missiles: average *combat radius* for aircraft, assuming high-level transit, low-level penetration of air defences and average payload unrefuelled.
[b] Production runs will continue for up to 10 years from first in-service date.
[c] Approx. percentage thought likely to be allocated to nuclear role against Europe. For USSR, assumes about 25% generally deployed in East (except where noted) and some 50% of bbrs and some 25% of FGA ac retained in nuclear role.
[d] Given by: Inventory × Warheads × Utilization × Serviceability.
[e] Survivability is a function of weapon system characteristics, tactics and location in relation to attacking force.
[f] Estimated likelihood of system functioning as planned after launch.
[g] Dependent on effectiveness of defence against specific system and ECM fit. For NATO assumes Moscow ABM defences not targeted or after ABM suppression.
[h] Given by: Warheads available × Survivability × Reliability × Penetration.
[i] Total nuclear-capable systems available.
[j] Assumes 33% in Western USSR, 33% in 'swing-zone' in the Central USSR and with range to threaten NATO and Far East.

[k] All assumed in Western Sea Areas (primarily Baltic), H-II SSB/SALT-counted.
[l] Takes account of approximate submarine refit time and missile serviceability.
[m] Numbers in nuclear strike role reassessed from 1981–82.
[n] Some authorities give 3 as average warhead loading.
[o] ASM could be carried instead of free-fall bombs, and this would improve the penetration figure substantially.
[p] MRV counts as one regardless of dispersal pattern (warheads not separately targetable).
[q] F-IIIE could be reinforced by F-IIID (not SALT-counted and might be assumed available to reinforce Europe), but these are not available on day-to-day alert. FB-IIIA not assumed available for theatre use.
[r] Only 80 nuclear-capable aircraft in Anglo-French inventory of 219. Half of these assumed retained for nuclear role.
[s] Assumes 2 carriers in US 6th Fleet (Mediterranean); temporary redeployment not allowed for. Half strike inventory retained for nuclear role against land targets.
[t] Assumes one out of two French carriers in range.
[u] Figure assumed to be available to SACEUR for NATO targeting SALT-counted systems.

Source: The Military Balance, 1982–83. (London: IISS)

Table 8.2

Strategic Nuclear Capability Vehicles of the United States and the Soviet Union

Category and type	First year deployed	Range (km)	Throw-weight (000 lb)	CEP (m)	Launcher total 7/84	Warhead details and comments
UNITED STATES						
LAND-BASED						
Strategic						
ICBM						
LGM-25C *Titan II*	1962	15,000	8.3	1,300	37	1 × 9MT W-53/Mk 6. Being phased out.
LGM-30F *Minuteman II*	1966	11,300	1.6	370	450	1 × 1.2MT W-56/Mk 11C. (442 launchers if 8 are comms vehs.)
LGM-30G *Minuteman III*	1970	14,800	1.5	280	250	3 × 170KT W-62/Mk 12 MIRV.
	1980	12,900	2.4	220	300	3 × 335KT W-78/Mk 12A MIRV.
SEA-BASED						
Strategic						
SLBM						
UGM-73A *Poseidon C-3*	1971	4,600	3.3	450	304	10 × 40–50 KT W-68. Max 14 MIRV.
Trident C-4	1980	7,400	3.0+	450	288	8 × 100KT W-76 MIRV.
AIR						
Strategic						
Long-range bombers						
B-52G	1959	12,000	0.95	45	151	12 ALCM, 4 SRAM, 4 × B-28/-43/-57/-61 bombs.
B-52H	1962	16,000	0.95	45	90	4 SRAM, 4 × B-28/-43/-57/-61 bombs.
SOVIET UNION						
LAND-BASED						
Strategic						
ICBM						
SS-11 *Sego* mods 1/2	1966/73	10/13,000	2	1,400	} 520	1 × 1MT.
mod 3	1975	8,800	2.5	1,100		3 × 100–300KT.
SS-13 *Savage* mod 1	1968	10,000	1	2,000	} 60	1 × 750KT.
SS-17 (RS-16) mod 1	1975	10,000	6	450	} 150	4 × 750KT MIRV.
(cold mod 2	1977	11,000	3.6	450		1 × 6MT.
launch) mod 3	1982	10,000	—	—		4 × 20KT MIRV.

Table 8.2 (continued)

Strategic Nuclear Capability Vehicles of the United States and the Soviet Union

Category and type		First year deployed	Range (km)	Throw-weight (000 lb)	CEP (m)	Launcher total 7/84	Warhead details and comments
SS-18 (RS-20)	mod 1	1975	12,000	16.5	450	} 308	1 × 20MT.
(cold	mod 2	1977	11,000	16.7	450		8 × 900KT MIRV.
launch)	mod 3	1979	10,500	16	350		1 × 20MT.
	mod 4	1982	11,000	16.7	300		10 × 500KT MIRV.
	(mod 5)	(1985)	(9,000)	(16)	(250)		(210 × 750KT) MIRV.
SS-19 (RS-18)	mod 2	1979	10,000	7.5	300	} 360	1 × 5MT.
(hot launch)	mod 3	1982	10,000	8	300		6 × 550KT MIRV.

		First year deployed	Range (km)	Max speed (Mach)	Weapon load (000 lb)	Launcher total 7/84	Warhead details and comments
AIR							
Strategic							
Long-range bombers							
Tu-95 *Bear B/C*		1956	12,800	0.78	40	100	1–2 AS-3/–4 ALCM, 2–3 bombs.
Mya-4 *Bison*		1956	11,200	0.87	20	43	4 bombs.
Medium-range bombers							
Tu-16 *Badger*		1955	4,800	0.8	20	410	1–2 AS-2/–3/–6 ALCM, 1 bomb. (*Badger* G carries (?6) AS-5.) Air Force (220), Navy (190).
Tu-22 *Blinder*		1962	4,000	1.5	12	160	1 AS-4 ALCM, 1 bomb. Air Force (125), Navy (35).
Tu-26 *Backfire*		1974	8,000	2.5	17.5	235	1 or 2 AS-4 ALCM, 2 bombs. Air Force (130), Navy (105).

Category and type		First year deployed	Range (km)	Throw-weight (000 lb)	CEP (m)	Launcher total 7/84	Warhead details and comments
SEA-BASED							
Strategic							
SLBM							
SS-N-5 *Serb*		1964	1,400	n.a.	2,800	45	1 × 1MT.
SS-N-6	mod 1	1968	2,400	1.5	900	} 368	1 × 1MT. Liquid-fuel.
Sawfly	mod 2	1973	3,000	n.a.	900		1 × 1MT. Liquid-fuel.
	mod 3	1974	3,000	1.5	1,400		2 warheads. Liquid-fuel.
SS-N-8	mod 1	1972	7,800	1.5	1,300	292	1 × 1MT.
	mod 2	n.a.	9,100	8	900		1 × 800MT.
SS-N-17		1977	3,900	2.5	1,500	12	1 × 1MT. Solid-fuel.
SS-N-18	mod 1	n.a.	6,500	5	1,400	224	3 × ?200KT. Solid-fuel.
	mod 2	1978	8,000	n.a.	600		1 × 450KT.
	mod 3	n.a.	6,500	n.a.	600		7 × 200KT MIRV.
SS-N-20		1981	8,300	n.a.	n.a.	40	9 × ?200KT MIRV.

Source: *The Military Balance, 1984–85* (London: IISS)

9

SDI and Peace in Europe

ROBERT C. RICHARDSON III

In March of 1983, President Reagan announced his plan to abandon the United States strategic strategy of Massive Retaliation in favor of a new strategy called Assured Survival. The new strategy required that we develop effective defenses against Soviet ballistic missiles. Since the President's announcement, a debate has raged over the impact of this decision not only on United States security but also upon that of NATO Europe.

Following the announcement of the President's intention to change United States strategy, a research-only program was established to determine the feasibility and optimum technological configurations of the proposed missile defense systems. This Strategic Defense Initiative, variously called SDI, Star Wars, or Peace Shield, although primarily aimed at ICBM and SLBM defenses, included consideration of Tactical Missile defenses (ATBMs) for use in Europe and elsewhere overseas. The principal focus of the United States SDI program, however, has been and remains on strategic missile defense, as implied by its title.

Before the President made his 1983 speech announcing the SDI program, key defense officials, alert defense analysts, and the public were exposed to a preview of the new concept and its pros and cons by a project called High Frontier (HF). This project was established by Lt. Gen. Daniel O. Graham in 1981 in order to evaluate the technical feasibility, economic viability, military soundness, and political acceptability of the proposed new strategy, a strategy which he had recommended to President Reagan in 1980 when he was one of the President's pre-election advisors.

In order to assess its political acceptability High Frontier took the new strategy public in late 1982. This involved a 42-state press, TV, and radio tour sponsored by the Conservative Caucus. It resulted in validating the program's political acceptability, in surfacing all conceivable objections and concerns, and in creating a constituency for the proposed new strategy prior to the President's speech of March 23, 1983.

The publicity this tour gave to the High Frontier proposals prepared the American public for the President's March 1983 speech. It also generated a sizable amount of mail to the White House and the Defense Department indicating extensive U.S. public support for the building of defenses against Soviet missiles. Unfortunately, it was not possible to undertake a similar public education program in Europe at that time. As a result, our allies, along with many United States bureaucrats and pundits who ignored the High Frontier presentations, were caught unaware and unprepared by the President's announcement.

Since Europe had not been consulted by Washington officialdom, or even alerted by High Frontier type presentations, the initial overseas press reaction to the President's 1983 speech tended to be negative. It was based more on "gut feelings" than on any real understanding of the pros and cons of his proposal. Terms such as "disaster," "Marginot Line concept," "Fortress America," appeared in the European press and threatened to set the tone for subsequent government to government consultations. They also resulted in both High Frontier and administration spokesmen rushing in to limit the damage.

On Understanding the Purpose of SDI

To assess the applicability of SDI and its proposed missile defenses to the future security of Europe one must first understand why this change in strategy is the only affordable solution to the security of the United States in the present Soviet threat environment.

The primary purpose of President Reagan's SDI program is to perpetuate deterrence of nuclear wars and, should deterrence ever fail or accidents happen, to provide as much protection as possible for the people and resources of America and its allies. So long as the military balance continues to shift in favor of the Soviets, and their military buildup remains unconstrained by verifiable arms control agreements, the credibility of Mutual Assured Destruction (MAD) as a deterrent cannot but decline. While MAD might have been a credible, if not a desirable, way in which to deter Soviet aggression when the United States enjoyed strategic nuclear superiority, or, at least parity, it no longer is now that the Soviets are acquiring a first strike capability to destroy our ability to retaliate.

In his historic speech announcing SDI, the President made it quite clear that the continued Soviet buildup now made it necessary to adopt a new approach to maintaining a credible deterrent. He said: "The strategy of deterrence has not changed. It still works. But what it takes to maintain deterrence has changed. It took one kind of military force to deter an attack when we had far more nuclear weapons than any other power—it takes another kind now that the Soviets, for example, have enough accurate and powerful nuclear weapons to destroy virtually all our missiles on the ground." The SDI program is designed to provide this "other kind of force."

Ever since 1981 the only alternatives to a change in strategy have been either to accept increasing United States nuclear inferiority or to try to keep up with the Soviet buildup in a multibillion-dollar offensive nuclear arms race (MAD). The first alternative, United States inferiority, is clearly unacceptable. Economic and social considerations soon made it clear that the second alternative—which requires throwing ever more money at defense—is also unacceptable. We had started down that road in the Carter years with plans for some 200 or more MX missiles, 70 billion-dollar mobile shelter systems, or 35 billion-dollar Dense Pack schemes.

The defense debate initiated in 1982 and 1983 by High Frontier brought about a public understanding of the MAD strategy, and the people had not liked what they learned. The MAD strategy risks everything on deterrence only. It gives the military the primary task of avenging an attack rather than defeating it. MAD was introduced by a few, would-be, defense experts and academicians in the 1960s. These architects and proponents of MAD were obviously a minority who had assumed that they knew best what was good for the country regardless of whether or not the majority of Americans agreed. The debate over MAD versus SDI, and the polls associated with it, show that most Americans expect their government to defend them, if at all possible.

When MAD was explained to the American public, it was found that approximately 65 percent of the people actually thought that their government was providing them with the best possible defenses against Soviet missiles. From 75% to 85% of those polled indicated that they expected and wanted their government to protect them. The proper role of the military is to protect the nation, not merely revenge acts of aggression as is the case under MAD. Revenge is also perceived by most informed people to be an informal strategy that violates the civilized rules of warfare, including those we agreed to in the 1946 Geneva Conventions.

In considering the applicability of SDI to European security an understanding of the basic deterrent and defense goals of the SDI program is essential. Europeans who were erroneously led to believe that the sole purpose of SDI was to "build a protective bubble" over America, or "reduce the role of nuclear weapons" have difficulty identifying their security with the President's proposal. On the other hand, those who understand the need for the SDI in order to perpetuate nuclear deterrence, and provide some protection should deterrence ever fail or accidents occur, as well as those who understand that the alternative to SDI is more offensive nuclear weapons and higher defense spending, can easily identify with President Reagan's new strategy of Assured Survival.

Unfortunately, from the beginning, many of SDI's proponents have mixed together the basic goals of the program with some of its fringe benefits. The fact that the new strategy may lead to a reduction in the dominant role now played by nuclear weapons in defense plans; that it is more morally acceptable than MAD; that it would use primarily non-nuclear weapons that can only kill other weapons, not people; and that it will be a far cheaper way to maintain a credible deterrent than would a continued MAD arms race in offensive systems have led some people to lose sight of the main objective of the whole effort which is to sustain deterrence in the new environment in which the Soviets now have, or will soon have, a decisive superiority in offensive nuclear ballistic missile systems, and a credible first strike war winning capability.

On Applicability of SDI to European Security

Since the formation of NATO, peace and security in Europe have been guaranteed by a combination of conventional and tactical nuclear forces deployed in Europe and by the American commitment to use "any and all forces, if necessary" to repel a Soviet aggression. "Any and all forces" is a political euphemism for United States tactical and strategic nuclear forces.

NATO's European-based forces have never enjoyed the size or sustainability needed to defend Europe against a major Soviet offensive. But such an offensive has been effectively deterred over the years by Soviet recognition that the United States NATO commitment, if honored, would lead to a global nuclear exchange which they would be unlikely to survive, let alone win. This deterrent to limited aggression in Europe worked so long as the United States enjoyed strategic nuclear superiority, or at least was able to retain a credible ability to inflict acceptable damage in retaliation under any circumstances, including a Soviet first strike.

In somewhat simplified terms, the classic scenario that the NATO nations have relied upon in the past for deterrence of, or defense against, limited Soviet aggression calls for: first, sufficient conventional forces to delay Soviet advances in Europe in order to allow time for political intercession; second, a tactical nuclear response; and, third, assuming these do not arrest the attack or bring the Soviets to the conference table, escalation to a strategic nuclear exchange. This "drill," however, can produce a credible deterrent only so long as the strategic exchange remains unacceptable to the Soviets.

In a worst case scenario, peace and security in Europe have thus been dependent on the United States' ability to retaliate with strategic forces. The credibility of the American commitment to NATO is likewise dependent on this strategic ability. It is obvious that any degradation of United States ability to survive a Soviet first strike, and retaliate, not only weakens the general war deterrent and United States security but also the credibility of the American commitment to Europe and therefore of NATO's ability to deter limited aggression against Europe. Since the shift in the strategic balance that has gradually been taking place over the past twenty years threatens United States ability to retaliate effectively under all conditions, and since SDI was initiated primarily to arrest and reverse this trend at a cost we can afford, it follows that SDI is as vital to peace and security in Europe as it is to America security.

It now appears that defenses against Soviet tactical missiles may be more urgently required, and easily provided, than can defenses against Soviet ICBMs. SS-21s now facing Europe, and other forward areas such as Israel (from Syria) pose an immediate threat to conventional defenses in these areas. Since the nations threatened by these tactical missiles are not party to the ABM Treaty, and do not need all the space based elements envisioned for SDI layered defense, they can test and deploy missile defenses as soon as these can be developed. Their efforts to provide for their own survival will thus both benefit from SDI technology and may also provide major inputs to some aspects of United States SDI program. A *Wall Street Journal* editorial on 13 March 1986 entitled: "A New SDI Perspective" made public this important new requirement.

Deterrence of a Soviet strategic nuclear first strike against the United States will, therefore, not only reinforce deterrence of general nuclear war but also reinforce deterrence of limited conventional wars.

Strategic defenses will also provide some protection for America in the event of a strategic exchange initiated by either side. This makes the United States commitment to escalate on behalf of NATO, if necessary, far more credible than it is now under MAD where, without such protection, implementing our commitment would be tantamount to suicide. As such, missile defenses are essential to the defense of Europe in Europe as well as to the perpetuation of a credible United States commitment to come to the rescue of Europe.

There are some in Europe who are concerned that the establishment of effective defenses against ICBMs by both the United States and the Soviet Union might result in a strategic stalemate that would preclude useful resort to strategic nuclear weapons by either side. They then suggest that the Soviets, feeling relatively secure from escalation involving their homelands and ours, would be encouraged to exploit with impunity their conventional Warsaw Pact superiority. Were this to come about they then believe that it would lead to demands for additional, costly, divisions and tactical air forces as necessary to provide a self-sufficient "horizontal" deterrent and defense in Europe.

While theoretically plausible, this argument assumes an asymmetry in strategic offensive and defensive capabilities unlikely to ever come about in the real world. To assume that either side would accept the loss of a major war in Europe rather than escalate, or that the Soviets would risk surrendering the strategic or tactical nuclear initiative to the United States, regardless of the American commitments to NATO allies, makes little sense.

It may also be possible to exploit SDI and EDI technologies to offset Warsaw Pact quantitative force superiority in conventional anti-tank defenses. This was recently proposed by Dr. Kai-Uwe von Hassel, the former president of the Western European Union (WEU) and former and West German minister of Defense.

SDI and Peace in Europe

A scenario of current concern is one in which the Soviets would present the United States with a *fait accompli* European conventional grab. To do this they would have to make a first strike on some 300 or less critical targets that make possible NATO's conventional defenses in Europe. French strategists such as General Pierre Gallois argue that they can do this today with their SS-21 missiles using only chemical or other non-nuclear warheads since all these targets are "soft." The Soviet goal would be to defeat NATO in Europe by paralyzing its conventional defense capabilities quickly enough to preclude a useful resort to nuclear escalation at any level. Defenses based on SDI technology make any scenario such as this too risky to attempt.

In summary, SDI would lead to improved European security by almost any criteria. It will do this by perpetuating deterrence of major Soviet acts of aggression at the strategic level. It would also do this by providing the technology essential to the survival of NATO's conventional forces. It would preclude any "quick grabs" based on theater level, non-nuclear first strikes—a threat that the ATBMs that will spin out of the SDI program, and the accompanying European Defense Initiative (EDI) discussed below, will make impossible. Furthermore, SDI could result in technical developments that could improve conventional, non-missile defense capabilities sufficiently to more than offset any superior Soviet mass in the Warsaw Pact.

Evolution of European Reactions to SDI

Europe has gone through four phases in reacting to SDI. The "knee jerk" negative reaction previously discussed was followed by a phase of "understanding" of the logic of the proposal from the United States point of view, qualified by expressions of concern over possible adverse impact they foresaw on NATO. This was generally expressed as: "We see why America needs to adopt the new Reagan strategy to perpetuate deterrence and respond to demands for defenses if deterrence fails or accidents occur, but (1) this is a threat to our national nuclear forces, (2) it may invite limited conventional aggression by stalemating the strategic commitment, (3) it will lead to a technological gap within the alliance that will decouple Europe from the United States economically and militarily, and (4) it may require an increase in NATO's conventional defense capability.

Once the above concerns were addressed, partly after further analysis and partly after the paradigm nature of the proposed shift in United States strategy surfaced secondary considerations that negated some of these, the fourth and hopefully last phase of Allied reactions began to develop. This fourth phase consists of a recognition among European strategists and politicians of the need for defenses against those missiles most threatening to Western Europe, specifically the SS-21s, 22s, and 23s. Given the highaccuracy of these new Soviet missiles, and the threat that they pose to NATO's vital airbases, stockpile sites, ports, radars, and strike forces with either conventional, chemical, or very low yield atomic warheads, effective defenses against these is now vital to the effectiveness of NATO's conventional defense forces. Fortunately, such defenses can now be developed and deployed as a result of the United States SDI research program.

This conclusion led to the establishment in Rotterdam in 1984, of a European counterpart to High Frontier, called High Frontier Europe (HFE). HFE was organized by a Dutch lawyer and former member of the European Assembly, James Jansaan van Raay. Its chairman is Dr. Kai-Uwe von Hassel, the former president of the Parliament of the Western European Union; former President of the Bundestag and former defense minister of Germany. Its board and planning group members include: General Pierre Gallois (FR), Air Vice Marshal Stewart Menaul (UK), Commissioner Carlo Ripa de Meana (IT), and Dr. Klause Heiss (Austria). High Frontier Europa was established in an effort to bring together these European defense experts in a collective approach to determining how Europe's security could best benefit from the United States SDI program and to make certain that Europe's defenses against Soviet ballistic missiles are given the priority they deserve. In a preliminary report released in November 1985, High Frontier Europa proposed a European Defense Initiative (EDI). This report will be followed in 1986 by recommendations as to how EDI might best be implemented.

In 1984, America asked its major NATO allies to participate in SDI research and development. As yet there has been no official collective response to this offer either in terms of reacting to the value of the concept to their collective security, or in terms of coordinating their participation. The French rejected the United States offer and countered with their Eureka proposal. The British were the first to accept the American offer and have entered into a bilateral research agreement on SDI. The Germans are still discussing participation in SDI research on a bilateral basis as of this writing. Most of the bilateral agreements between governments or firms and SDI have so far been motivated more by economic than defense considerations. With the recognition of the growing tactical missile threat, this is beginning to change.

During HFE's evaluation of strategic defenses for European security the difference between threats to the United States and to Europe led Dr. von Hassel, the Chairman of HFE, to also suggest that EDI should study the application of missile defense technologies, and possibly even SDI and EDI space-based systems, to offsetting Warsaw Pact conventional force superiority. His idea was that some of the new systems under development by SDI— such as lasers using "pop up" mirrors or rail guns in the alps— could not only engage tactical missiles but also target tank and other conventional force formations. It is argued that this would resolve the concern that a strategic stalemate from the adoption of defenses by both sides would establish a requirement for additional build up in NATO Europe conventional defenses in order to maintain deterrence. Whether or not this is practical or cost effective remains to be seen.

Relationship between EDI, SDI, and Eureka

The existence of three different organizations presumably having a role in missile defense in Europe, EDI, SDI and Eureka, has resulted in some confusion. In my view these three entities are neither duplicative nor mutually exclusive. European nations or individual corporations may, should they desire, participate in all three.

EDI and SDI must be closely coordinated and mutually supportive. SDI, by definition, will give primary attention to the strategic threat and to those systems that can deal with ICBMs. To the extent that there is overlap in technologies, SDI will also pursue systems to deal with tactical missile threats, though on a lesser priority. SDI is funded exclusively by the United States.

EDI would give priority to the missile threat to Europe. It would ensure that systems applicable to Europe, but not necessarily applicable to intercontinental defenses, are adequately pursued. And it would develop concepts and strategies for the integration of the missile defense system in Europe with the NATO and national defenses now responsible for dealing with any conventional attack, namely, the Warsaw Pact land/air threat.

Whether EDI is funded by European governments and charged with managing research in Europe for European defenses, or whether its role is limited to that of a coordinating and planning activity, it would not duplicate SDI research. What it would do is keep current on SDI activities, both in the United States and overseas, and identify and exploit applications of these to Europe's defense problems. EDI could also be an activity under NATO should the participating governments so decide.

The exact role of EDI remains to be determined, but some collective entity among NATO countries interested in developing defenses primarily for Europe (ATMs) appears to be an essential requirement. Participation in EDI does not preclude national or corporate participation in SDI. Those who wish to work for the SDI office, and United States dollars, can do so. Those who wish to work for the SDI office, and United States dollars, can do so. Those who wish to work on European priority systems can get their guidance, and possibly even contracts, from EDI.

Once the American and European-based systems become operational, command and control in Europe would no doubt pass to NATO. The European missile defense capability will undoubtedly have to be dependent on some elements of the United States defense capability such as satellite tracking and/or boost phase or midcourse intercept of long range missiles aimed at Western European targets.

As for Eureka, I do not see that it has any role in either the SDI or EDI activities. Eureka emerged from a French concern that SDI would generate a great leap forward in United States technology leaving a growing gap between the United States and Europe. This would be destructive of both economic and military cooperation in NATO. Since the Mitterrand government did not wish to participate in SDI, but was concerned about this perceived gap, it proposed certain collective European research in similar, non-defense technologies. Coming at the time of, if not in response to, the American offer to participate in SDI, Eureka was seen by some as a French alternative to SDI—which it is not, except in terms of advancing technologies somewhat similar but for their non-defense potential.

Looking Forward

The principal implication of the SDI and EDI programs for Europe is that they should lead to strengthening deterrence of aggression at all levels. Both programs will give the people of Europe protection should deterrence fail or accidents occur. And neither need create a requirement for any additional conventional build-up. On the contrary, SDI/EDI, when implemented, should restore confidence in NATO's existing defense regardless of any increases in Soviet forces in Eastern Europe or of the deployment of additional or new Soviet tactical missiles.

A capability to defend against missiles aimed at Europe could, and should, be developed and deployed during the next two or three years. Tactical missile defenses are not inhibited by the ABM treaty as are ICBM defense, nor are the Europeans a party to the treaty. Furthermore, the Soviets have already deployed early generations of ATBMs in Eastern Europe. The next generation European-based defenses need not initially have any space-based elements but would probably look to United States space systems for help in tracking and target identification.

The European nations will hopefully reach agreement soon on a collective effort to plan and manage the development of missile defenses in Europe and to coordinate the contribution of European industry to their acquisition. While SDI will no doubt contribute as best it can to this effort, European missile defense should not be SDI's priority consideration, especially where the systems applicable to Europe are not equally useful to ICBM defenses, or where the European systems are designed for both missile and selective conventional forces defense purposes which the von Hassel proposal referred to earlier.

High Frontier Europe will continue to define the European interest in, and argue for the need to manage collectively, the development and acquisition of European missile defense systems—always in close coordination with SDI. If NATO does not do so, HFE will recommend how EDI should be constituted, what its terms of reference should be, and where and under what European management organization, if any, it should be established. If NATO authorities assume responsibility for getting this done, as they may well do now that the requirement for these systems has been stated by Mr. Mansfred Worner, Germany's Minister of Defense, then HFE will assume an expediting and public education role similar to that of High Frontier in the United States.

Finally, a word about the technological gap issue, for this is an important matter for the future of NATO and one that has not as yet been given adequate attention. I am convinced that President Mitterrand's concern over a growing technological gap between the United States and Europe is valid. However, this gap is not a by-product of the SDI effort, as the French President seemed to believe, nor is it being driven solely by SDI research. The gap was inevitable with or without President Reagan's SDI plan.

We are about to witness a great leap forward in American technology, especially in communications, computers, materiels, laser and particle beam capabilities, and other space oriented technologies. This was getting underway long before SDI as a result of a combination of common sense and new generations of managers who have broken free from the technological plateau notions imposed in the 1960s on "cutting edge" advances, especially in space and weapon systems. No longer influential are the misguided views of the 1960s to the effect: that technology is bad; that it drives costly innovations; that politicians can't control its products; that it is provocative and produces arms races by obliging the Soviets to compete; and, worst of all, that the United States has to be slowed down so the Soviets could catch up as a prerequisite to the arms control agreements.

Fortunately, the United States and its major NATO allies can again look forward to great advances in space and defense technologies in the 1990s and beyond. We will also reap extensive economic spinoff benefits from these, as was the case with missile, jet, and atomic technology research in the 1950s. The SDI technologies will provide tremendous opportunities for economic growth and improved standards of living, as well as for affordable security for the entire Free World. As one example, space communications advances, if and when coupled with Japanese made cheap receivers could spell an end to closed societies. This prospect could explain to some extent why the Soviets view with such emotion the progress being made in SDI.

Instead of SDI's creating the technological gap that the Mitterrand government expressed concern about, SDI should be seen as an opportunity to prevent it.

Were it not for President Reagan's Defense Initiative, and the need for collective collaboration among NATO nations on defense matters, the technological advances now underway in America would most likely not be shared even with our closest allies. Historians may well write that SDI gave the European nations a window on a private-sector technological surge in America that was inevitable and that without this window there would have developed differences in economic growth likely to have split up NATO more effectively than Soviet propaganda or subversion.

10

The Moralizing of Foreign Policy: The Condition of America's Acceptance of Its Superpower Destiny

LEO SANDON

I

Hail Land of light and joy! thy power shall grow
Far as the seas, which round thy regions flow;
Through earth's wide realm thy glory shall extend,
And savage nations at they scepter bend.
Around the frozen shores thy sons shall sail,
Or stretch their canvas to the Asian gate.

Timothy Dwight, 1771

Why, were other reasons wanting, in favor of now elevating this question of the reception of Texas into the Union, out of the lower region of our past party dissensions, up to its proper level of a high and broad nationality, it surely is to be found, found abundantly in the manner to which other nations have undertaken to intrude themselves into it, between us and the other parties to the case, in a spirit of hostile interference against us, for the avowed object of thwarting our policy and hampering our power, limiting our greatness and checking the fulfilment of our manifest destiny to overspread the continent allotted by Providence for the free development of our yearly multiplying millions.

John L. O'Sullivan, 1845

These lofty words of Timothy Dwight and John L. O'Sullivan contain the essential concepts upon which nineteenth-century American expansionist policy was based. Dwight, the grandson of Jonathan Edwards and president of Yale College, first expressed the millennial vision in which America's destined role became "manifest."[1] O'Sullivan, editor of the *Democratic Review* and the *New York Morning News* first used the actual phrase, "manifest destiny."[2] Dwight celebrates Columbia's power and glory "through earth's wide realm." O'Sullivan and his colleagues combined the possibilities of territorial expansion, the general postmillennial theology of the Protestant establishment, and the idea of America's messianic commission and destined greatness.

Postmillennialism, the idea that under divine guidance the kingdom of God on earth—a holy utopia—is to be established as a precondition of Christ's second coming, is virtually an American theological invention. Rooted in English Puritan thought, first suggested by Cotton Mather, later articulated by Jonathan Edwards, and fully developed by Samuel Hopkins, a postmillennial perspective became—by the republican period— "the common and vital possession" of evangelical American Christians.[3]

According to the prevailing postmillennial world view, the millennium probably would be established in the West, that is, in the "new world" or, in later terms, the United States. "Westward the course of empire takes its sway," said Bishop Berkeley in 1752. This mystique of the westward course was still strong in 1890 when Washington Gladden could speak of universal history as God's plan for westward movement. Gladden, in a sermon, articulated the essentials of the millennial doctrine: By divine ordination "the great mass of these inhabitants of the New World belong to the Aryan race, whose teeming millions have been hurrying westward ever since the dawn of time." For Gladden, even though the expansion had halted in California, "here, upon these plains, the problems of history are to be solved; here, if anywhere, is to rise the city of God, the New Jerusalem, whose glories are to fill the erath."[4] The idea of America's millennial role in world history is treated fully in Ernest Lee Tuveson's book *Redeemer Nation.*[5]

Early American expansion was not understood as a matter of empire for empire's sake. In our doctrine of Manifest Destiny, there was an exceptionalist rationale: territorial expansion was essential to freedom. We must annex new territory as a requirement for the extension of freedom. As Albert K. Weinberg wrote: "Americans were destined to develop themselves as subjects in the great experiment of liberty and federated self-government entrusted to us."[6] Thus we were able to wed millennial exceptionalism with democratic idealism as our reason for territorial expansion.

It is important to note, then, that the obviously self-serving aspects of the doctrine of Manifest Destiny are mixed with genuine commitment to democratic ideals. Weinberg wrote:

[O]ne must begin by recognizing that the egoism of the American's philosophy of the destiny of democracy did not exclude a love of democracy for its own sake. When the American spoke of extending the area of freedom he had in mind not only freedom for Americans but also greater freedom by means of Americans. This impersonal element in the American's attachment to the cause of freedom is abundantly illustrated in the expansionist listerature.[7]

Sincerity notwithstanding, there were elements of ideological rationalization as we placed our land hunger under the rubric of Manifest Destiny. As Reinhold Niebuhr pointed out, "we began our history by claiming the sanction of a democratic ideal for an imperial impulse."[8] This was the first instance of what was to be a pattern in American thought and policy: the moralizing of the imperial enterprise. In Niebuhr's words, it was the "first intimation of the formation of a unique national characteristic or trait of character, namely, the expression of a vital impulse in the name of an ideal."[9]

It is important to point out that our earliest experience with imperial policy did not require the testing that frequently prepared nations for empire. Our national ordeal—the agony of the Civil War—was internal rather than external in nature. There was little agony and even less genuine trial in America's westward expansion. George Liska notes the absence of serious struggle in early American expansionism.

> The American expansion westward does not, therefore, elicit the image of the wrestler propelled forward into the void created by the felling of the adversary. It supports, instead, the metaphor of an advancing current receiving sufficient momentum from its tributaries to effortlessly flatten minor natural obstacles. In the American expansion, the incoming waves of immigrant populations were the tributaries; and the presumed (European) defenders against the expansionist current were most of the time busy removing the artificial barriers from before the momentum as part of pursuing their competitive and individually immediate self interests.[10]

While the doctrine of Manifest Destiny provided the moral legitimation for our settlement across the continent, the Monroe Doctrine—a statement of United States resistance to external European threats and encroachments—provided the opportunity for the pursuit of American interests in the Western Hemisphere, particularly in the Caribbean. By the end of the nineteenth century, as American imperialist endeavors became more explicit, the Monroe Doctrine was used, not only to oppose European power in the Soviet Union, but to justify the extension of American hegemony in the area. Theodore Roosevelt brought the complete imperialist interpretation to the Monroe Doctrine by insisting that continued instability in a Latin American country might necessitate United States involvement in order to prevent European intervention.

When American empire became explicitly colonial in the late nineteenth century, the moralizing of the foreign policy was required. The incredible development of American industry during the Gilded Age and the disappearance of the North American frontier in 1890, led us to look to expansion across the Pacific and to engage in the political and economic domination of Central and South America. The Spanish American War—John Hay's "splendid little war"—left the United States in possession of Puerto Rico, the island of Guam, and the Philippines. The acquisition of a colonial empire disturbed the conscience of many Americans, but President McKinley bolstered the case for the annexation of the Philippines by an appeal to American destiny: "There was nothing for us to do but take them all, and to educate the Filipinos, and uplift and civilize and Christianize them, and by God's grace, do the very best we could by them, as our fellow-men for whom Christ also died."[11]

American entry into World War I was dictated by the fact that in 1917 defeat was staring Britain and France in the face and the United States could not afford a triumphant Germany dominating the continent. Economically and politically, American intervention proved inevitable: Militarily, American intervention proved decisive.

In order to gain public support, Wilson injected a moralistic justification for American intervention. The war was really an altruistic crusade "to serve and save the world at whatever cost for America," an ennobling war to end all wars and make the world safe for democracy.

In the wake of World War I and the Treaty of Versailles, there was a period of isolationist retreat. World War II signaled the end of any more "protracted periods of isolation" because the North American continent was, by means of technological developments and world politics, now too close to Europe and Asia. The option of isolation was obsolete. World War II was more easily understood as a just and necessary war than was World War I: There was a very real monster to destroy. Intervention was more obviously justified. By 1945, the United States would be too great a power to even consider avoiding international politics.

II

. . . It is my duty to place before you certain facts about the present situation in Europe.

From Stettin in the Baltic to Trieste in the Adriatic an iron curtain has descended across the continent. Behind that line lie all the capitals of central and eastern Europe. Warsaw, Berlin, Prague, Vienna, Budapest, Belgrade, Bucharest, and Sofia, all these famous cities and the populations around them lie in what I must call the Soviet sphere, and all are subject, in one form or another, not only to Soviet influence but to a very high and in some cases increasing measure of control from Moscow. . . .

I do not believe that Soviet Russia desires war. What they desire is the fruits of war and the indefinite expansion of their power and doctrines.

Winston Churchill
Westminster College
March 5, 1946

In late 1945, Winston Churchill accepted the invitation to deliver the annual Green Foundation lecture at Westminster College in Fulton, Missouri. The invitation came to Churchill through President Truman at the request of General Harry Vaughn, a Westminster alumnus. America had emerged from World War II as virtually the only world power which was stronger than it had been before the war. The new center of Western power was now the United States. In January 1946, the leading democrat of Europe came to offer advice. "I think I can be of some use over there," he told Sir Charles Wilson, "they will take things from me."[12] In Fulton, Missouri, Churchill offered his famous and controversial "iron curtain" address, an address that one New York periodical called an "ideological declaration of war against Russia."

Churchill's warning proved to be prescient counsel. It was delivered by the former prime minister of a nation used to exercising power it no longer possessed to a nation "in possession of world power without either the experience or the inclination to exercise it."[13] In 1945, the United States was capable of imposing a *pax americana* and to approximate Henry Luce's dream of "the

American Century." The armies of the United States were quickly demobilized, our fleet put in mothballs, while our economic power was deployed in behalf of consumer goods and services. It was two years before, with the aid of Winston Churchill's warning, we began to respond to Russian expansionism.

In 1947, Truman announced a new doctrine which was virtually a declaration of global war against Communism. Henceforth, the United States would come to the aid of any nation which faced either internal or external threat from totalitarian conspiracy or aggression. The Cold War began in earnest when the Truman Doctrine was used to commit American troops to fighting North Koreans who had invaded South Korea. A widespread public support for the Korean "police action" in 1950 became public disgust over the stalemated war by 1952.

The Truman administration built a network of alliances designed to contain Soviet expansion: the Rio Pact, NATO, ANZUS (committing the United States to the defense of Australia and New Zealand), and SEATO. A bilateral security arrangement was also negotiated with Japan.

The Eisenhower administration added to these alliances (CENTO, 1954; bilateral security arrangements with South Korea, 1953 and the Republic of China, 1954; and the Middle East Resolution, 1957) and, generally, continued the Cold War policy of the Truman years. The fighting in Korea was stopped, but a full-scale war in Southeast Asia was to follow. John Foster Dulles escalated the rhetoric of the Cold War with his interpretation of the state of world affairs, his apocalyptic statements about the future, and his langauge of liberation. Covert operations by the CIA in Iran and Guatemala overthrew two governments and stabilized those nations. By the end of the second Eisenhower term, there was an increasing "dis-ease" regarding the threat of Soviet strength. Sputnik, the world's first space satellite, aroused our anxiety concerning Soviet technological superiority. In 1959, Americans were stunned by the loss of Cuba to the Communists. In the presidential election of 1960, John F. Kennedy campaigned on a foreign policy platform of waging the Cold War with more "vigor" than the Republicans.

American globalism reached its apex in the early 1960s. Kennedy, in what is still the most memorable inaugural address of this century, described our commitments in the most expansive terms: "Let every nation know whether it wishes us well or ill, that we shall pay any price, bear any burden, meet any hardship, support any friend, oppose any foe to assure the survival and success of liberty." For Kennedy, who surrounded himself with "action intellectuals" who took pride in their "hard-headed realism," their "tough-mindedness," and their "lack of sentimentality," these were words of excessive idealism in complete continuity with America's nineteenth-century and early twentieth-century moralizing of foreign policy. Simon Serfaty reminds us that these words were not merely rhetoric, for by the end of that fateful decade Kennedy's promise was largely fulfilled: "The United States had over 500,000 soldiers stationed in approximately 30 countries, not including the troops fighting in Vietnam and the Atlantic and Pacific fleets that amounted to 650,000 men, and operated 429 major bases that cost approximately $4.8 billion a year."[14]

Both Kennedy and Johnson waged the Cold War with what, in retrospect, has come to be seen as too little concern for the consequences. The explicit escalation of American involvement in Vietnam began with Kennedy and continued under Johnson's leadership. Analysis of America's longest, most divisive war has occupied and continues to occupy social historians and political scientists. The ordeal of Vietnam became too intense to be endured by either the general public or by members of the bipartisan Cold War/political elite. The Vietnam War became both the source and the symbol for the dissolution of the postwar foreign policy consensus which was based on global interventionism.

III

Let us be honest. Most of us are holding together in our own little groups for comfort's sake. It is natural, of course, for people to like their like, and to be easier with those who have the same associations as themselves. Most people, as they grow older, get support from those few they have known for a long time. That is natural. But we often use natural feelings as an excuse. We are turning inward more than is really natural. As I said before, we draw the curtains and take care not to listen to anything which is going on in the street outside. We are behaving as though we were in a state of seige.

C.P. Snow
Westminster College
November 1968

That 1968 was an important year in modern American history is a commonplace observation. While it is more or less arbitrary to select a specific year as the beginning of an epoch, the case can be made that 1968 signaled the end of most of those movements identified with the 1960s. In another paper, I argue that indeed 1968 signaled the end of the postwar period and the beginning of the time in which we now find ourselves.

To bring 1968 to mind is to recall a year of painful historical judgments: Tet; the assassinations of Martin Luther King, Jr., and Robert Kennedy; the Chicago Convention. These and other events set the year apart. I wish, however, to refer to two events as particularly revelatory. The first event is yet another of the Green Foundation Lectures, this one offered by the late C.P. Snow. Lord Snow's lecture was as prescient as Winston Churchill's "iron curtain" address twenty-two years earlier.

Snow began his lecture by observing that he had traveled widely in 1967 and that, on the basis of many conversations with friends and acquaintances, he had found a strange uneasiness everywhere he went. This uneasiness had an edge of fear and it seemed to have been deepening in 1968. Snow said that the people sensed "that our world is closing in."

> What is going wrong with us? Of course, we are not the first people in history to have this kind of experience or ask this kind of question. But we can deal only with our own time and speak only with our own words. It does seem . . . and though the feeling is subjective it is strong and one can hear it expressed by the very young—that our world is closing in. It gives us the sensation of contracting, not of expanding. This is very odd. It is very odd intellectually. For, after all, ours is the time of all times when men have performed some of their greatest triumphs. It is, or ought to be, exciting that there will soon be the first voyage round the moon: there is a technical triumph, and for many, I suspect, a release from some of our day-by-day unease.[15]

The sense of the world closing in was the result of telecommunications and the immediacy of information. We know what is happening. "We know so much: and we can do so little. We turn away." Here Snow used an interesting and very British metaphor as he spoke of the general tendency toward enclave making in 1968:

> Yes, we turn away. We don't project ourselves outwards: we turn inwards. We draw what in England we call the curtains, and we try

to make an enclave of our own. An enclave, a refuge, a place to shut out the noise. A group of one's own. Enclave-making: that is one of the characteristic symptoms of our unease.[16]

Snow observed that one could see enclave-making occurring "in bigger and smaller forms." The larger forms were expressed in the revival of nationalisms and the building of "language walls" along ethnic lines. Youth were turning inward, into their own customs and their own private language. People were, in essence, creating privacies, huddling together into personal refuges.

Snow allowed that there were objective and psychological reasons why persons in cities of the advanced world should behave as though they were in a state of siege. The incidence of crime was increasing exponentially. The complexity of the modern industrial state weighed upon many persons. Even more important, Snow argued, were the world population problems and the gap between the rich and poor countries: "The two problems are interconnected. They are among the noises that we don't want to hear." Snow worried that the population flood was "already making us more callous toward human life." These two crises were two of the most important causes of our sense of a state of siege.

> The fact that half our fellow human beings are living at or below subsistence level. The fact that in the unlucky countries the population is growing faster than the food to keep it alive. The fact that we are moving—perhaps in ten years—into large-scale famine.[17]

Snow maintained that the gap between the rich and poor countries was growing and that many millions of people in the third world were going to starve to death before our eyes, that is, "we shall see them doing so upon our television sets." These were the most important questions in 1968, Snow argued, more important than the events with which those of us in Western societies had been preoccupied—student power, racial conflicts, and the disaffection of youth. The population-hunger problem was international in scope and catastrophic in nature. There would first be local famines beginning around 1975–80. These local famines would spread into a sea of hunger. Only concerted effort would stave off a major catastrophe before the end of the century.

> We shall, in the rich countries, be surrounded by a sea of famine, involving hundreds of millions of human beings, unless three

tremendous social tasks are by then in operation. Not just one alone, but all three. They are:

1) A concerted effort by the rich countries to produce food, money and technical assistance for the poor.

2) An effort by the poor countries themselves, on the lines of India and Pakistan, to revolutionize their food production.

3) An effort by the poor countries—with all the assistance that can be provided under (1)—to reduce or stop their population increase: with a corresponding reduction in the population increase in the rich countries also.

Those are the three conditions, all necessary, if we are to avoid social despair.[18]

Snow thought that it was unlikely that the tasks would be engaged successfully. Both individuals and entire societies were looking inwards. In order to cope effectively with the coming catastrophe, three "quantum-jumps" in human endeavor would have to occur: (1) Poor countries would have to make a major effort to limit population increase; (2) the superpowers would have to agree to collaborate for humane ends; and (3) rich countries would have to sacrifice to a degree which they had never contemplated before, except in major war.

This extreme estimate is that, to make the world safe while there is time, the rich countries would have to devote up to 20% of their G.N.P. for a period of ten to fifteen years. Obviously that would mean a radical decrease in military expenditure: it would mean that the standard of living would stay still, and then decrease. It sounds a fantastic estimate: yet I believe it is nearer the truth than more comfortable ones. In the whole of this exercise of seeing our dangers, most of us—and this is certainly true of me—have been complacent. We have been playing at it.[19]

Snow did not think that the quantum jumps would be taken. Political memory lasts about a week; political foresight stretches about another week ahead. It was not realistic, Snow concluded, to believe that such efforts would be made.

The alternatives to the above prescription were gloomy. Model A, the most likely scenario according to Snow, would see no significant alteration of relations between the superpowers. They would continue to coexist, avoiding major war. Increasing sums would be spent on armaments, anti-ballistic missiles, and so on, without either side's gaining greater security. Both the American and the Soviet societies would get richer. The food-population collision would occur on schedule. Famine would become the primary reality in many countries.

Model B was a bit more cheerful. There would be some relaxation between the superpowers. There would be success in some initiatives such as the Indian agricultural effort. Serious suffering would not be averted, but time could be bought to "give mankind a generation's breathing space to think and plan."

Model C, the most unlikely scenario, would be for citizens to act on the assumption that the only decent way to respond to a state of siege is to break out of it. Intelligence has been the strength of our species, and it would be our only hope now. The facts would have to be told by high officials, scientists, teachers, and churchpersons of all kinds. Great sacrifices would need to be made. Snow concludes:

> One hears young people asking for a cause. The cause is here. It is the biggest single cause in history: simply because history has never before presented us with such a danger. It is a very difficult cause to fight, because it will be long-drawn-out, it is going to need using political means for distant ends.

> We have to stop being trivial. Many of our protests are absurd, judged by the seriousness of the moment in which we stand. We have to be humble and learn the nature of politics. Politics is bound to be in essence short-term. That is to no one's fault. Politicians have to cope with the day's tasks. American governments have to try to keep their country safe, in the short term as well as the long. Soviet governments have to do exactly the same. But, it is in the nature of politics that the short-term duties come first. It is the duty of all the rest of us, and perhaps most of all generations which are going to live in what is now the future, to keep before the world its long-term fate. Peace. Food. No more people that the earth can take. That is the cause.[20]

If Lord Snow's address was the first, the second revelatory event of 1968 was the flight of *Apollo 8* in December, 1968. On December 23, the capsule sent photographs of earth from approximately 180,000 miles in space. Three astronauts, Frank Borman, William Andrews, and James A. Lovell, Jr., viewed the earth from the depths of space and commented on their impression. Captain Lovell saw the earth as a "grand oasis in the big vastness of space." Lovell also remarked to the flight's commander, Captain Borman, "Frank, what I keep imagining is if I am some lonely traveler from another planet what I would think about the earth from this altitude. Whether I think it would be inhabited or not." The astronauts described the royal blue of the earth's waters, the bright whiteness of cloud formations, and the land areas in various shades of brown.[21]

On Christmas Day, 1968, Archibald MacLeish wrote a 506-word meditation which appeared on the front page of *The New York Times*.[22] In his reflection, MacLeish noted that our conceptions of the human situation have always depended on our notions of the earth. For the first time, human beings have *seen* the earth: "Seen it whole and round and beautiful and small."

The photograph of the earth from space provided humankind with a new *Weltbild*, a new world picture. After 1968, McLuhan's "global village" and the metaphor of spaceship earth were standard terminology. There was a prevailing Malthusian concern about the fragility of the planet as scientists and philosophically oriented economists brooded over the depletion of finite natural resources and the continued ability of the earth to support future human civilizations. Environmental pollution and the state of the atmosphere as well as the overall health of the biosphere were part of the agenda of those concerned with "the care and maintenance of a small planet."

Soon after 1968, the United States joined the global economy. Of course, we have had "foreign trade" from the colonial period onward. Foreign trade, however, had not been crucially important. We led industrial revolutions in steel and mass production and then in electronics. America had such a large internal market that we did not worry too much about foreign markets. Then, in the early seventies, we noted that West Germany and Japan had become fierce competitors. Simultaneously, trade became more important: Exports almost doubled and the imported part of the internal market more than doubled in the seventies. The West Germans and Japanese began turnkey plants in South Korea and other third world countries. Multinational corporations flourished. There was, in a word, an unprecedented internationalization of the United States economy in the seventies.

C.P. Snow's remarkable Green Foundation lecture turned out to be a prescient description of the seventies. Snow's concepts of a siege mentality and enclave making, moreover, provide a hermeneutic for much of American social history in the 1970s and the 1980s. For over eighteen years, there has been an oscillation between efforts toward engaging global issues, on the one hand, and tendencies to "draw the curtains," to build enclaves, on the other hand. The cultural manifestation of drawing the curtain on the world outside has been described by Christopher Lasch in what he termed "the Culture of Narcissism," and by Tom Wolfe as "the me decade."[23] Economically, enclave building has been and is being expressed in fitful gestures of protectionist policy in the face of an increasing global economy. Politically, enclave building has been expressed in several versions of neo-isolationism and the temptation to revert to a "Fortress America" foreign policy.

The Nixon-Kissinger years began what was to be a decade-long process of oscillation between the opening of new international fronts and disengagement. Disengagement is used here, not only with regard to our withdrawal from Vietnam, but to our more general drift away from an active and forceful role for the United States in international affairs. On the one hand, the American public evidenced a weariness with both allies and adversaries. The vicissitudes of history finally overtook nature's nation and we were tempted to draw the curtains on the world outside and to avoid the responsibility of empire.

On the other hand, the opening to China in 1971–72 was a bold venture and strategic success for the Nixon-Kissinger foreign policy. Detente as an international policy seemed to wind down the intensity of the Cold War. The SALT agreement, a large wheat sale to the USSR, and a cordial presidential visit to Moscow conveyed a sense of easing tension. But disillusionment with detente was widespread by the 1976 presidential election year.

The world had demonstrably changed by the 1970s. Robert Schulzinger describes the change:

> Twenty years of rapid economic growth in Western Europe and Japan allowed those industrial nations to produce twice as much as the United States. Robust expansion stopped, however, in the wake of a tripling of energy costs. Poorer nations, concentrated mostly in the Southern Hemisphere, demanded greater shares in the world's posterity. Some Americans, stung by the bad memory of Vietnam, also hoped to focus attention on social and economic issues rather than military confrontation.[24]

The Carter administration emphasized "leadership without hegemony" and "the management of interdependence." From 1977 to 1979, the United States concentrated on human rights as the centerpiece of its foreign policy and moved to limit the global arms race. Neither of these objectives was achieved nor even approximated. Carter's two foreign policy successes were the Panama Canal Treaty and the mediation of a formal peace between Israel and Egypt. Russia's invasion of Afghanistan led to a new anti-Soviet line by Carter; America's Iranian hostage crisis led to an anti-Carter line by the American voters in 1980.

IV

The neo-internationalist does not deny that the spread of these values, pluralism, (human) rights, and democracy supports American power, nor that American power is needed to support the spread of these values. He does deny the central realist premise: that the purpose of such foreign exertions is the increase of America's power for its own sake.

He denies it because he does not believe it. He believes that the American conflict with the Soviet Union is not simply the blind struggle of two imperialisms, but a struggle with a moral meaning and a moral purpose; that, the emergence of political liberty being an episodic and unusual historical phenomenon, we live in a rare historical moment; that because of the historical accident (the exhaustion of Europe in two world wars) the United States is the one nation on whom the success of liberty most depends; and that such a fragile commodity, which provides the philosophical basis of the American polity itself is a good worth defending in and of itself.

Charles Krouthammer
"The Poverty of Realism"

I conclude this essay by speaking in behalf of a neo-internationalist foreign policy for America in 1987. Neo-internationalism is chosen from the options of neo-isolationism (George Kennen) or some form of "realism" (Christopher Lange). Charles Krouthammer's trenchant article in *The New Republic*, "The Poverty of Realism," contains a lucid description of the neo-internationalist position.[25]

A neo-internationalism stance is appropriate, in the first place, because it recognizes that our fate is wrapped up with the world's. This is a given. Economic isolationism is no longer an option. The *Apollo 8* photograph is an icon that symbolizes the reality of an increasingly international system.

Neo-internationalism is a fitting concept for United States foreign policy, in the second place, because it does not avoid the issue of values. Americans have no real affinity for mere balance-of-power politics. We have always insisted on the moralizing of foreign policy. This is just another way of saying that Americans are uneasy with the notion that power is an end in itself. Power must be in the service of some higher value. Power is never morally neutral except in the abstract considerations of academic realists. Power always is more closely related to value than realists sometimes realize, and Americans characteristically have believed that intervention must be morally justified. That is precisely the reason that American leaders have consistently resorted to moral interpretations of foreign policy.

The values in behalf of which Americans should exercise power in 1987 are food and freedom. A responsiveness to world wide hunger is in keeping with America's heritage and character. Viewed from the standpoint of our struggle with the Soviet Union to secure the allegiance of emerging nations, there is no other area in which the non-Communist countries can demonstrate the superiority of their system than in the production and distribution of food. The cause of engaging hunger was correctly identified as a major problem by C.P. Snow in his Green lecture. Food policy, to be sure, is as complex as other aspects of foreign policy and the United States must be certain that good intentions are not thwarted by authoritarian regimes which use food for their own interests.

Freedom as a central value really includes the Western social norms of pluralism, human rights, and democratic institutions. Stated negatively, this means America defends stable governments against Marxist-Leninist takeovers whenever possible. Positively stated, we will encourage democratic revolutions against Communist regimes. In practice, this policy means not only United States support for the contras in Nicaragua, but also for "third forces" in countries like the Philippines which are ruled by pro-American despotisms. One could celebrate such a third force victory in Chile even as we now nervously celebrate the success of the Aquino movement in the Philippines.

In speaking in behalf of the necessary moral component to interventionism, we of course do not mean some notion of moral purity or total innocence. We do not mean moral pretension or the claiming of more virtue in our actions than the facts warrant. An assumption of neo-isolationist foreign policy is the understanding that the exercise of power in the nuclear age means guilt and a certain degree of dis-ease.

An activist neo-internationalist policy must likewise be prudent and aware of the limitations of power. Lessons learned during the past two decades must be applied with care to the complexities of a volatile and fragile global arena. But it is time, after a period of disengagement and frustration, to seize the initiative in behalf of the Western alternative to increased Soviet hegemony in an unstable world. Our problem today is not so much the arrogance of power as it is the avoidance of its use.

For the foreseeable future, America's destiny is obvious, that is, manifest: shouldering the burden of a superpower in a "long twilight struggle" with a totalitarian adversary. For forty years our nation has engaged the responsibilities of a superpower in a dangerous world. In our recent past we showed signs of fatigue and declension. Now there seems to be a readiness to resume the initiative in the interventionist enterprise. The condition of American acceptance of this role is a conviction of the relationship of such international activism to American values.

NOTES

1. Quoted in Ernest Lee Tuveson, *Redeemer Nation: The Idea of America's Millennial Role* (Chicago and London: University of Chicago Press, 1968), p. 105. See Leon Howard, *The Connecticut Wits* (Chicago: University of Chicago Press, 1943), pp. 83ff.

2. Albert K. Weinberg, *Manifest Destiny: A Study of Nationalist Expansionism in American History* (Gloucester, Mass.: Peter Smith, 1958), p. 112.

3. H. Richard Niebuhr, *The Kingdom of God in America* (New York: Harper & Row, 1937), p. 43.

4. Washington Gladden, "Migrants and Their Lesson," *Publications of the Ohio Archeological and Historical Society* 3 (1891): pp. 180–95.

5. Tuveson, *Redeemer Nation.*

6. Weinburg, *Manifest Destiny*, p. 129.

7. Ibid., p. 126.

8. Reinhold Niebuhr and Alan Heimert, *A Nation So Conceived* (London: Faber & Faber, 1963), p. 9.

9. Ibid.

10. George Liska, *Career of Empire: America and Imperial Expansion Over Land and Sea* (Baltimore and London: The Johns Hopkins University Press, 1978), p. 110.

11. Margaret Leech, *In the Days of McKinley* (New York: Harper, 1959), p. 345.

12. Robert H. Pilpel, *Churchill in America, 1895–1961* (New York and London, 1976), p. 213.

13. James P. Warburg, *The United States in the Postwar World* (New York: Atheneum, 1966), p. 30.

14. Simon Serfaty, *American Foreign Policy in A Hostile World: Dangerous Years* (New York: Praeger Publishers, 1984), p. 16.

15. Charles P. Snow, *The State of Siege*: The John Findley Green Foundation Lectures, Westminster College, November, 1968. (New York: Charles Scribner's Sons, 1969), p. 5.

16. Ibid., p. 9.

17. Ibid., p. 23.

18. Ibid., p. 31–3.

19. Ibid., p. 37.

20. Ibid., p. 43.

21. *The New York Times*, Dec. 24, 1968, p. 6.

22. Ibid. MacLeish used the meditation as the lead essay and title of his anthology. *Riders on the Earth: Essays and Recollections* (Boston: Houghton Mifflin Company, 1978).

23. Christopher Lasch, *The Culture of Narcissism: American Life in an Age of Diminishing Expectations* (New York: W.W. Norton and Company, 1979); Tom Wolfe, "The Me Generation and the Third Great Awakening," in *Mauve Gloves & Madmen, Clutter and Vine* (New York: Farrar, Strauss, and Girous, 1976), pp. 126–167.

24. Robert D. Schulzinger, *American Diplomacy in the Twentieth Century* (New York: Oxford University Press, 1984), p. 316.

25. Charles Krauthammer, "The Poverty of Realism," *The New Republic*, February 17, 1986, pp. 14–22.

NOTES ON CONTRIBUTORS

Gordon C. Bjork is the Jonathan B. Lovelace professor of economics at Claremont McKenna College. A consultant to government and private corporations, he is also the author of *Private Enterprise and Public Interest: The Development of American Capitalism* (1969) and *Life, Liberty, and Property: The Economics and Politics of Land Use Planning and Environmental Control* (1980).

Armand Clesse is professor of political science at the University of Saarlandes in West Germany and a member of the International Institute for Strategic Studies in London. His publications include *Technology Transfer: Opportunities, Risks and Limits* (1983, editor) and *Pacifism and the Search for a European Security Order* (1983, editor).

Peter van den Dungen is lecturer in peace studies at the University of Bradford, UK. He has received the Fulbright Travel Award (1971) and the British Academy Award (1978). His recent publications include *West European Pacifism and the Strategy for Peace* (1985, editor).

P. Edward Haley is professor of political science and the director of the Keck Center for International Strategic Studies at Claremont McKenna College. He is chairman of the International Relations Committee. His books on United States foreign policy and international affairs include *Revolution and Intervention, Qaddafi and the United States since 1969* and *Nuclear Strategy, Arms Control and the Future* (co-editor).

Klaus Hornung is professor of political science at the University of Freiberg in West Germany. He has also been a visiting professor at Cairo University. His main publications include *The*

Fascinating Delusion—Karl Marx and the Consequences (1978), *Political–Pedagogical Handbook* (1980); *Peace Without Utopia* (1984, editor); and *Freedom in our Time* (1984).

Morton A. Kaplan is professor of political science and director of the Center for Strategic and Foreign Policy Studies at the University of Chicago. He is a frequent consultant to government on foreign policy questions and author of more than twenty books, including *Strategic Thinking and Its Moral Implications* and *Science, Language and the Human Condition.*

Robert C. Richardson, a retired USAF Brigadier General, is deputy director of High Frontier and director of the American Foreign Policy Institute. He is also president of Global Activities Ltd. and author of numerous articles on atomic warfare, NATO and strategy.

Richard L. Rubenstein is the Robert O. Lawton Distinguished Professor of Religion at Florida State University and president of The Washington Institute for Values in Public Policy. He is the winner of the *Portico d'Ottavia* literary prize in Rome, 1977, for the Italian translation of *The Religious Imagination.* He has authored or edited nine books, including *After Auschwitz* (1966), *My Brother Paul* (1972), *The Cunning of History* (1975), *The Age of Triage* (1983), and *Modernization: The Humanist Response* (1985).

Zdzislaw M. Rurarz was formerly Polish Ambassador to Japan and professor of economics at the Central School of Planning and Statistics in Warsaw, Poland. He was also a former economic adviser to the Polish cabinet. Dr. Rurarz is the author of seven books, including *Energy Crisis—Myth or Reality?* (1978), *Dilemmas of Development* (1977), and *Foreign Trade—Problems and Perspectives* (1971).

Leo Sandon is Director of the program in American Studies and Professor of Religion at Florida State University. He was the founder and executive director of the Institute for Social Policy Studies, 1974–79. Dr. Sandon has received the AMOCO Foundation Award for excellence in undergraduate teaching. He has authored over eighty monographs, articles and review essays and co-authored a widely used textbook, *Religion in America*.

Hans-Martin Sass is professor of philosophy and coordinator of the European professional ethics program at Bochum University in the Federal Republic of Germany. He is also a senior research fellow at the Kennedy Institute of Ethics at Georgetown University and adjunct professor at Georgetown University Medical School. His recent publications include *Responsibility with Risk* and *Arnold Ruge: Works and Letters* (ed.), both in German.

INDEX

The index is of persons, major themes, and tables. A number in brackets [ ] after a page number refers to a footnote on that page. Numbers in **bold face** type refer to pages written by the person indexed.

Index